"MY FATHER WAS A JEW. THIS DID NOT SEEM TO HIM A GOOD IDEA, AND SO IT WAS HIS NOTION TO DISASSEMBLE HIS HISTORY, BEGIN AT ZERO, RECREATE HIMSELF."

THE DUKE OF DECEPTION

"An engrossing, often moving search for the troubled bond between fathers and sons that is known as love."
—*TIME*

"An unusually pleasurable book, a memoir of a vagabond childhood spent in the company of the author's conman father. Wolff writes with care and craft, and also with a certain exhilaration, as if this were a story he had wanted to tell for a good long time."
—*ATLANTIC MONTHLY*

"Conscientious and intimate: as lucid and complicated a story as a good novel."
—*NEW YORK TIMES*

A Selection of the Book-of-the-Month Club

"HE WAS A LIE THROUGH AND THROUGH. THERE WAS NOTHING TO HIM BUT LIES AND LOVE."

THE DUKE OF DECEPTION

"An engaging story, principally because Wolff so clearly loves the terrible man whose biography he is writing."

—*BALTIMORE SUN*

"In this extraordinary memoir, Wolff brings to the full complexity of life a most exceptional man, and tells of the indelible effect the deplorable Duke had on him. It is an achievement of a high order."

— *NEW YORKER*

"It is not a novel. It may very well outlive a lot of the novels being written at the present moment."

—*NEW YORK POST*

"I HAD THIS FROM HIM ALWAYS: COMPASSION, CARE, GENEROSITY, ENDURANCE."

THE DUKE OF DECEPTION

"A remarkable book, as exciting as a good novel, shocking in its related cruelties . . . a book that reveals a deep love for a flawed parent."
—MEMPHIS COMMERCIAL APPEAL

"Duke was not only a con artist. He was also a father — a loving one — and his son's book is more than a chronicle of the old man's scams and deceits. It is the story of an intense relationship between father and son."
—SATURDAY REVIEW

"For those of us who are the sons of fathers and the fathers of sons, there is much to ponder in this story."
—CHICAGO TRIBUNE

THE DUKE OF DECEPTION

MEMORIES OF MY FATHER

GEOFFREY WOLFF

BERKLEY BOOKS, NEW YORK

*Grateful acknowledgment is made to the following for permission to
reprint previously published material:*

The excerpt from *Certain Half-Deserted Streets* by Geoffrey Wolff
was originally printed in *The Nassau Literary Review*.
The material from *Bad Debts* by Geoffrey Wolff
was first published by Simon & Schuster.
Copyright © 1969 by Geoffrey Wolff.

This Berkley book contains the complete
text of the original hardcover edition.
It has been completely reset in a type face
designed for easy reading, and was printed
from new film.

THE DUKE OF DECEPTION:
Memories of My Father

A Berkley Book / published by arrangement with
Random House, Inc.

PRINTING HISTORY
Random House edition / August 1979
Berkley edition / August 1980

ISBN: 0-425-04660-5

A BERKLEY BOOK® TM 757,375
Berkley Books are published by Berkley Publishing Corporation,
200 Madison Avenue, New York, New York 10016.
PRINTED IN THE UNITED STATES OF AMERICA

I wish to acknowledge the generous help given to me during the writing of this book by the John Simon Guggenheim Memorial Foundation.

G. W.

This story is for
Justin and Nicholas

Opening the Door

On a sunny day in a sunny humor I could sometimes think of death as mere gossip, the ugly rumor behind that locked door over there. This was such a day, the last of July at Narragansett on the Rhode Island shore.

My wife's grandmother was a figure of legend in Rhode Island, a tenacious grandam near ninety with a classic New Englander's hooked and broken beak, six feet tall in her low-heeled, sensible shoes. A short time ago she had begun a career as a writer; this had brought her satisfaction and some small local celebrity. She spent her summers in Narragansett surrounded by the houses of her five children and by numberless cousins and grand-children and great-grandchildren. One of these, my son Nicholas, not quite four, had just left for a ride with her. As old as she was she liked to drive short distances in her black Ford sedan, but she maintained a lively regard for her survival, and had cinched in her seat belt, tight.

Nicholas's little brother Justin was with his mother at the beach. I was with my wife's brother-in-law on a friend's shaded terrace. Kay's house was old and shingled,

impeccably neglected. It was almost possible to disbelieve
in death that day, to put out of mind a son's unbuckled
seat belt and the power of surf at the water's edge. I looked
past trimmed hedges at the rich lawn; beyond the lawn a
shelf of clean rocks angled to the sea. Sitting in an
overstuffed wicker chair, gossiping with Kay and a couple
of her seven children, protected from the sun, glancing at
sailboats beating out to Block Island, listening to bees
hum, smelling roses and fresh-cut grass, I felt drowsy,
off-guard.

We had been drinking rum. Not too much, but enough;
our voices were pitched low. Usually the house was loud
with laughter and recorded music—all those children,
after all—but this was a subdued moment. We were
drinking black rum with tonic and lime; I remember
chewing the lime's tart flesh.

In my memory now, as in some melodrama, I hear the
phone ring, but I didn't hear it then. The phone in that
house seemed always to be ringing. My wife's brother-in-
law John was called to the telephone; I guessed it was my
wife's sister, fetching us home to our mother-in-law's. We
always lingered too long with Kay.

John returned to the terrace. He stood thirty feet from
where I sat supporting my drink on my shirt. I remember
the icy feel of the glass against my chest. John was
smirking, shifting from one foot to the other. John was a
man to stand still, with fixed serenity, and my chest
cramped. As I stared down the terrace at him, Kay and
her children quit talking, and John's cheeks began to
dance. I looked at the widow Kay, she looked away, and I
knew what I knew. I walked down that terrace to learn
which of my boys was dead.

Justin was as sturdy as a fireplug: he once ate an
orange-juice glass down to its stem; it didn't seem to
trouble him. Another time was different: Running across
a meadow he tripped, gave a choked cry, nothing out of
the way. We walked toward him casually, paying no
attention. We were annoyed to find him face forward in
the mud. His mother said, "Get up," but he didn't. He

liked to tease us. I rolled him over, and his face was gray patched with pale green. His eyes had rolled back in his head: His brother began to cry; he had understood before we had, and his rage was awful. I tried to breathe life into my son, but in my clumsiness I neglected to pinch shut his nose. I blew and wept into his mouth, and tried to pry it open wider, just to do something, but mostly I wept on his face. My wife shouted at no one to call a doctor, but she knew it was useless. He was dead, any fool could see, and we didn't know why. Then he opened his eyes, went stiff with fear, began to cry. We are naked, all of us, I know, and it is cold. But Justin, it seemed then, was invulnerable.

So it was Nicholas.

John said: "Your father is dead."

And I said: "Thank God."

John recoiled from my words. I heard someone behind me gasp. The words did not then strike a blow above my heart, but later they did, and there was no calling them back, there is no calling them back now. All I can do now is try to tell what they meant.

1

I listen for my father and I hear a stammer. This was explosive and unashamed, not a choking on words but a spray of words. His speech was headlong, edgy, breathless: there was neither room in his mouth nor time in the day to contain what he burned to utter. I have a remnant of that stammer, and I wish I did not; I stammer and blush, my father would stammer and grin. He depended on a listener's good will. My father depended excessively upon people's good will.

As he spoke straight at you, so did he look at you. He could stare down anyone, though this was a gift he rarely practiced. To me, everything about him seemed outsized. Doing a school report on the Easter Islanders I found in an encyclopedia pictures of their huge sculptures, and there he was, massive head and nose, nothing subtle or delicate. He was in fact (and how diminishing those words, *in fact,* look to me now) an inch or two above six feet, full bodied, a man who lumbered from here to there with deliberation. When I was a child I noticed that people were respectful of the cubic feet my father

4

occupied; later I understood that I had confused respect with resentment.

I recollect things, a gentleman's accessories, deceptively simple fabrications of silver and burnished nickle, of brushed Swedish stainless, of silk and soft wool and brown leather. I remember his shoes, so meticulously selected and cared for and used, thin-soled, with cracked uppers, older than I was or could ever be, shining dully and from the depths. Just a pair of shoes? No: I knew before I knew any other complicated thing that for my father there was nothing he possessed that was "just" something. His pocket watch was not "just" a timepiece, it was a miraculous instrument with a hinged front and a representation on its back of porcelain ducks rising from a birch-girt porcelain pond. It struck the hour unassertively, musically, like a silver tine touched to a crystal glass, no hurry, you might like to know it's noon.

He despised black leather, said black shoes reminded him of black attaché cases, of bankers, lawyers, look-before-you-leapers anxious not to offend their clients. He owned nothing black except his dinner jacket and his umbrella. His umbrella doubled as a shooting-stick, and one afternoon at a polo match at Brandywine he was sitting on it when a man asked him what he would do if it rained, sit wet or stand dry? I laughed. My father laughed also, but tightly, and he did not reply; nor did he ever again use this quixotic contraption. He took things, *things*, seriously.

My father, called Duke, taught me skills and manners; he taught me to shoot and to drive fast and to read respectfully and to box and to handle a boat and to distinguish between good jazz music and bad jazz music. He was patient with me, led me to understand for myself why Billie Holiday's understatements were more interesting than Ella Fitzgerald's complications. His codes were not novel, but they were rigid, the rules of decorum that Hemingway prescribed. A gentleman kept his word, and favored simplicity of sentiment; a gentleman chose his words with care, as he chose his friends. A gentleman accepted responsibility for his acts, and welcomed the liberty to act unambiguously. A gentleman was a stickler for precision and punctilio; life was no more than an inventory of small choices that together formed a man's character, entire. A gentleman was this, and not that; a *man* did, did not, said, would not say.

My father could, however, be coaxed to reveal his bona fides. He had been schooled at Groton and passed along to Yale. He was just barely prepared to intimate that he had been tapped for "Bones," and I remember his pleasure when Levi Jackson, the black captain of Yale's 1948 football team, was similarly honored by that secret society. He was proud of Skull and Bones for its hospitality toward the exotic. He did sometimes wince, however, when he pronounced Jackson's Semitic Christian name, and I sensed that his tolerance for Jews was not inclusive; but I never heard him indulge express bigotry, and the first of half a dozen times he hit me was for having called a neighbor's kid a guinea.

There was much luxury in my father's affections, and he hated what was narrow, pinched, or mean. He understood exclusion, mind you, and lived his life believing the world to be divided between a few *us's* and many *thems*, but I was to understand that aristocracy was a function of taste, courage, and generosity. About two other virtues—candor and reticence—I was confused, for my father would sometimes proselytize the one, sometimes the other.

If Duke's preoccupation with bloodlines was finite, this did not cause him to be unmindful of his ancestors. He knew whence he had come, and whither he meant me to go. I saw visible evidence of this, a gold signet ring which I wear today, a heavy bit of business inscribed arsy-turvy with lions and flora and a motto, *nulla vestigium retrorsit*. "Don't look back" I was told it meant.

After Yale—class of late nineteen-twenty something, or early nineteen-thirty something—my father batted around the country, living a high life in New York among school and college chums, flying as a test pilot, marrying my mother, the daughter of a rear admiral. I was born a year after the marriage, in 1937, and three years after that my father went to England as a fighter pilot with Eagle Squadron, a group of American volunteers in the Royal Air Force. Later he transferred to the OSS, and was in Yugoslavia with the partisans; just before the Invasion he was parachuted into Normandy, where he served as a sapper with the Resistance, which my father pronounced *ray-zee-staunce*.

His career following the war was for me mysterious in its particulars; in the service of his nation, it was understood, candor was not always possible. This much was clear: my father mattered in the world, and was satisfied that he mattered, whether or not the world understood precisely why he mattered.

A pretty history for an American clubman. Its fault is that it was not true. My father was a bullshit artist. True, there were many boarding schools, each less pleased with the little Duke than the last, but none of them was Groton. There was no Yale, and by the time he walked from a room at a mention of Skull and Bones I knew this, and he knew that I knew it. No military service would have him; his teeth were bad. So he had his teeth pulled and replaced, but the Air Corps and Navy and Army and Coast Guard still thought he was a bad idea. The ring I wear was made according to his instructions by a jeweler two blocks from Schwab's drugstore in Hollywood, and was never paid for. The motto, engraved backwards so that it would come right on a red wax seal, is dog Latin and means in fact "leave no trace behind," but my father did not believe me when I told him this.

My father was a Jew. This did not seem to him a good idea, and so it was his notion to disassemble his history, begin at zero, and re-create himself. His sustaining line of work till shortly before he died was as a confidence man. If I now find his authentic history more surprising, more interesting, than his counterfeit history, he did not. He would not make peace with his actualities, and so he was the author of his own circumstances, and indifferent to the consequences of this nervy program.

There were some awful consequences, for other people as well as for him. He was lavish with money, with others' money. He preferred to stiff institutions: jewelers, car dealers, banks, fancy hotels. He was, that is, a thoughtful buccaneer, when thoughtfulness was convenient. But people were hurt by him. Much of his mischief was casual enough: I lost a tooth when I was six, and the Tooth Fairy, "financially inconvenienced" or "temporarily out of pocket," whichever was then his locution, left under my pillow an IOU, a sight draft for two bits, or two million.

I wish he hadn't selected from among the world's possible disguises the costume and credentials of a yacht club commodore. Beginning at scratch he might have reached further, tried something a bit more bold and odd, a bit less inexorably conventional, a bit less calculated to please. But it is true, of course, that a confidence man who cannot inspire confidence in his marks is nothing at all, so perhaps his tuneup of his bloodline, educational *vita*, and war record was merely the price of doing business in a culture preoccupied with appearances.

I'm not even now certain what I wish he had made of himself: I once believed that he was most naturally a fictioneer. But for all his preoccupation with make-believe, he never tried seriously to write it. A confidence man learns early in his career that to commit himself to paper is to court trouble. The successful bunco artist does his game, and disappears himself: Who *was* that masked man? No one, no one at all, *nulla vestigium* [*sic*] *retrorsit* [*sic*], not a trace left behind.

Well, I'm left behind. One day, writing about my father with no want of astonishment and love, it came to me that I am his creature as well as his get. I cannot now shake this conviction, that I was trained as his instrument of perpetuation, put here to put him into the record. And that my father knew this, calculated it to a degree. How else explain his eruption of rage when I once gave up what he and I called "writing" for journalism? I had taken a job as the book critic of *The Washington Post*, was proud of myself; it seemed then like a wonderful job, honorable and enriching. My father saw it otherwise: "You have failed me," he wrote, "you have sold yourself at discount" he wrote to me, his prison number stamped below his name.

He was wrong then, but he was usually right about me. He would listen to anything I wished to tell him, but would not tell me only what I wished to hear. He retained such solicitude for his clients. With me he was strict and straight, except about himself. And so I want to be strict and straight with him, and with myself. Writing to a friend about this book, I said that I would not now for anything have had my father be other than what he was, except happier, and that most of the time he was happy enough, cheered on by imaginary successes. He gave me a great deal, and not merely life, and I didn't want to bellyache; I wanted, I told my friend, to thumb my nose on his behalf at everyone who had limited him. My friend was shrewd, though, and said that he didn't believe me, that I couldn't mean such a thing, that if I followed out its implications I would be led to a kind of ripe sentimentality, and to mere piety. Perhaps, he wrote me, you would not have wished him to lie to himself, to lie about being a Jew. Perhaps you would have him fool others but not so deeply trick himself. "In writing about a father," my friend wrote me about our fathers, "one clambers up a slippery mountain, carrying the balls of another in a bloody sack, and whether to eat them or worship them or bury them decently is never cleanly decided."

So I will try here to be exact. I wish my father had done more headlong, more elegant inventing. I believe he would respect my wish, be willing to speak with me seriously about it, find some nobility in it. But now he is dead, and he had been dead two weeks when they found him. And in his tiny flat at the edge of the Pacific they found no address book, no batch of letters held with a rubber band, no photograph. Not a thing to suggest that he had ever known another human being.

2

When I was a boy my father introduced me, with ceremony, to a couple of family treasures. There was my great-grandfather's medical degree from Leyden and a worn leather case, my grandfather's, fitted with surgical devices. These totems are gone now, lost during one or another last-minute, dark-of-night escape from a house where the rent was seven months overdue, or from a town where a rubber check had just bounced to the D.A.'s desk. But I recollect well enough those gleaming instruments set in blue-velvet cavities.

Not long ago I bought a set of compasses and dividers solely because, snugged in their own blue velvet nests, they returned me to evenings when I sat beside my father at his desk, and he showed me the clamps and probes and trepan and lancet and scalpels. I would hold a piece and examine it, and then return it to its fit place, and promise never again to touch it without my father's supervision. I was warned that germs and microbes deadly beyond imagining still lurked on the blades, but there was no need to scare me away from them: I had never seen things so mysterious, cold, or menacing.

It was characteristic of my father to impress upon me his family's artifacts rather than its history. He was reticent about his background. He would mention, with more awe than love, his father's skills, his huge medical library, his ease with foreign languages. These references had an abstract quality because my father could not afford, given his wish to unmake his origins, to place Dr. Wolff in the world among kindred named Samuels and Krotoshiner.

I first heard the inventory of family names as I stood with my cousin Bill Haas, a stranger, in Hartford's Beth Israel Cemetery, above the bones and markers of Beatrice Annette Wolff (August 19, 1894–April 9, 1895) and Harriet Krotoshiner (1867–1944) and Arthur Jacob Wolff (June 5, 1855–June 22, 1936). I was thirty-eight, a latecomer to my family. Bill Haas, and two Ruths—his sister and his cousin—led me through names and places and dates. They showed me photographs; I had never seen a likeness of my father younger than forty, or any at all of my grandmother, grandfather, their parents. For years I had feared them, had thought maybe my father had just cause to hide them. But they looked fine, just like ancestors.

My father Arthur was delivered by his father Arthur at home on Spring Street in Hartford, November 22, 1907. Dr. Wolff took pains to bring his son safely into the world, and then to ease him through it. He was meticulous, almost as exacting with himself as with others, and he and his wife Harriet were unlikely to enjoy another opportunity to perpetuate themselves. She was forty, he was fifty-two. They had had a daughter when Dr. Wolff was thirty-nine, still young enough to believe he could mend anyone. But Beatrice Annette's scarlet fever was beyond his power to heal, and she died at eight months of life.

My grandfather was born in London in 1855, but some restlessness brought his father to America. He served during the Civil War as surgeon to a French regiment, and after the war moved to Brownsville, Texas, where he practiced medicine for the Army at Fort Brown, across the Rio Grande from Matamoros.

When my father was a schoolboy—and from his inexhaustible reservoir of Micawberisms applying for admission to Yale—he was asked to confide a few particulars of his background. He told Yale that his father had been educated at "Balioll" [*sic*] College, Oxford, and this was not so. My grandfather was removed from high school at fourteen, and from that age was educated in science, medicine, mathematics, literature, and languages by his father. Four years later he entered Texas Medical College in Galveston, and was graduated in 1876. My father also told Yale that his father had interned at Bellevue. This was true, Bellevue—like Oxford—being an approved institution.

Yale asked for my grandmother's maiden name, and my father gave them Harriet K. Van Duyn. The "Van Duyn"—in other applications "Van Zandt"—he did not enclose in quotation marks, but it is a fiction. "Harriet" was accurate, and some vestigial attachment to his source caused my father to return to his mother that remnant of her identity in the character *K*, the abbreviation of her name.

Krotoshiner: the family took its name from Krotoschin in the Prussian province of Posnán, "the nice part of Prussia" my cousin Ruth Atkins told me. Now the place is called Krotoszyn by the Poles, who own it. Samuel and Yetta Krotoshiner emigrated from Prussia to Glasgow, where my grandmother Harriet was born. (Ruth Atkins still owns the thistled pin that once secured the folds of the Krotoshiner tartan.) From Glasgow the family sailed to Canada, where Mr. Krotoshiner set up as a "gentleman farmer," which is what they still call a farmer who knows nothing about farming, and loses his shirt. They moved again, to Brooklyn, where Harriet fell in love with young Dr. Wolff, an *alrightnik* with soft brown eyes and an appetite for excellence who was attracted to the sixteen-year-old girl's soft good humor.

When Samuel Krotoshiner died, Yetta sold his wine-importing business and moved her three daughters to Hartford, where she established, against the custom of the time, her own business, a fine china shop. Dr. Wolff married Harriet in 1893 in a double wedding with her younger sister. Yetta was doing well enough to give each of her newly married daughters a fur coat and a Bechstein grand piano.

My grandfather was a wonderful doctor, everyone agreed. When Mt. Sinai Hospital was established in Hartford in 1923 he was chief of the medical board and of the medical staff. A sense of his range may be taken from the fact that he was also the chief of its surgical staff, chief of gynecology and chief of the laboratory. Coincidentally he was municipal bacteriologist of the Hartford Health Department and a medico-legal expert whose microscopic analyses of criminal evidence broke open murder trials in Connecticut and New York.

Yet there were people, and my grandmother was one, who believed that this man, known invariably as The Doctor, should never have practiced medicine. Not that he lacked compassion, but that he lacked humility. The year after he was chosen chief of staff of Mt. Sinai he severed his connection with the hospital. The reason is among the records of his successor: "On opening of the hospital Dr. Wolff assumed a dictatorial attitude and he would allow no one to do major surgery without his consent. This was resented and he resigned."

His temper was explosive. People have described his rages as "terrifying," "wild," "beyond control." He was brutal with patients who disregarded his instructions. He had a sharp tongue, and from the time he began his association with Hartford's St. Francis Hospital the year after his marriage, he became notorious for baiting nuns and priests—the former about their absurd and unsanitary costumes, the latter about their preposterous beliefs, and both for interfering with his patients.

His own religious preference was simple: he was an

atheist. He believed in evidence and natural law and in Occam's razor, the principle of parsimony developed six hundred years ago by William of Occam that holds that what can be proved with few assumptions is proved in vain with more. He was, that is, an enemy of complication and mystification, yet he held throughout his life to a single irrational (and wonderful) conviction: that every word ever spoken continued, as he said, "to kick around out there in the atmosphere," and that some day, by the agency of some instrument, could be recovered, like money from a bank. My grandfather was especially eager to attend the conversations of Voltaire with Frederick the Great, and Sir Francis Bacon with anyone at all.

My grandfather was venerated by people who knew him, and he was no enemy of their respect, but his preference was for solitary work. He took up photography because he liked the quiet of his darkroom. He cherished gadgets, built model steam and internal combustion engines from scrap metal, lavishing months of his old age on them, tapping and turning, drilling and polishing their small, precise parts. He built his own microscopes except for their lenses, and liked to correspond with the Royal Society of London about what he saw looking in them. I have one of the contraptions into which he poured time and money, a device to custom-fit eyeglasses.

His family and friends thought of The Doctor as a whiz of an inventor, but his Big Ideas had the Wolff stamp of improbability upon them. The fixer in him provoked his improvement on the pneumatic tire. He had bought one of Hartford's first automobiles (and installed one of Hartford's first telephones, gramophones, X-ray machines), and it offended his sense of economy to replace the car's tires every thousand or so miles. It is now a family legend that The Doctor's tire was a good one, and that its design was stolen from him, that he "could have made a million" had he only had "a smart lawyer."

The fable of the lost million, every family's staple! For Wolffs the refrain was repeated, with threnodic variations, right to the jailhouse door. There's the story of the Travelers' Insurance Company stock, offered in lieu of a fee for a timely job of cutting on the Travelers' president's daughter. The Doctor preferred cash, and later the cry was cried, from generation to generation, *if only*. Other Hartford doctors became millionaires, perhaps by the customary expedient of saving. My grandfather, by contrast, grew poorer as he lived richer, and for this he paid dearly in gall.

He and Harriet began married life on North Capital Street in a handsome clapboard house, and then moved to a formidable stone structure on the corner of Spring Street and Asylum Avenue, a valuable location contiguous with St. Francis Hospital. When the Wolffs traded up again, moving to a huge establishment on Collins Street, the hospital pestered The Doctor to sell the Spring Street house to those nuns and priests he had so unmercifully bullied, and they hornswoggled my grandfather—*Jewed him down, as a relative put it, without irony* and there went another million. If only he had hung on to that property...can you imagine? Priceless! *If only...*

If gentiles suspected Jews of sharp practices, my family now believes that The Doctor was chiseled and finally undone because he was at the mercy of cynical Yankees who used him when he could save their skins, and never fairly paid him for his service. Dr. Wolff is said to have left the staff of St. Francis because a Jew couldn't get a fair shake from the Catholics.

Neither were the Jews of my grandfather's background very tolerant of greenhorns, Jews with accents, Jews from Eastern Europe. German and Western European Jews did not mingle with what a cousin has called "Johnny-come-latelies." They had different congregations, different lives, different prejudices. Another cousin, stunned that my father would repudiate his blood's history, can also tell me that "there were only a few old Jewish families like ours in Hartford. The Wolffs were old-timers, here before the Gold Rush; we weren't proud to mix with gentiles, but newcomers were proud to mix with us."

Exclusion and discrimination were in the air my father
breathed.

He told me one story only that touched the Jewish
experience. Dr. Wolff and Harriet were in an Atlantic
City hotel, and Dr. Wolff—"incredibly," in my father's
words—was "mistaken" for a Jew by a desk clerk. This
suspicious monitor of the hotel's reputation as a
sanctuary from the bothersome *Hebraic element* (known-
even in tour guides of the time as *our Israelite brethren*)
must have observed something extreme in the topography
of Dr. Wolff's nose. He said something, asked something,
that offended The Doctor. Who checked in, plugged up
the sink and tub, turned on all taps full force, and
departed without checking out. My father loved this
story. It perplexed me, and caused me to study the size
and contour of my father's nose, and mine.

But I dwell too morbidly on my grandfather's losses,
disappointments, vices of temper and arrogance. His
curiosity, boyishly exuberant to the end, was his
signature, and when he died at eighty-one it was what *The
Hartford Courant* remembered in an editorial:

"Dr. Wolff's death recalls to many persons a man
whose youthful zeal in his exacting work belied his years.
The test tube and the microscope were as toys in his
hands, so absorbing was their use to his searching mind."

Harriet could make him laugh at himself; he was
evidently a good laugher, especially at his own jokes. He
liked to tease people close to him with diagnoses of
fantastical ailments that required fantastical remedies.
Was the symptom a runny nose, slight cough, muscle
ache? An obvious case of *catootus of the cameenus*,
calling for the force-feeding of oatmeal and amputation
of an ear.

He liked practical jokes, and was known as a wit to his
friends in an informal convocation called The Saturday
Night Crowd. These friends played bridge, or listened to a
recital of music by one or another of them. My
grandfather despised gossip, so there was no gossip.

Sometimes there was a poker game, husbands and wives playing for high stakes, bets a dollar minimum, pot the limit. But at the game's end everything was settled a penny on the dollar, a scale of debt resolution that satisfactorily impressed my father, who proposed it to many merchants.

A couple of years before my father was born a large wedding was given at the Touro Club for my grandmother's niece, Hannah Samuels, who was marrying William Haas. This was a sunny occasion, and the program for that evening is all I have of a material nature to suggest the comfortable and generally good-willed quality of my grandparents' lives in their middle age, in 1905. The meal was lavish: oysters and hors d'oeuvres, poached salmon with hollandaise, a filet of beef followed by sherbert. This was followed by roast capon and champagne, then a green salad and *glacés fantaisies variées.*

During cordials and cigars the guests listened to The Doctor perform an air of his own composition, done to the beat of "Tramp, Tramp, Tramp," a ditty innocent of application to the bride.

> There once was a happy maid,
> Quite stupendous, so they said,
> She always had a smile to give you too;
> She was loving, she was true,
> She could kiss, I think, do you?
> But those were "handed" only to a few.

This was followed by a chorus:

> Good-bye, Hannah, you must leave us,
> We'll all miss you, when you're gone;
> Now, Sweet William, have a care,
> Of our girl, so sweet and rare,
> And return with her to those you've left at home.

Here was no short-winded doggerel: there were six

more stanzas, followed by as many repetitions of the chorus, but then who needed to rush? There was all the time in the world to spend on a simple expression of affection. Time for love, time for play, and after passing The Doctor's nice turns on *William* and *will*—Hannah now had a "strong Will of her own"—I'd like to linger for a final stanza:

> From summer dances at the docks,
> She sought seclusion at the rocks,
> Where she watched the tide in ebbing and in flow,
> How much Billing, how much cooing,
> How much time used up in wooing,
> The rocks won't tell, and we will never know.

The tide and summer dances were rhythms of Crescent Beach, on Long Island Sound at Niantic. Now the place is seedy, hard by the Boston–New York railroad tracks. The Doctor had begun going there in the nineties, brought by Dr. John McCook, a Hartford personage and friend with whom he established the first laboratory at Saint Francis Hospital. Every summer the Wolffs came down the Connecticut River by steamboat from Hartford to Old Lyme, and traveled (in the early days) the fifteen miles along the shore by oxcart.

The Samuels families also summered at Crescent Beach, and William Haas built a house next door to The Doctor's. My grandparent's house still stands, large, with cedar shingles and a shake roof, with green shutters and a sun deck above a shaded porch furnished with wicker chairs, a rocker and a hammock. The nights there were cool, and the days lazy but sociable. Activities with members of these close-knit families cut without self-consciousness across generations.

When I was nine and ten and eleven my father would take me on fine winter weekend mornings to Crescent Beach. The place was desolate then; the houses—set close together and helter-skelter back from the beach—were boarded up, and often as we made our way to the rocks at the northeast rim of the beach, below McCook Point, we would kick through ice and snow-crusted seaweed.

Ostensibly we had come to shoot tin cans my father would fill with sand and set at the water's edge. When I turned nine he had bought me a bolt-action single-shot Remington .22, and he would let me spend my allowance on a fifty-round box of rim-fire shorts. I would shoot them up in a couple of hours while my father kept one eye on me and the other on a book. Later, walking down the beach, my father would point to the huge gabled McCook house, shared by the families of Dr. John McCook and his brother Anson, a lawyer; my father would tell of its fabulous rooms, and what had passed there and in the gazebo that overlooked the rocks below the point, where we had come to sit. I wanted to climb the rocks and see the house close up, but my father respected the integrity of that property, and would not let me.

Sometimes in my line of fire, if I raised my sights to lead a seagull (a forbidden practice), was a small prominence called Crystal Rock, and my father told me that he was once nearly drowned swimming to it on a dare, but when I pressed him for particulars—where had he lived then, how old was he, what was his connection with the McCook house?—he would distance himself from my curiosity.

My father did tell me, laughing dryly, that he had once taken his father for a ride in a motorboat Dr. Wolff had just the week before given him. My father, showing off, had brought no oars and had shut off his Johnson Sea Horse to clean its carburetor filter, which fell overboard. Young Arthur had been obliged to face The Doctor's red and furious face as the tide lapped them toward McCook Point.

We must have been alone on that beach twenty times, perhaps forty. And we walked each time past the house where my father spent every summer of his life, happily, until he thought he would rather be elsewhere, and was old enough to drive himself away from Crescent Beach. And never did my father tell me that we were together near a sacred family place, or point to the house—its architecture and dimensions less imposing than the McCook Place—that had given his father such pleasure and pride. Of my father's serial repudiations I find this the most perverse and sad.

3

My father's cousin Ruth Atkins was thirteen when he was
born, and she stood for a time as his older sister. Her
father—Louis Samuels—had died when she was four,
and The Doctor, fond of his niece, treated her like a
daughter. She spent every Saturday night at the Wolff
house, and on Sunday mornings he would read the
funnies aloud with verve, losing himself in their
complications, doing all the voices. "He smelled of cigars,
but clean."

She recollects especially the big house on Collins Street
to which The Doctor and Harriet moved after my father
was born. (Cousin Ruth's brother, Arthur Samuels, a
New York editor and wit, had been named for The
Doctor, and my father was called Arthur Samuels Wolff
to return the compliment; he upclassed this to Arthur
Saunders Wolff.) Ruth's favorite room was the library,
dark and formidable, dominated by The Doctor's huge
desk. There was also a music room, a drawing room
paneled in oak, and a kitchen in the care of a Norwegian
cook. There was a maid, and a chauffeur in charge of

several Pierce-Arrows and a couple of Rolls-Royces as the years passed. When The Doctor drove himself he drove at a constant speed, whatever he encountered; people were meant to move aside for him.

As Ruth grew older she ceased spending every Saturday night in The Doctor's house, but she would stop off most afternoons after school to find him reading the *New York Journal.* If she had missed a couple of days between visits my grandfather would pout: "I didn't know you were still alive."

Probably better than anyone, she understood my father's childhood: "Duke was beyond imagination spoiled. I remember going to his room, filled with every single thing made for a child, and the room looked like a hurricane had come through it; you couldn't walk across it without breaking a toy because there was no room on the floor for them all. It was grotesque, and cruel."

And then Ruth, shaking her head, recollecting her love for my father and the anger that caused her to tear to shreds every photograph she owned that included him—grinning in a sailor's suit, rolling a hoop, catching a baseball, Beau Brummel in a white three-piece suit among fraternity chums—looked down, and dropped her voice: "He never had a chance."

Why not? To be born the third Arthur Wolff didn't seem to be bad luck. His parents were comfortable and respected. My father's health was studied and maintained, he was petted and adored. The little boy was even allowed to attend his father in his laboratory and workshop, providing he held his tongue. Yet almost from the beginning there was trouble. Bill Haas, six months younger than my father, remembers him as a "toy-breaker." The Haas and Wolff families celebrated Christmas, presumably as a secular occasion, to exchange gifts: "If I got to Collins Street on Christmas afternoon or early the next day, there'd be something left to play with. A couple of days later, all broken."

Perhaps my father was an unexpected boon to a busy professional man past middle age. Certainly The Doctor begrudged his son time, and instead of time preferred to give him things, forgetting the attention and education lavished on him by his own father. For whatever reason, an old and sad story began to unwind, of love's shortcut through stuff. My father spent time, the truly precious gift, on me; but even so he thought of possessions as the fundamental, material manifestations of love. If I mentioned that I would like to collect tin soldiers I would the next day have a hundred tin soldiers. If coins or stamps were my interest of the moment I would get albums, the things already fixed in place. Thus was the nature of desire blindly perverted. To be thrust upon as my father was thrust upon, as he thrust things upon me, was crucially unsettling.

Yet I knew that my father poured goods on me because he loved me. Did my father think of himself as similarly loved? I don't know. Ruth believes that her cousin's dominant sensation in the presence of The Doctor was fear. That he stammered from fear. Ruth and Bill both recollect The Doctor's insane tantrums around his son: they remember him chasing the boy, trying to hit him with a chair, threatening to kill him with it, but they don't remember why.

My grandmother Harriet doted on her little boy, dressed him like a doll and praised him ceaselessly in her low, gentle voice. Her son loved her back, but he was awful when he was crossed or denied, capable of tantrums, pipsqueak imitations of his father's. These she would hide from The Doctor. It was not that she was afraid, or mousy—she knew her mind as her husband knew his—but that she liked to keep the peace.

My father was thought by his friends and cousins to be generous, talented, bright and charming. His charm disarmed them and his mother, but never his father. To please The Doctor required attainments his son was too young to possess, plotting ways around the judgment and daunting standards of someone sixty-five when he was thirteen.

How hard it must have been to grow up under the

measuring gaze of that father! From the beginning my father heard talk about the best of this, the best of that: the best neighborhood, school, automobile, mind, family. And if Jews with educations and without accents were better than Jews with accents and without educations, couldn't it follow that best of all was to be no Jew at all?

Even as a child my father expressed an amused disdain for the Jews he had chanced to fall among, and Bill Haas remembers Duke, only nine or ten, overhearing The Doctor remark that Temple Beth Israel had been built too close to the sidewalk; my father gestured at the Gothic structure on Charter Oak Avenue and muttered: "Yeah, about a m-mile too c-c-close."

Bill was treated generously by my father except on the single occasion when he mocked his stammer, and my father hit him, hard. They played together at Crescent Beach, where they lived summers next door to each other, and Duke taught him dirty jokes, and bragged to him about fictional sexual conquests, and to the best of his ability led the younger boy astray. Duke was an excellent swimmer; he was courageous and amusing. He was also moody, eager to lose himself in fantasies of accomplishment, and in books. "Your father read real stuff, not crap like I read but literature, Melville and Dickens and Swift."

He was thought by The Doctor's neighbors to be a "wild boy." He broke windows, and charged petty items to his mother's account at the neighborhood drugstore, without her permission. At grade school he cadged petty cash from his classmates. As he grew worse, but surely not awful, his mother withdrew into a pacific acceptance of his condition, and his father gave more time to his inventions and medical research.

Today my father's punishments are more vividly remembered than his crimes. What did the child do? He wasn't a bully, didn't steal, was kind to animals, loved his mother, was awed by his father. Because he exhibited none of the superiority so precious to The Doctor, he pretended to it. My grandfather finally gave up on his son when my father was thirteen.

Duke's first boarding school was Deerfield Academy, sixty miles up the Connecticut River Valley from Hartford, in Deerfield, Massachusetts. Headmaster and usually benevolent tyrant from 1902 till 1968, Dr. Frank Boyden had a reputation for tolerance, for mending boys rather than tossing them aside. It was the legend that he would not kick any boy out of Deerfield, but my father was sent packing after a single semester in 1921.

He was brought by Dr. Wolff to see the school and be seen by Dr. Boyden. Among the headmaster's notes from the time of my father's first visit to the school are his impressions of another applicant, with "a funny head. It comes to a peak. Lips. A silly boy. Too fine-bred for us. Mother has too many ideas about education." (So did The Doctor. His son had previously studied at Hartford's public West Middle School whose teachers, responding to Dr. Wolff's theories of educational practice, often visited my grandfather at home in Hartford, and spent weekends with him at Crescent Beach. Dr. Boyden was not one to place himself on so intimate a footing with a Hartford surgeon, no great personage by Deerfield's measure.)

Another contemporary applicant revealed himself to Dr. Boyden's judgment: "stubby fingers. Sloppy. A big nose." What the headmaster thought of young Arthur— who stammered and wore glasses, whose curly hair was unruly, who sometimes wore a goofy Groucho Marx-like leer—can be imagined. My father was neither cute nor assured. He was young, but had already been trained to believe he wasn't of much use to the world. Dr. Boyden described the child's semester at Deerfield offhandedly: "He was a well-meaning boy who had practically no preparation. Also, he had never done any real work."

So he was sent along to the Eaglebrook Lodge School for younger boys, also in Deerfield and established coincidentally with my father's entrance in 1922 by Howard B. Gibbs, who had taught for Dr. Boyden. The main building was set high up on Mount Pocumtuck, beside a brook. It had been built as a private retreat in the 1890s, and during a stay there of several weeks Rudyard Kipling wrote *Captains Courageous,* a circumstance retailed to the boys to inspire them.

My father was one of twenty-six students, and happy, at first. The inaugural year was easygoing, and the school nurse remembers that "if Mr. Gibbs decided he wanted to eat dinner in town we all went to eat dinner in town." Gibbs knew boys to be savage as well as noble, and for all that managed to love them. He obliged them to shake hands firmly, to speak audibly and with candor. A graduate recollects that Gibbs was "of the old school. If someone did something wrong, he would haul off and bang him one."

My father once ran away from school with another boy, probably from motives other than homesickness, and the matter was reduced to a boy's scale, with a boy's punishment given for a boy's crime. Mr. Gibbs collected the pair by car and brought them back to the Lodge, and remarked that as they seemed to enjoy long-distance hikes, they could hike five hours, nonstop, around the school's circular driveway.

Very early each morning, fall and winter and spring, the boys were led in sets of exercises. At night ghost stories were told beside the fireplace. In the spring there were hikes to the summit of Mount Pocumtuck, and in the winter the children descended iced chutes on toboggans, and skied downhill and cross-country and off jumps.

The children came from families of all quantities and conditions (many with old New England surnames), who had in common mostly their ability to pay the tuition. (This was evidently a hardship for The Doctor, who sold the Collins Street house in 1922, and built a smaller place at 217 North Beacon Street that nevertheless had a huge workshop out back.) Eaglebrook boys were wealthy orphans, children of divorce, children of Americans abroad. The son of a Boston mortician arrived for the first time at Eaglebrook in the back of a hearse, asleep, and a fourteen-year-old Japanese boy with an allowance of twenty thousand a year always took an instructor with him to Bermuda during the holidays.

Before my father went home for his first Christmas break the boys and their masters walked to Deerfield, the paradigm of New England villages. They walked on snowshoes, carrying lit candles, and stopped at each house to sing carols. When I think of my father, an old man in a California prison, I sometimes think of him too as a young boy singing a celebration in the snow.

His grades at Eaglebrook were for the first and almost last time almost respectable: he flunked math, which would plague him from then on, whether he was pretending to draft an airfoil for Lockheed or listing his assets and liabilities; he got a 65 in French. But his 78 in Latin was fine, and his grade in English was the highest in his class.

But something happened; I don't know what, and Eaglebrook either can't or won't tell. My father was sent home to his father, who sent him away to St. John's School, a military academy in Manlius, New York, near Syracuse. This was the kind of place that advertises in the back pages of *The New York Times Magazine*, showing a stiff-backed adolescent cadet with his chin jammed against his chest. Duke was sent there by the intercession of his uncle Lambert Cain, the husband of one of The Doctor's sisters, a West Point graduate and career Army officer. My father appeared at St. John's in the autumn of 1923, at fifteen, to have his character built, or beaten, into him.

During my father's first few weeks at school he burst out of the blocks, doing excellently in all his subjects, even algebra and geometry, winning a reputation as a bright young man. Once his intelligence was beyond dispute, he began to backslide. He despised the grinding earnestness of the place, and chafed at St. John's regulations. The upperclassmen—cadet officers—were bullies, and the teachers taught by the principle of rote. By late November of my father's first year The Doctor had received a letter from St. John's principal, General William Verbeck, complaining about the boy's indolence and concluding with a threat: "If he will not respond to our demand for a good grade of scholastic work he is really wasting time at Manlius."

What a lament this caused in Hartford, what virtuoso hand-wringing! The Doctor wrote his son:

> You may easily understand my astonishment in finding that you are repeating the great source of serious trouble you are giving both your mother and myself. I had been hopeful that you would try to be a dutiful son, and be faithful to the trust we have all put in you, and it is very disappointing. You are now a young man, and you have not much time to make good. I am so sad about it all that I hardly know what to say to you. You promised so much to us all, and fair words and loving kindness do not seem to impress you in the least. My heart is so full, and my disappointment is so great that it is difficult to put in words what I feel is the result of your thoughtlessness and the wicked manner in which you are using up the patience I have had with you. Now, my dear boy, I want you to ask yourself if it is not time to leave your wicked and foolish ways. You will never have another such chance to make good, and to be properly prepared for the life you must follow when I am gone, and if you will not do what you should do with the chances we have given you, what will the result be then? It makes me sick at heart every time I think of it.

After much more of the same, The Doctor signed off "your affectionate Father," and then added a grim postscript, reminding his boy that in a few weeks it would be "just one year ago that you were sent home from Eaglebrook, and I beg of you not to have this repeated."

It is important to restore some proportion to this matter. The Doctor's letter followed a slip in his son's academic standing from very high to medium rank. At the time it was written my father had had no disciplinary troubles, but he soon would. At the time it was written he played the banjo in the school band, swam on the team, and was conspicuously good-willed. The school barber, called Mac, still remembers him: "Sure, Duke Wolff, big boy, handsome, plenty smart. His dad would get mad as blazes at him, he'd tell me about it. Say this for him, all the boys liked him, he could always raise a laugh at something silly or himself. That counts for something, you know, to be able to lift people out of the dumps with a laugh."

But The Doctor and The General fed each other's appetites for rancor, and devised increasingly sophisticated methods of settling Duke's hash. If he wouldn't do his work "as a soldier should do it," as The Doctor told his son, he must not be allowed trips with the other boy-soldiers to Syracuse, as The Doctor told The General. This particular punishment, if that is the description for an embargo on Syracuse, had a further purpose: The Doctor explained that he would like his son kept on campus "because of Arthur's impulsive nature and extravagant ideas, and I feel that it is time now to teach him something of the value of money, and the commodity it may purchase."

When my father returned to St. John's in 1924 he set about failure with a will. By year's end he had flunked or dropped every subject he took, and spent three weeks in April hospitalized for "nervous exhaustion," even then a euphemism for deep distress, and had run away from school three times.

My father mentioned St. John's to me only once, calling it "Manlius," as though he could not bring himself to say its proper name. From those crucial years of his boyhood he retained a single memory he would share, and it was appropriately bleak. Two cadets—was he one?—had set a small fire in the school gymnasium, and The General gathered the boys there at night, with the fire out but still smoking. He knew two boys had done the deed, and asked them to come forward and confess. When they did not he told the assembled cadets that they would remain in the gymnasium till he had a confession; they were free to mill about as they pleased, but not to leave the building. He watched them for several hours and then, as though by magic, named the guilty ones, two who had stuck fast to each other, speaking to no other boy. I guess I believe my father set fire to that gym, but whether he did or not, St. John's expelled him by the spring of 1925.

Under the influence of his cousin Arthur Samuels, an idol, my father had always assumed he would go to Princeton, where Samuels, '09, had been president of both the Triangle and Cottage Clubs. But now something drew him to the simplicity of Dartmouth as a first choice. Accordingly, The Doctor exiled his son in the fall of 1925 to The Clark School, in Holderness, New Hampshire, a place of even lower academic prominence than that from which he had just descended, a school where many dense Dartmouth hopefuls had been prepped.

The Clark School's memory of my father's academic year there is not happy. The headmaster wrote the headmaster of Duke's next institution (one school's trash is another school's treasure): "I am sorry that it is necessary for me to send you the grades of Arthur S. Wolff as they do not reflect much credit upon his work with us." (English: 62; geometry: 46; French: 28.) To add to the mess, The Doctor had a financial dispute with Dr. Clark, the school's owner and headmaster, over the recovery of fees after his son was sent down from Holderness.

At home at 217 North Beacon Street the summer of 1926, by now aged eighteen, my father got in hot water with the neighbors for making passes, some successful, at their maids and daughters. But his most serious offenses were financial: "He had gorgeous taste," Ruth remembers, and he liked to exercise it.

When he was as young as sixteen my father would travel to New York for "the best." He'd buy hand-knit sweaters and socks, have his shirts custom-tailored at

Saks or Brooks Brothers or Triplers, and bill what he bought to his mother. He was generous, would give his friends expensive clothes they, like their benefactor, would soon outgrow. He'd also bounce checks, but in amounts small enough for his mother to cover from her household account. As usual, he pushed his scams past the limit, and his father caught him. The Doctor frequently used gold in his laboratory, and one day his supply house received a call from someone who, after identifying himself as Dr. Wolff, placed an unusually large order, saying his son would soon appear to take delivery of it. Young Arthur got the gold, and his father got the bill.

After this incident my grandfather decided that he could not, would not, have his son at home, it was out of the question. At seventy-one he had earned some peace and self-respect, he wouldn't have under his roof a boy who troubled the neighbors' daughters and maids, who dressed like a popinjay and stayed out till all hours, who stole from his own father. So, after a few hard summer months in 1926, Dr. Wolff bundled up his son one last time and essayed to install him in a place where he would be someone else's problem, and might even be reformed.

The school this time was near home, in Cheshire, Connecticut, and was called Roxbury Academy, now Cheshire Academy. It had been established in the eighteenth century and had educated such Hartford personages as J.P. Morgan, but in the past few years had been in the hands of a venerated headmaster named Arthur Sheriff, who had turned the place into a tutoring school. Roxbury was especially popular with boys bound for Yale, and many of these were thick-headed but quick-footed and clever-handed scholar-athletes whose very high tuition was paid by loyal sons of Eli. Students received instruction from tutors one-to-one, so Roxbury was mostly a school for the rich.

My father—now known to his friends as Duke, for his noble airs—was offered to Mr. Sheriff in August of 1926, and he told the headmaster that Princeton, not Yale,

would suit him. After his interview it was noted that
Arthur S. Wolff II (as he chose to know himself, despising
the modifier *Jr.* even as his father must have despised it,
with its suggestion of close kinship between the men) "has
not studied but now means to get to work. The boy
stutters somewhat, though not badly enough to effect his
success, I think."

Soon Mr. Sheriff and Dr. Wolff were communicating
on friendly terms regarding the fate of the delinquent
young Duke. The Doctor was invited to lecture Roxbury
boys on his work as a medical expert at murder trials, and
he made a hit, showing lantern slides of the most grisly
details of man's inhumanity to man. Mr. Sheriff
frequently dined in Hartford with The Doctor, whose
principal ambition was that the headmaster serve as my
father's father.

Mr. Sheriff felt obliged to consult with The Doctor on
many matters touching the school's policies toward the
boy, now, at nineteen, almost a young man. One of these
was delicate, a matter involving Jesus Himself. My
grandmother, devout as she was, would impose her beliefs
on no one, and my father had not been inside the Temple
Beth Israel since he was a child. At Deerfield and at
Eaglebrook he had assimilated, or assimilated himself,
attending with more regularity than fervor the Congregational Church in Deerfield where Dr. Boyden chose to
worship. At St. John's my father announced himself to be
a Unitarian, and now at Roxbury had asked to attend the
Episcopal church in Cheshire. Mr. Sheriff asked to know
my grandfather's wishes regarding his son's religious
preferences. Dr. Wolff said the boy should worship where
he wished, should "have some discretion in this matter."

(During my fifth-form year at Choate I joined a
confirmation class offered by the headmaster, Rev.
Seymour St. John, to the end of leading his sheep into an
Episcopal heaven, that most exclusive of elective clubs. I
may have been brought every Sunday morning to the
reverend headmaster's feet by some sensation approx-
imating faith, but I was certainly there to enjoy the

God-sent opportunity to challenge his authority. This, then, was no small pleasure, to be licensed to argue fine letters of ecclesiastical law and chop logic—putatively as his equal—with The Head. One Sunday, however, a piper was to be paid, and I found myself on my knees at the altar of the Choate Chapel spouting the Apostle's Creed, testifying to my faith in the Trinity, and the Resurrection, even as a congregation of boys who knew me better than did the Lord giggled and made fart noises at my rigid back. In the front row sat my father, showing a thin smile. After the ceremony, the performance, he gave me a silver cigarette case, curved like a flask, a thoughtful gift for a new communicant at a school where smoking was punished by instant banishment from Choate's campus, records, and memory. Inscribed on the gold-washed interior of this case was a sentiment: *For Christ's Sake!*)

One of the first items to enter my father's file at Roxbury was an IOU scribbled in pencil on a calling card: *Received of Eddie O'Donnell 1 Yale vs Harvard football ticket—November 20, 1926.* Documentation of my father's liabilities multiplied, and by June of 1927 the motto captioning Duke's photograph in the yearbook *Rolling Stone* (O tempora! O mores!) was this, perhaps itself on loan from another: "All that he fails to borrow is knowledge."

A New Haven haberdasher, White, one of many who traveled to such schools as Roxbury to seduce boys with a display of garments, wrote Mr. Sheriff bluntly: "We have tried and tried but without success. He has never kept any of his promises. I believe he will never pay this bill. In the five years we have been showing at the Roxbury School I can safely say that he is the only boy who doesn't want to pay his bills."

Remedies were tried. My father was immediately put on a tight allowance, administered by Mr. Sheriff. But before The Doctor had an opportunity to settle his son's account at White's, only twelve days after the letter was mailed, Duke responded to that merchant's wavering faith with a procedure that became his signature. He called it, after one of the Oxbridge locutions he favored, "flogging the wogs": When a creditor whined too bitterly or rudely about one's debt, a chap had to show the flag, turn the screws a bit more, wot? So my father entered White's emporium across from the Taft Hotel for a bit of shopping the afternoon of a Yale baseball game, and drove up his debt from $45.50 to a bit over seventy-three dollars. White wrote again to Mr. Sheriff that young Mr. Wolff "wanted to purchase a pair of hose. He actually took the hose without the permission of our salesman and left the store. In other words, he took the hose without our permission."

There were suchlike episodes at Joseph Hardy, Inc., J. Press, John Howard, Inc.—plenty of places. There were letters like White's in great number in my father's Roxbury file, and I could read them with my eyes closed: there was astonishment that a cheeky pup would break his word to his elders, anger that he played his game even after its transparently unfair rules were known, wonder that he couldn't be chastened, wouldn't learn his place, continued to trick himself out like a gentleman fastidious about his person while he remained careless of his character. Among his classmates he made an impression as a "natty dresser."

As I read about the debts of that "natty dresser" I felt shame, decided he was merely a bad man, with shabby, canted values. Not complicated, simply off base. Or rather that is what I felt I ought to feel. It was my father, though, who taught me that we should distinguish in this life between what we feel and what we feel we should feel. That if we can distinguish between these things we may have access to some truths about ourselves.

The truth is that as I moved through the record of my father's debts and evasions I felt less shamed by it than diminished by its predictability. And then I fell on a letter from a clothier, Langrock, that put a new spin on my experience of my old man, and took my breath away. At first glance the thing looked run of the mill, a letter to Mr.

Sheriff asking him to dun The Doctor for about seventy-five dollars. My grandfather got the letter but, at the end of his string, refused to pay the debt. Mr. Sheriff then wrote my father's father: "So far as I can see the Langrock people took a chance and have only themselves to blame."

Thirty years later, an undergraduate at Princeton, I had run up a bill of several hundred dollars at Langrock, and couldn't pay it. I had other debts, quite a few, and was not too innocent to have an inkling where this would end. So, with the encouragement of several deans of behavior, I left college for a year of manual labor, to earn money to settle my accounts. Settle them, after misadventures, I did; my good name was restored to the books at Langrock, but I made no use of my account there. Nevertheless, one day I returned to my room to find a bill from Langrock. I opened the envelope and whistled: the bill was a leviathan, more than a thousand dollars. Less angry than amused I telephoned to explain that here was a case of mistaken something-or-other.

No, Langrock assured me, here was a simple case of debt. Certain suits and shirts and outer garments had been purchased from the Nassau Street store by Arthur S. Wolff III (he had now grown beyond those skimpy double pillars—*II*—yet accurately judged *IV* to be patently bogus, and mocked a classmate of mine who fashioned himself the *IVth* Someone of Akron), who wished them charged to his son.

My father, with his purchases, was long gone, to parts unknown to me. And so I made my speedy and unhappy way to the office of William D'Olier Lippincott, Princeton's Dean of Students. And Lippincott decided that I owed Langrock neither a legal nor a moral debt, and told me, with the adjustment of a word or two, "so far as I can see the Langrock people took a chance and have only themselves to blame."

Soon after my father began his studies at Roxbury he sat for an examination in English history, and I have a blue book with "Duke" scribbled in his hand at the top. The first sections were questions of fact, asking for place names and dates, and these he got wrong. Then he turned to a required essay on a British prime minister: "Benjamin Disraeli was a Jew, born in London in 1809. He was the son of a Jew who had turned Christian and received a careful private education. Disraeli was an English gentleman, and even the Queen, the late Victoria, thought well of him, even if he was a Jew…"

My father's studies, despite his own "careful private education," were not going well. So Mr. Sheriff wrote The Doctor one of those letters he was by now so used to reading:

Arthur's instructors, in general, report that he has a good mind woefully lacking in training. His understanding and his power of original thought are good. On the other hand, in concentration and thoroughness he is poor, and his memory is unreliable. This means that if he makes a conscious effort to overcome his mental weaknesses he can certainly be successful; but if he does not make the effort he must reconcile himself to having second-rate ability for the rest of his life.

I am writing this frankly, knowing that you will show the letter to Arthur and have a chance to discuss it with him. I wish to say for Arthur that I have found him always willing—almost too willing—to accept criticism, even though adverse; and have found also that the mistakes he has made are due more to thoughtlessness than to premeditation. Nevertheless, in his case, the very amiability of his faults is a bad thing, because it is largely indicative of instability of character. I have tried my best to impress this upon Arthur during the past two or three months, and do believe that to some extent I have succeeded.

It perhaps would be good for Arthur to know the impressions he makes upon his instructors, and to a certain extent upon the boys. One master, for example, says that "in the classroom he is inattentive and unstable." Another states that he is perhaps unintentionally rude in manner and lacks discipline of mind and tongue, and that he has superior ability but fails to do himself justice. Another states that he insists upon bluffing his way through and does not use his ability. Still another mentions the fact that he has ability but that he is hazy and inaccurate because of superficiality. And from another instructor I find that Arthur is "noisy, restless and too assertive."

I quote these impressions of the masters so frankly so that Arthur may be able to see cold written the impressions he gives of himself. It would be comical if it were not also tragic to think how far Arthur has allowed himself to be led astray by his instinct for buffoonery. It is not only among the masters that he makes such impressions as these but among many of the boys as well, much as they like him in spite of his faults; certainly not for the reasons he may think. I think that fundamentally he is a boy well worth saving. I think that he has it in him to be a very good, capable man...

The headmaster, winding down his summary of my father's prospects and vices, did not neglect the usual issue: "This carelessness of Arthur in incurring debt is perhaps his worst fault."

In short, Duke wouldn't climb aboard the train. He never would. Nothing in Mr. Sheriff's report sounds to me out of character except the words "amiability" and "buffoonery," and these represent, I think, a misreading of Duke's manner. My father was capable of violent anger when he was faced with someone's cruelty, or what he perceived as cruelty. But his deepest rebellion was quiet, a Bartleby-like refusal to play ball, a preference for the declined gambit. So untroubled was he by negation that he could afford his amiable manner, which came not from an eagerness to please but from a cooling, in early age, of those fevers that provoke young men to run fast to mount that very train my father had no wish to ride.

And what did his schoolmates think of him? The motto accompanying his photograph in the 1928 *Rolling Stone* describes him as "a slave to all the follies of the great." But he had standing, was a member of Lamba Phi, the snappiest school fraternity. He swam crawl on the school

team, and was a tackle on the football team; he played
banjo for the jazz band and the orchestra, and was an
editor of the yearbook. One classmate remembers "a
friendly and likable guy, sociable and humorous."
Another looks at a photograph of the assembled school
and finds "Art in the front row, sitting on the ground in
knickers and argyles, in his usual sartorial splendor." His
stammer is recalled, and the way he would joke about it.
He is remembered as tall, self-assured, articulate and—
above all—generous and warm.

He spent weekends in New York with Sidney Wood, a
classmate and tennis champion, and at King's Point with
another classmate, Walter Chrysler, Jr. With these and
Hartford friends he traveled to Vassar and Smith and
Bryn Mawr, and often there were parties in the houses of
absent parents whose children were wealthy, idle and
without variation Christian, bearing the surnames
Griggs, Rice, Glover, Smith, Lester and Gillette. Among
these affluent drifters my father was a leader, and where
he led trouble followed.

The Doctor's rhetorical manner has been observed: it was
avuncular and aggrieved, laden with the vocabulary of
disaster. The martyr's lament has been a family affliction.
It's bad tradition: blaming, whining, scolding; my father
would indulge in it when he was drunk, which was seldom
but memorable. From before the age when my voice
changed till after I was old enough to vote I knew there'd
be hell to pay if midnight passed and he was not yet home.
I'd lie tensed in bed waiting for his return from a party,
listening for the crunch of tires on our gravel drive, or the
low growl of his voice as he stumbled hanging up his coat.
Then I'd hear ice rattle in a glass, and lugubrious mutters,
angry cries of unspecified pain. I'd hear my father come
toward my room, stand in front of my shut door. I'd lie
with my back to the door, feigning sleep, but he'd hear me
catch my breath from fear when he opened it and spilled
light on me. He'd stand there looking down at me, and
grunt a nasty laugh, and then sit heavily at the foot of my

bed. He knew I was awake; he knew me inside out. That I was counterfeiting sleep inflamed his resentments, and he'd begin to talk to me, never raising his voice from its exhausted monotone, slurring his words, throwing off static: *worse than your mother...kicked my ass... did everything for you, got nothing back...not worth a nickel, never will be...sorrow and abuse...I'm finished...what's the point...nibshit kid...nibshit...*

The next morning, desolate and hungover, he'd recollect what he'd said, joke about it, promise it would never again happen, that what he said when he was drunk was plain crazy, would I forgive him? Please? Of course, of course. Because I believed it *was* plain crazy, a fever he had caught that had now cooled. And because I knew that while it would happen again, it would not happen soon, and so I was relieved, even grateful.

Now, looking over letters about my father from his father, I think I see the source of that awful vitriol, that cruelly inappropriate language of woeful condemnation. Shortly before a Christmas vacation from Roxbury, my father borrowed some money from a school friend to whom he already owed money and hired a car and drove it to Hartford with another friend to meet a couple of girls at a hotel. He broke, that is, a few school rules, and for this he was punished by Mr. Sheriff, who wrote The Doctor about the episode and its aftermath.

My grandfather was beside himself with fury, and with something else, a lacerating self-pity from which my father could have no possibility of appeal. The Doctor wrote Mr. Sheriff about "my son Arthur's unmanly and disgraceful conduct. It is more than humiliating to me...I do not know what to say more, for this is such a disgrace to me, and it troubles me so much, as it causes me so much sorrow."

The headmaster sought to calm The Doctor: "We don't feel that the boy was guilty of anything but just foolishness." He was, after all, twenty. But Duke's father would not hear a word in the boy's favor, and soon even my grandmother indulged a rare display of temper and anguish: "I cannot bring myself to say Dear Arthur to you." After this salutation she told her son "your father says that he doesn't want you home for the Holidays, not after your behavior. He is through with you. I doubt that you are gaining anything out of this treatment of your parents. Perhaps you are happy, we are not." Then a signature, without valediction: "Your Mother, Alas."

The matter did not end there. A crime had been committed against The Doctor, who sprayed lamentations and complaints at Mr. Sheriff:

> This whole thing greatly mortifies me, and to be in a position such as this is very painful, for I assure you I do not deserve it, and it seems I have no shelter to which I can apply for comfort, for I fear that Arthur by his lack of attention to what is right shuts his heart to the echoes of those sounds against which he shuts his ears. His disobedience still becomes more poignant when it is conducted in such a manner as to give no opportunity of protest until it is a fait accompli, or when it is so blended with good humor and external decorum as to think that no one can see it but the conscious victim.
>
> This troubles you, however, and I should not pour out my soul to such a busy man as you are, and I hope you will forgive this outcry against the pain my wounds are causing me.

What does this mean? Sense and syntax break before this storm of grief, at once overwrought and stuffy, self-conscious and self-lacerated. These locutions are less the effects of a cause than pathological symptoms. I wonder if such exaggerated expression was ever turned toward my father in praise, pleasure, love? I listed in mute terror as my father listened my torts against him, real and fancied. But I listened, too, when he called me the best, brightest, most loving, most loved, apple of his eye, pride of his life, one to whom all things were open. I wonder if The Doctor ever said healing words to his patient, his son? I want to argue my father's case to Dr. Wolff, to beg that monster of rectitude, not so terribly injured by his son as his letter imagines: *Ease up a little, old man.*

4

Mr. Sheriff gave Yale his opinion of my father, an applicant: "Wolff is a boy with considerable ability and very little backbone. He is amiable and good-natured, but lacks determination and steadfastness." Perhaps Duke could follow Arthur Samuels (by then editor of *Harper's Bazaar*, and a personage in the worlds of music, theater, and publishing) to Princeton? Mr. Sheriff was candid—"I wish some way could be found to impress upon him the ridiculousness of his present attitude. He seems to be quite contented to be a featherweight and a buffoon when he might well be intellectually in the van"—and Princeton thought he'd be better off in some other college's van.

Well, what place *would* have him? One, at least, the classic catchall for sun-struck, rich dumbbells, the University of Miami. Duke entered in the fall of 1928, Miami's third year as an institution, and right away he was in trouble. Enrolled in seven courses his first semester—three of them in literature, the others Spanish, French, history and economics—he flunked them all—or rather he was obliged to withdraw from them "on account non-attendance classes" in the registrar's abbreviated style. He managed to exceed even Miami's liberal notion of fit deportment: my father and some half dozen friends occupied apartments in an off-campus building, where their activities soon scandalized community proprieties, to the extent that the college president, B.F. Ashe, after warning the scholars that it was "entirely improper" to entertain "young women" in their rooms, sacked my father and three of his friends on the first day of 1929.

Eight weeks later President Ashe was again at his typewriter, this time assuring Miami's chief of police that Duke and his accomplices, "who did not conduct themselves in a proper fashion," had no association with his college. The president had been made fretful by word that "these boys are still in town" and by "reports, which may be exaggerated, about their actions."

The reports were not exaggerated. My father did his first overnight in jail in Miami, for setting off fire alarms, driving drunk in his Chrysler convertible (a gift from The Doctor to celebrate Duke's admission to Miami) and being a "public nuisance." While The Doctor and my grandmother were spending a year in Europe, my father remained in Florida. When he wasn't up to mischief he swam with Buster Crabbe and Johnny Weismuller in an aquatic circus, playing exhibition matches of water polo. He also speculated in racing greyhounds: my father's ran fast as dogs went, but slower than other greyhounds.

When his parents returned from Europe, Duke, twenty-one, allowed himself to be brought home to Hartford. On the night of the Wolff family reunion my father drove his Chrysler along a sidewalk, and brought it to rest with its grille poking about eighteen inches through an Elm Street shop window. He lived at home the next two years, and what that was like for his parents and for him may be imagined.

During this time Duke began to read with a consuming appetite, which he never satisfied. His first love was French and English fiction of the eighteenth and nineteenth centuries, but he also took up the work of

Joyce and Williams and Eliot and Stein and Hemingway; his sense of them as belonging to him in a comfortable way was not the least of his legacies to me.

In late 1930 he had another go at formal education. To paper over his Florida disgraces he or someone got a family friend at G. Fox & Co., Hartford's best department store, to write *To Whom It May Concern* that during the exact period of his stay in Miami "Mr. Arthur Wolff has been in the employ of this Corporation. I am pleased to say that he has been most industrious, and shown great application to his work. He is leaving of his own accord." This was signed, putatively, by Moses Fox, President. The letter accompanied my father's application to the University of Pennsylvania.

He was not admitted to the university proper but to a program taught by its regular faculty called College Courses for Teachers. He matriculated in January of 1931, enrolled in seven courses. Six of these were divided between English and history, and he received credits (and mediocre grades) in four. The seventh course was in philosophy. Ethics. Duke flunked it.

He lasted a semester, and may or may not have wangled his way into DKE. Duke's Hartford friend, a bona fide student at the bona fide University of Pennsylvania, thinks he was a Deke: "It was very unusual for a Jew in those days to get into a non-Jewish house. Maybe he didn't get around to telling anyone he was Jewish."

I wonder what he wanted. Not simply to be liked, though he was. To partake of the excellence so much discussed at home? Probably. But he had attained nothing, and it must have seemed he never would. Still, he knew how to dress, speak, and carry himself like a gentleman. He stood tall and erect, and wore soft tweeds and a waistcoat with its bottom button undone (fat Henry VIII had begun the custom, he told me) and a gold watch chain looped through its middle buttonhole. (It would have been like a Duke Wolff watch chain to have no timepiece secured to its end.) My father was well-read, sardonic, informed, a declared expert on everything. He had physical courage, collateral to his general disregard of consequences, but not much stamina.

His roommate at the University of Pennsylvania thought he was "just a great guy. He was a good friend to me. I loaned him money, and he always paid it back."

(I was told this in front of a cousin, Ruth Fassler, and when she heard it she said: "Come off it! He paid you back! Who are you kidding?" But the roommate added encomia to my father: "He took my fur coat once, disappeared with it; I thought it was a goner, but at the end of the weekend he brought it back. He was okay, really." And my cousin said: "Great, he wasn't a thief. A regular gent we have here.")

While he was loose in Hartford during the Depression many people felt his touch. (Ruth Fassler said: "Duke wasn't poor. He was broke.") Bill Haas walked into a downtown shoe store one afternoon and found the usually dour manager grinning ear to ear.

"Why so chipper?" Bill asked him.

"Duke Wolff just borrowed a sawbuck from me."

"Jesus, that's nothing to lift a man's spirits. You'll never see it again."

"Yeah, but now I've given, he can't ask me again. I got off cheap, most guys go ten or twenty."

One of my cousins said: "I always trusted him, and he treated me well. He was a good-looking guy, and good company."

Another cousin in the room that day said: "He was my friend."

And a third cousin looked straight at me, and said: "He was a gonif, a schnorrer. He was just a bum. That's all he ever was."

No: he was more than that. A college friend recalls that when he told my father his troubles, Duke listened patiently, and gave good advice. Duke loved to give advice. When Bill Haas was in his prime—running a large tobacco business, raising a family—and my father was down and out, on the run from the law and "flat bust" (as he liked to say), Bill saw him, for the first time in years, sitting out a red light on State Street in Hartford. My father waved to his cousin, a man who had his number if anyone had it, and told him: "Your hair's wrong. Don't try to cover that bald spot. When you lose hair on your crown you should cut short what's left, like I do." The light went green, the old man put his unpaid-for MG in gear and shot a last instruction over its stern: "Don't let them use electric clippers. Shears only." And that day Bill Haas had his hair cut short, and it is short today.

I know little about my father's doings after he left the University of Pennsylvania and before he met my mother five years later. He divided his time between Hartford and New York, with a runaway trip in 1933 to Europe. Years later a raffish character, a bass player, approached my father in a seedy Los Angeles jazz club, where I had been taken to hear Jack Teagarden. I was thirteen, and interested in the musician's story, which embarrassed my father. It seems the musician and Duke had shipped out as deckhands on a cattle boat bound for Bremerhaven from Boston. They carried their instruments, bass fiddle for the friend, banjo and four-string guitar for my father. They arrived in Europe broke, without papers, and jumped ship; the plan was to find work as jazzmen. It was not a sound plan, and soon my father collect-wired The Doctor for passage money home. In place of money he got a reply, also sent collect: DID NOT RECEIVE YOUR CABLE STOP WILL NOT RECEIVE YOUR NEXT CABLE EITHER STOP FATHER.

My father borrowed his way home, and worked at menial jobs around Hartford, even picking tobacco for cigar wrappers with stoop-labor migrants for a few weeks. Broke, he nevertheless learned to fly, and fell in love for good with airplanes, but again his father, without malice or intention, diluted his pride. The week after my father's first solo flight there was a headline in the *Hartford Times:* PHYSICIAN PILOTS PLANE AT 77: "Always possessed of an adventurous and inquiring spirit, Dr. Wolff piloted an airplane at the age of 77 without any previous instruction. While riding in a plane over Brainard Field, he took over the controls."

Not long after, Bill Haas heard Duke tell someone he had had a trying day, flying the mail from Hartford to Boston through a thunderstorm. Haas called my father on his fiction, told listeners that Duke could fly, but not that well, and had never flown the mail. My father exploded at this betrayal with the hurt anger of someone truly wronged, and he left Haas with the burden of believing that, yes, he *had* wronged his cousin: "I shouldn't have butted in," he told me.

The closest Duke could come to a job in aviation was to clean engine parts at Pratt & Whitney for two bits an hour. While he was at this work Duke's comrades struck the plant, and my father was used, successfully, as the workers' and managers' go-between. He was not in later life ashamed of this work, so I learned of it from him, but that is almost all of his Hartford life I do know from him. He worked elbow-deep in bins of gunk that cut grease and carbon from odds and ends of airplane engines due for overhaul. He'd then take his lunch from a fitted wicker picnic basket that held sandwiches with their crusts removed by the Norwegian cook, a linen napkin, and a fruit knife to pare an apple's scrubbed skin. He did not discourage these dandy airs, just as he liked to be called Duke and allowed himself to be driven to a strike meeting by his father's chauffeur in his father's Rolls-Royce.

In 1932, at twenty-four, he tried to enlist in the Navy, and was rejected for his stammer. Two years later he was tentatively accepted for Army officers' training school until a major in the personnel office at Governor's Island, New York, where Duke had enlisted, received a reply to his routine query to Manlius for confirmation of my father's accomplishments there: "Mr. Wolff did not complete four years of R.O.T.C., nor was he a Second Lieutenant of the machine gun company while at this institution."

So until 1936 my father mostly drank too much at parties, played the banjo and piano, read novels and poems, became a fabled clothes-wearing man, and waited for something to happen to him.

5

Rosemary Loftus, my mother, met Duke during the great Hartford flood of March 1936. The Connecticut River's excitement had stopped the city dead, and my father with half a dozen of his sidekicks had holed up in a couple of suites at the Hueblein Hotel, where they ran out of girls before they ran out of gin. My mother was nineteen, with time on her hands. After Sunday mass a "fast" friend asked if she'd like a blind date and my mother, bored, said sure, she'd take potluck.

The first time my mother saw him, my father was sitting in the back seat of a friend's new convertible, with a handsome girl giggling on his lap. My father was too informal for my mother's taste: "He seemed tight, and he needed a shave. He was wearing battered sneakers and white flannels and no socks. He was not an impressive figure."

My mother was put off by a car filled with people—Walter and Nervy and Piggy and Jack and Duke—who seemed to have known one another forever, who traded private jokes that excluded her. They had all been drinking, and my mother didn't much like to drink.

Still, she went with them to the Hueblein. Rosemary liked to be a good sport.

When she got to the hotel, and went upstairs to Duke's room, he offered her a drink. Was he her blind date? She never found out. To my father's astonishment Rosemary declined a cup filled with warm gin, just as an Air Corps colonel emerged from an adjoining bedroom buttoning his fly and grinning. Rosemary said she would like to be returned home.

Her innocence, pep, and girlish beauty—alone or in combination—powerfully attracted my father, and he asked to see her again, named a night. She said she would be baby-sitting then, so he asked if he could sit with her and talk. Without knowing exactly why, Rosemary accepted this proposal.

When my mother told me this story a couple of years ago, speaking with her measured, flat, accentless voice, I had just finished reading "In Dreams Begin Responsibilities," Delmore Schwartz's autobiographical imagining of his parents' courtship, a premonition of their bitter divisions. The story's narrator slumps in a shabby theater, where he watches his parents come together in a crude movie which he tries betimes to interrupt, disturbing the audience. He calls out to the figures jittering across the screen: "Don't do it. It's not too late to change your minds, both of you. Nothing good will come of it, only remorse, hatred, scandal, and two children whose characters are monstrous."

As my mother began her story of disappointment, humiliation and want, infrequently relieved by affection and satisfaction, I didn't feel that way at all. I sat across from her, cheering my father on, cheering her on, marveling at the chance conjunction that joined them, made my brother, made me, shaped us all. My mother talked, her voice low, even, calm and resigned, anxious to get the facts right.

(Before I began to work on this book there had for many years been a great distance between my mother and me, a chilling formality. My mother is not cold, and she is not stiff. She has been unfailingly warm and loving with my boys, and with my wife. She laughs a lot, teases, likes to be teased. But neither of us, I think, trusted the other's love.

There is much we don't know about each other. Between the ages of twelve and fifteen I saw my mother three times, for a total of about ten days. Between the ages of fifteen and twenty-six I never saw her. When I was twelve my mother was thirty-two, still unfinished, not yet what she would become. I had known her under terrible pressure, but when the pressure was relieved, or she learned to live with it, my mother returned to her natural gaiety and energy. During the years I did not see my mother she was a community leader, a joiner, an advice-giver, a sportswoman, a political activist.

When my mother and I had discussed my childhood in the past, we had never gotten very far before one did the other some unintended injury. I once mentioned to my mother a barbecue restaurant "we" had liked, and my mother replied: "I used to go there, too." To her *we* meant simply my father and me, which is what it usually meant to me, but not at that moment. Against such stupid barriers, then, we stumbled, again and again, and we learned, despite mutual good will, to defend ourselves with distance.

When my mother agreed to help me with this book, when she put her life in my hands, I decided to interview her with a tape recorder, in the hope that by talking to it my mother could lose sight of me, forget that a judge sat listening. This cold instrument worked wonders for us. My mother opened up while the spools turned, reached into her memory with self-assurance and ease, relaxed her defenses.

It wasn't until I transcribed her words, twelve hours of talk, that I appreciated the full force of her gift to me. I had been prepared to save my mother from those little gaffes of speech that everyone commits, errors of tense and number and parallelism, the *ahs* and *ughs* and

I-means and *you-knows* that deface interviews. And because my mother is not an articulate woman I had expected to give her special protection against her infelicities of speech. But I was wrong about what I thought I had heard her say to my tape recorder; perhaps I have been wrong about what I heard her say as long as I have known her. For here were finished sentences and paragraphs, calculated and precise. We have no documents in our family to restore my mother's past with my father to the present, and that was what my mother wished to do. She had thought hard about it, and wanted me to have it, as it was, plain. When I asked a hard question, my mother paused, and tried hard to answer it. If I didn't know what to ask, my mother asked for me.

I believe she may have paid a heavy toll for her precision and honesty, that her speech in this book may appear cold, unfeeling. It is no such thing. It is respectful of particulars, without false piety or sentiment. What my mother told me of our history brought us together again, and we had a long way to journey from there to here.)

Duke appeared at the house where Rosemary was baby-sitting, and behaved himself. He sat across a coffee table from her and told stories at his own expense, entertained and charmed her. "But he didn't attract me."

When my mother met him, my father was living at home. The Doctor was dying of stomach cancer, and Duke spent much time with him. What could they have said to each other, so late in the season? Duke got by on a dollar a day and all he could borrow; his friends Gifford Pinchot and Nervy Smith and Wellington Glover and Jack Lester and Piggy Gillette all had plenty, enough for everyone, and soon my mother began going with my father and these people to parties in Hartford and New York and Boston and New Haven.

"Although I was not what you'd call innocent, I had never run around with people who were quite so open about their mischief. Your father led this group; he seemed, then, to prefer weak friends.".

If Rosemary's feeling for Duke was so tepid, why did she bother with him?

"The pressure at home was terrible."

Yes, it was. At the funeral of Commander Stephen A. Loftus my brother wept. My mother, his mother, the commander's only daughter, asked why. "What's so sad?" (In fact my brother was moved to tears not by a dead man in a box but by the occasion, a military ceremony at Arlington National Cemetery. My brother was in the Army, and liked the guns and uniforms and flags, was moved to tears by rows of crosses.)

My mother's father was a time-serving prig and bully; he was narrow, envious, bigoted, self-important, pea-cock-proud and snake-mean. His parents had come to America from Ireland during the potato famines, and he and several brothers were born here in awful poverty.

A family photograph taken at the turn of the century, where they fetched up, shows weathered peasants, the teenagers looking forty, dressed in shiny black worsted church clothes. The brothers' wrists hang from frayed, stiff jacket cuffs, and the sleeves are too short. Everyone but the eldest brother wears a hand-me-down, and far down the line comes Mother's father, the only Loftus with clean fingernails. My mother pointed to his brothers: *This one died in Ludlow in the mines, a strike or a cave-in, can't remember which; that one killed a railroad bull, and went to prison; this gentle-looking boy just disappeared...*

The second youngest, Stephen, went to sea in 1903 as a cabin boy, and came out of the Navy a commander in 1944. He was what they call a Mustang, a man with brilliantly spit-shined shoes who pulled himself up through the ranks. He served during two world wars and never, whether from luck or cunning, heard a shot fired in anger. Once he was court-martialed for having cut with water a few thousand bottles of ketchup. He was a chief mess officer at Pearl Harbor then and had found a way to shave costs. For his offense he got a reprimand: he hadn't

pocketed the savings, wasn't venal, was just a bootlicker.
He was hated by his men and a joke to his fellow officers,
who endured him for his efficiency and unwavering
conviction that military regulations were divinely inspired.

And what a tyrant he was at home! He married Mary
Lucille Powers in 1915, a year before my mother was
born. My grandmother, called Mae, was sweet, with
gentle Irish good looks, raven hair, high color on high
cheeks, blue eyes. She was twenty-five—a Denver
telephone operator with a weak heart from rheumatic
fever—when she married the up-and-coming sailor.
Rosemary's mother was the daughter of a domestic
servant and a manual laborer on the Denver and Rio
Railroad who had stowed away from Ireland, where he
got himself in political trouble.

The heart has its mysteries. Stephen Loftus, awful as he
was, was handsome in a frosty, stiff-backed way. He was a
good dancer, ambitious, cocksure. My only memory of
him is set near Atlantic City, in Margate, New Jersey,
where he had retired from the Navy. I was nine, and he
had just taught me to tie my shoes the Navy way. I am in
his debt for this, only this. My shoes have never come
untied since. Pleased with his powers of instruction, he
took me for a brisk stroll, what he called a "constitution-
al," along the boardwalk. His shoes were tiny, and he
clicked his heels in a metronomic beat against the rotting
planks as we walked. I paused for a moment to watch the
Atlantic rollers break against the beach, and he gripped
my shoulder, just a bit harder than he should have gripped
it.

"You're like your father," he told me. "Wasting your
time, dreaming it away."

Then he sat me down on a bench, and gave me a stubby
pencil and a three-by-five spiral notebook, and instructed
me to record verbatim all that he was about to tell me, that
what he was going to say could turn my life off its
reef-bound course, out toward the open waters of success.
We sat hunched together. He was so clean, I remember, as

smooth as a new tombstone, and his skin was pale as
skimmed milk. He wore a thick, black wool greatcoat,
even on that sunny day. His breath was foul as he
confided in me, and corrected my spelling as I transcribed
his secrets. I didn't know what the hell he was talking
about, something about the tidal rhythms of the stock
market, and the nutritional benefits of uncracked wheat.
He would speak, and tap the notebook's pages while the
wind whipped at us, perceptibly lifting his hairpiece. I had
never before seen a hairpiece, didn't comprehend what
was happening to the top of this man's head. His fingers
were long and delicate, and their nails were manicured.
He was, perhaps, simply crazy. Later, when my mother
took me to see Roy Rogers' horse Trigger dive into a
swimming pool off a high board at the end of the Steel
Pier, I asked her why her father seemed so angry all the
time. When she laughed too long and too hysterically at
my question, I failed to guess that at that moment, so near
that awful man, she was probably a little crazy, too.

Later the commander tried to kill himself. He waded
into the reflection pool in front of the Lincoln Memorial
wearing dress blues and his sword. The water was ten
inches deep, and he came out wet and puzzled. The park
police told my mother he wept when they fished him out,
and helped dry him off. She wouldn't believe that her
father could weep. He died in a Navy hospital, sometimes
sticky with false and desperate sentiment, and sometimes
mean. He lay hooked up to pipes and wires by people
indifferent to his character, and threatened to cut
everyone out of his will when in truth he hadn't a thing to
leave, and he died without a friend, or even an enemy.

My mother was born with pneumonia in Chicago while
her father was at sea in the Dardanelles. The birth was
hard on her mother, but there was money for a nurse, and
later a maid, and my grandmother, a pacific woman,
didn't complain, and gave her daughter love in abundance
when they both recovered from the birth.

The Navy moved the Loftus family to San Diego,

Paterson, N.J., Bremerton (where my uncle Stephen was born eight years after my mother), and then, for a long stay, to Honolulu. Mrs. Loftus had been instructed to have no more children after my mother was born, but her husband wanted a son, and she wanted to oblige. The boy was delivered by the principles of Christian rather than medical science because her husband decided his wife's illnesses were symptoms of a failure of spirit and will.

My mother grew up a tomboy in Honolulu, and as happy as she would ever be. She mothered her baby brother, surfed, studied at Punaho and had boyfriends who put her to no other use than as a companion.

When she went to the Mainland at fourteen, and to Beverly Hills High, she was screen-struck. (My mother has always been a dreamer; this is not the least of her virtues; she believes in the Big Break, the bank-busting lottery ticket, the grand prize in the sweepstakes, the place with the perfect climate. Now, past sixty, she says that if her ship ever comes in she'll buy the biggest goddamned Winnebago anyone ever saw, and laugh herself to death wheeling it back and forth across the country.) While she was at Beverly Hills High, waiting to be discovered by the movies, boys discovered her. They didn't use her very well; few of them ever would. She was saucy and cute, made herself up to look like Carole Lombard, and at fifteen was queen of a Rose Bowl float; right there, head of the parade, was her pretty face in a newsreel close-up! She waited for a studio to call; none called.

When Rosemary was sixteen the family moved to Hartford, where her mother died. Mae never had the strength of other people. My mother would not flat out accuse her father of murder, but something awful went on in Hartford, some pain was permitted to continue because of that man's stubborn preference for Christian Science, and his lack of compassion. Oh, he was a special case: he spanked my mother after dinner every night on the principle that while he didn't wish to trouble himself with specifics, she must have been guilty of *some* misdemeanor that day. She soon learned to take advantage of the inevitability of her punishment by deserving it: having a smoke, fooling with the boys, stealing change from her father's pockets, lying to him.

When his wife died my grandfather insisted at once that Rosemary quit William Hall High School to care for his son and his household. So at a stroke, my mother lost everything—mother, love, school and hope. Even money: during the late twenties there had been plenty around, the fruit of her father's investments at a time when dancing bears could make stock market killings, but during The Great Sorting Out of 1929, he had been sorted out.

There was something else, too: "At night Daddy always wanted to kiss me goodnight, and he'd hold me much too close. The relationship was not at all what I thought it should be, between a father and daughter."

My mother persuaded this man to let her visit some old school friends in Hollywood for a couple of weeks. She went west by train, and meant never to come back. She dreamt of becoming a dress designer, but couldn't get a job even as a salesclerk in that Depression year of 1934. She moved in with some "fast" girls who advised her to sell herself. She thought about it, seriously. She was hungry. Her father had encouraged her to smoke to keep her appetite and the food bills in check, and one day in a drugstore she took a deep drag on a cigarette and fainted from hunger.

Then a man made promises he didn't mean to keep, and my mother discovered she was pregnant, and didn't know where to turn. So she came home to her father, who arranged an abortion. And he pushed his interest in his daughter even further than before:

"He excused what he did, what he tried to do, by saying he was just testing me after my trouble in California, to see how oversexed I was. I was eighteen. It was the sort of thing you just don't forget. Ever. Every time after that night when he came near me I stiffened, which is why when he was old and senile, helpless and dying and in pain, I didn't feel anything."

When she met my father, a couple of promising affairs

with young Hartford gentlemen had come unstuck. My mother didn't understand why, all she knew for sure was that she was anxious to live with a man other than her father, "any man." She had no ambitions now for a career: "In those days, the only way out was to get married and hope you got a better life than the one you had before."

By those standards my father was okay, marginal. Rosemary could see that he loved her, and she let him press ahead with a kind of courtship. The Doctor died in June of the year my parents met, and my mother never saw him, but soon after the funeral my grandmother Harriet invited Rosemary and her brother and father to dinner at 217 North Beacon Street. The Navy man, humiliated that his daughter would traffic with a Jewboy, went with contemptuous reluctance. My cousin Ruth was there; it was an important occasion for my father. Ruth despised my grandfather on sight, saw that he was a bully, that his young son was terrified of him. She noticed his awful table manners, at once fastidious and incorrect, and his banal conversation and the skinny, mean wrists poking from his starched cuffs.

Ruth liked my mother immediately, saw in her a relentless innocence and willingness to pick herself up to try again. "But there must have been something wrong with her if she would marry Duke." Ruth's too hard on them; they were trying for something better than what they had known.

They were married in January of 1937, rain-drenched, standing in the parlor of a Westchester County justice of the peace. My mother calls the occasion "that ridiculous ceremony." A gang of Duke's married friends had tagged along: "All they cared about was that Duke got married so that he'd be as bad off as they were, trapped like them."

My mother tells me this placidly, without bitterness or much regret, with no evident sense that it touches me, this "ridiculous ceremony." I ask my mother:

"Did you love my father, ever?"

She studies this question with a kind of disinterested

curiosity: "No, I never loved him. Not in the conventional sense. I never could understand what my feelings were toward him. We had some good times together, and there was some affection. But I never loved him. The act of making love, for example, I did not enjoy. So he probably didn't, either."

From some joyless union, a month after my parents were married, I was conceived. My mother once told me I was a "mistake," and another time she told me I wasn't, and then again that I was. I guess I was a "mistake." My mother seldom measures her words, is capable of the most startling bursts of candor, and I guess I was what she told me fifteen years ago I was.

This should not surprise me: Duke and Rosemary lived in a Milford apartment after they were married, and they were as close as close can be to flat broke. Duke worked for a while at Sikorsky Aircraft in Bridgeport; my mother doesn't remember what he did, only that he wore overalls to work, earned fifteen dollars a week and was fired for absenteeism. An employment agency then got him a job as a night rewrite man on *The Bridgeport Telegram*, and again he was fired for absenteeism, for which read hangovers. My mother earned a dollar a day from a Bridgeport welcome wagon, and threw up every morning.

My father stayed home reading, and waited for the settlement of The Doctor's estate. "I'm sure he was bored to death with me," my mother remembers. "Every night someone came down from Hartford to entertain him. I wasn't good company. I used to sulk and pout. He didn't like to be criticized by me. His friends didn't criticize him; they had no conversation except what had happened the night before. Nothing very interesting had happened the night before."

When my grandfather died his obituary ran down two columns of the front page of the June 22 *Hartford Times;* the following day the *Courant* ran an editorial memorializing The Doctor's "service to humanity."

The pallbearers were Hartford Jews, old-timers in the city, a drygoods wholesaler, a plumbing contractor and former health commissioner, a wine merchant, a tobacco grower. These men disapproved of my father. He understood. He told Bill Haas: "I've been a rotten son. I'm going to make it up to Mother." The funeral service was small and private, without flowers, and so was the burial at Beth Israel cemetery. I wonder if my father said *Kaddish,* the Hebrew prayer read by a son for his dead father? I wonder if my father knew what *Kaddish* was? He never told me, and so made certain I could never say such a prayer above his grave.

It was assumed that my grandfather's will, drawn when Duke was twenty, would reflect The Doctor's disapproval of his spend thrift son. This did not prove to be so. It was the least vindictive of documents. From the sum of his cash and securities my grandmother was to take the first fifty thousand dollars. My father was to have the next fifty, and all that was left was to go to his widow. When she died, her estate was to be held in trust for my father till he was thirty, and was then to go to him without condition.

Fifty thousand was then a mighty sum, and it seemed that my parents were presently to be elevated from their low estate in Milford. But when the affairs of The Doctor were plumbed, and their angles unraveled, it became evident that Duke's deliverance to Number One Easy Street was to be delayed. There was no fifty thousand, not for him and not for his mother.

He had without Harriet's knowledge mortgaged their house on North Beacon Street for twenty-five thousand dollars in order to treat them both to a final and very grand tour of Europe during 1929 and 1930. The house was sold, and the mortgage paid off. Then the toys and furnishings of a lifetime went on the block. When the sales ended there was enough to purchase my grandmother a modest annuity. She rented a tiny flat on Farmington Avenue, and was as ever chipper. So my father inherited fifty thousand dollars, but didn't, from his spendthrift father; he finally understood that he had no net beneath the wire he was walking.

Shortly after the estate was settled there was, in the way of these things, a bitter dispute between my father and some of his cousins. Duke had either sold some of The Doctor's optical equipment entrusted to him by his mother, or he had taken it without her permission. Whatever happened (and even now the principals won't discuss it) caused my father to look west. My mother, no lover of Connecticut and a dreamer of sun-dreams, was happy to try her luck elsewhere.

My grandmother bought them a new car, a Ford phaeton, and sent them away with her blessing. And so they lit out for the Pacific—with me in my mother's belly, making her sick—without reason to hope that anything good could possibly come of their move. But as both would later tell me, they were almost happy.

6

I was born in Hollywood. Was a baby in Redondo Beach and a little squirt in Palos Verdes. Drove east at four in a twelve-cylinder Packard convertible to New York. Father went to England. I heard the radio tell about Pearl Harbor, my second or third memory, at the Elm Tree Inn, Farmington, Connecticut. Mother drove us to Colorado Springs, to see her brother. The mountains bored her, we returned to California, Hermosa Beach. Father came home. He bought a tract house in Chula Vista, where we lived a few weeks. Cross-country to Birmingham, Alabama, a huge, four-columned Greek Revival manse. I began school. Mother took me away, north to Oak Bluffs, south to Dallas. Then Atlanta, a rooming house on Peach Tree Battle where Mother interrupted Father, who was reading *Treasure Island* aloud, to tell him a bomb had been dropped somewhere, the war was over. Up to Niagara Falls, the honeymoon suite of the General Brock, on the Canadian side. Down to New York, a cold-water walk-up on East Fifty-seventh. Father went to Lima, Peru. School again in Connecticut, where we lived in a

Saybrook fleabag called The Pease House, and bought a domesticated farmhouse in Old Lyme. Father went to Turkey. Top-secret escape from creditors, south with Mother to Sarasota, a drafty, damp cabin. At twelve, flight alone cross-country to Seattle, where Father and I lived together in a tiny boardinghouse in the University District and where I lived with my father and stepmother in a huge house beside Lake Washington. Southeast by Buick Roadmaster to Bell Buckle and Shelbyville, Tennessee. Sent north to Choate. Home for vacations—a rambling shingled house in North Chatham on the Cape, to the Ritz-Carlton in Boston, One Fifth Avenue in New York, Weston and Wilton, Connecticut. At seventeen to school in England, and back to Princeton. After my mother dropped off the carrousel so did my stepmother. Father disappeared. I found him at the edge of the continent, slipping off the shelf of the first place he ran to after his father died leaving him only the eternal reproach of a well-lived life.

Some of this backing and forthing was simple flight; some was restless, in the ever-diminishing hope that yonder life was better, or maybe easier. During my first twelve years my father spent fewer than six at home. We moved from here to there when he changed jobs, usually trading up. He was good at his work, and his work required demonstrable skills; like The Doctor, my father chose work that was difficult to fake. He was an aeronautical engineer, and became one at a time when engineering was a profession especially inhospitable to Jews.

Of course by 1937 my father was no longer a Jew, in his or the world's eyes. Irving Howe has written in *World of Our Fathers* that the thirties were a season for fast breaks and self-creations. That the people who came to maturity with my father longed to cut away from their families and from received conventions, and that this will to repudiate "can be seen as either an idea drawn from American tradition or Jewish heresy," depending upon the beholder's vantage. Moreover, "upon its sons and daughters the immigrant Jews branded marks of separateness while inciting dreams of universalism. They taught their children both to conquer the gentile world and to be conquered by it."

My father's conquest was to be absolute. During the years of his education, science—and especially engineering—was boss. Marxists dreamt of political engineering, capitalists of consumer engineering, doctors of physical engineering. Breathing the air of technology, Duke yearned to by God finally *do* something: his history was made of fluff and filled with hot air; now he was drawn to motion, mass, metal, combustion, and—true to his spirit—flight, the conquest of natural law.

But how could he become, merely by wanting to become, an engineer? The device was simple: an application blank and a brassy indifference to consequence. His first *curriculum vitae* gave him a diploma from Deerfield (later he reached further, to Groton or St. Paul's) and a degree from Yale (the year omitted), Bachelor of Science, Mechanical and Aeronautical Engineering. Yale not enough? Then add this, a Bachelor of Science degree from the Sorbonne, located as Duke said in "Paris, France" but—as he perhaps knew, perhaps did not—a school only of the humanities.

The first manufacturer beguiled by my father's educational dazzle was Northrup Aircraft Company. Rosemary and my father had crossed the country on his mother's money, planning to visit a Loftus, an undertaker, in Denver. But the thought of watching Duke watch her kinsmen watch him was sufficient to overcome my mother's exhaustion, and she insisted they press on west. They arrived in Los Angeles with ten dollars remaining in their poke, and they spent it, to the last penny, on dinner at the Brown Derby, before they knew where they'd sleep.

"I was impractical myself," my mother said.

They found friends, Bob and Ruby Donovan, who took them into their house in the Hollywood Hills. Ruby had once been Duke's girlfriend, and knew him well enough to be especially considerate to my pregnant mother. The four got along: they'd return empty soda bottles, and use the proceeds on a movie, or a few beers. But the Donovans' hospitality was not long put to the test. The moment Duke presented his amazing bona fides to Northrup, he was hired. In 1937 the aircraft business was nothing like the slick aerospace industry of today. It was an enthusiast's vocation, run out of garage-like hangars by executives less like software specialists than like grease monkeys. It is probable that no one at Northrup would take time to write Yale, less Deerfield or "Paris, France," to authenticate a bright young man's claims.

So he was hired at forty dollars a week as a draftsman. Bob Donovan drove him to work because now Duke had no car. He had traded their new Ford as part payment for a used LaSalle, and the LaSalle for a Packard, which was repossessed. This was ever my father's course, from something to something more to nothing. Still, my father and mother were happy, living in the small house in the hills, near the Donovans.

Within a week Duke's supervisor looked over his employee's shoulder and saw that Yale and the Sorbonne had neglected to teach the engineer the language or symbols or methods of engineering. He told my father to find another patsy, by Friday. Then, in one of those starbursts of luck that sometimes lit my father's life, Northrup's engineers went on strike, and the company retained Duke to flesh out a skeleton staff. My father's supervisor instructed him not to show his work to anyone, and advised him to get promoted fast so that he wouldn't have to create engineering drawings, merely hire people who could. Then he promoted my father to such a position, because he liked him and saw that he was gifted, because my father *was* gifted, because his gifts were useful to Northrup. And so The Duke, a few months earlier fired from a job at Sikorsky to which he wore overalls, had become an aeronautical engineer.

During the next fifteen years he was fired by companies fed up with his debts, or his arrogance, or his insubordination; he was never fired for incompetence. When I was born in November of 1937 my father left Northrup for Lockheed—hired away, his salary doubled. He was a project engineer on the experimental version of the P-38, a flashy twin-engined, twin-tailed fighter, the first American plane to shoot down a German. Duke could make people produce for him; he was impatient with conventional procedures, liked to take shortcuts. He was a useful bridge between thinkers and doers, and he liked especially to work with the odd, inward men who fabricated mock-ups and prototypes, model-builders and tinkerers not unlike The Doctor. Duke was liked by these people, who listened to his brainstorms and willingly followed the novel approaches that could be pioneered only by a man innocent of experience.

Soon he rose again, moving to North American and the XP-51, giving the best performance of his life, as later in his life he, alas, knew. In 1940, before the Battle of Britain but after Dunkirk, the British Purchasing Commission sent pilots to America to develop a fighter to compete with Germany's fastest, most maneuverable and best-armed. Working with Lend-Lease credit and under mortal urgency, British pilots applied their experience in the air against the Germans to rough out a fighter with an in-line engine (like those of the Spitfire and Hurricane, and unlike those of the American Thunderbolt and Corsair), and eight machine guns. A prototype of this advanced airplane was to fly, according to the contract with North American, one hundred and twenty days after the go-ahead, four months from the first doodle on a scratch pad till flight.

North American rolled out the first plane three days ahead of schedule, in August of 1940, and my first memory is of sitting in its cockpit while pilots and mechanics and my mother and father cheered. During those four months of flat-out work my father was euphoric, and my mother was proud of him. His sufficiency was now beyond question, and the couple had money and friends. These were pilots and designers, not like my father's Hartford friends. They were serious men, capable of courage, stamina, and command, and they treated my father as their equal.

There was money enough to buy a house in Palos Verdes; it was comfortable and cool, with terra-cotta floors and a tile roof and a couple of palms in the patio and a long look downhill to the Pacific. My father had brought his mother to the house for a long visit, and a couple of RAF pilots also lived with us, and were wonderful friends to my father and mother, who remembers the men—two of whom would distinguish themselves in the Battle of Britain, one of whom would die above the English Channel—playing at mock dogfights with model planes, letting me make the engine noises.

My father spoiled me. Every night after work he'd stop somewhere to buy me a trinket, and as soon as he drove up in the new twelve-cylinder Packard convertible I'd leave my mother and run to him. "Daddy! Daddy! Where's my toy?" This troubled my mother, who thought my father was buying my love, and perhaps he was, but like everything between mothers, fathers, and sons, the case was not that simple.

"You were lovable, I guess. When you were really little you were cute. Quick-tempered, of course. Angelic-looking in the Brooks Brothers Eton jacket. I used to get angry sometimes, and spank you. But I don't remember serious problems." My mother paused then, and said to herself, not to me: "Even when I nursed you you seemed to judge me."

My mother was too much judged. Duke was sloppy in those days, dressing with studied carelessness in battered tennis shoes and cashmere jackets and rumpled linen or flannel trousers. But he was meticulous on my mother's account, choosing her clothes and having her hair cut and arranged according to his taste. My mother, still the undiscovered starlet, inclined toward the cute flamboyance of a Betty Grable, while my father preferred the elegant simplicity of a Joan Bennett. That my father's taste best suited my mother didn't much matter, that he managed to hurt her mattered a great deal.

"I didn't have a lot of self-confidence to begin with, and what I had he took away. Not that he didn't try to build me up. I'd say sometimes how inadequate I felt without an education, and he'd tell me I knew more than most women he had known. But when we were entertaining he'd check the table to see whether I'd set it right. He used to make me feel I wasn't really very smart."

My mother suspected Duke of casual attentions to other women, beginning with an upstairs neighbor in Milford, days after their wedding; she was suspicious of his continuing affection for Ruby Donovan, a striking redhead, and didn't always believe him when he called to say he'd have to work late at Northrup or Lockheed or North American. She was more annoyed than wounded by this, having no desire for my father.

Of course, it is an insult to intelligence to be deceived, and my father's infidelities angered her as deceptions. His more pathological deceptions troubled her less. About her husband's Jewishness my mother says she "wanted to be fooled. I was dumb, dumb, dumb to pretend he wasn't Jewish. I guess I accepted this view of himself."

The only thing Rosemary failed to play along with was my father's promotion of her father to admiral, and the education he bestowed on the pismire, *honoris causa*, a degree from Annapolis. Among Mike Crosley and Jimmy Little (his RAF friends), and Bob Chilton, a North American test pilot—people who respected him—my father alluded seldom to Wolff history; he was sufficiently vitalized by his present. But even so, my mother recollects that "Duke had a way of implying much, without elaboration."

My father never dropped the pretence with my mother that he had gone to Yale. He would make oblique references to the Harvard game every November, as though he had a stake in its outcome. And at Palos Verdes he bought the first of several English bulldogs I grew up with. I guess he bought them to suggest his connection with Old Eli, and the dogs' connection with Yale's Handsome Dan. But he loved them, for all that, and cared for them and was stricken when they died, every one before his time, from the respiratory diseases that afflict dogs bred for unnaturally stunted, un-Jewish snouts.

Once, driving with my mother near Santa Monica, my father was almost hit by a car that ran a stop-sign at an intersection. Duke piled out of the Packard to raise hell—he used justice fearsomely, like a roll of coins in his fist—and the other driver raised his hands in surrender. Seeing my father he grinned, and greeted him by name: "Art Wolff! Son of a bitch!" My father seemed to wish that he were not, seemed about to deny that he was, but the fellow pressed on: "We were at Penn together, remember?" My mother saw that this man was a Jew, beyond dispute. "Come on, Duke, we roomed next door, used to party together." My father shook his hand. A couple of weeks later the man stopped by our house for a drink, but Rosemary never saw him again.

Soon after this incident my mother grilled Duke about his trumpery résumés. At first he insisted he had transferred to Yale from Penn, and then to Penn from Yale, and then he refused to speak more of the matter. My mother decided for once to know one thing, for sure, about her husband. Duke's mother was staying in Palos Verdes, helping to spoil me, and Rosemary asked her, bluntly: "Did Duke go to Yale?"

"What did he tell you, dear?" my grandmother asked my mother.

"That he went to Yale."

"Then I imagine he must have gone to Yale."

7

A few days before Pearl Harbor my father flew to London by way of the Azores and neutral Lisbon, where he dropped a few hundred dollars of expense money betting against a Luftwaffe officer shooting craps at the Estoril Casino. His plane was shot at when it crossed France, and the night my father landed in England bombs fell on the East London docks, raising huge columns of fire into the searchlight-crossed sky. He was afraid, he confessed, but not enough afraid to want to be any place other than where he was.

North American had given my father the title of Assistant Chief Designer, and the responsibility to work gremlins out of the RAF's new Mustangs. He was installed in a four-room flat on Park Lane, a block from the Dorchester and overlooking Hyde Park. Officers of the American embassy had dubbed my father an Air Corps major, a common practice that protected him with military privileges under the Geneva Convention were England invaded and occupied. The honorary rank mattered to him, crucially, for the rest of his life.

When Father left us in New York Mother drove the cream Packard with its red interior aimlessly around America, and settled finally into a California shorefront apartment at Hermosa Beach. Shortly after Pearl Harbor a midget Japanese sub had lobbed a few rounds at the Santa Barbara Biltmore, missing it but depressing waterfront rents. There were soldiers and heavy artillery pieces set beneath the boardwalk on the beach in front of our place, ready to blow away the Nips when they waded ashore, any minute now. The soldiers were friendly; they teased me and gave me candy and chevrons, which Mother sewed on my T-shirts. They flirted with her, innocent kid stuff, and Mother was friendly to them, and let the soldiers buy her a beer or a coke while I filled a beachside jukebox with their nickels, playing "Pistol-Packin' Mama" and "Deep in the Heart of Texas" till I ran them out of coins.

My father stayed fourteen months in London, until early 1943. Duke liked being part of those nights of Blitz and days of Churchill. He was proud that his father had been born in London, and in short order he found Mullins of Bond Street, a genealogical boutique where he bought a book bound in soft red calf, *A History of the Name Ansell,* tracing the family of his grandmother Sarah Ansell back to the *Domesday Book,* and from it he chose a coat of arms for the "Ansell Wolff" line.

He liked British manners and the mumbly, marble-chewing accent of the upper class. He couldn't get enough of understatement, the self-deprecation of the squadron leader who had just returned from his ninth flight of the day with his Spitfire shot full of holes and three ME-109s confirmed killed, *Fox gave us rather of a chase, never mind, rum job for him.*

I wonder how much he tried to sneak past them. Americans, socially insecure, will believe anything. Hints about "Sent Pawl's" and "Bones" register without challenge; I heard my father tell a Yale man that they were together in the same class at Yale, in the same entry of the same college, and the man was ashamed of his memory lapse rather than suspicious. The English work differently: *Duke, is it? Duke of what, old man? Oh quite, I see, Duke of nothing then, rilly. At Eton were you? What years? Then you know Bamber Lushington? No? Then you weren't at Eton, were you?*

If Arthur III stepped delicately through the minefields of British social complication, he ran amok with easy credit. Field boots from Lobb, lighters and pipes from Dunhill, tobacco from Fribourg & Treyer, a collapsible silver drinking cup from Garrard. Hawes & Curtis made his shirts, Huntsman his hacking jacket. Holland and Holland contributed a matched pair of guns, Foyle's threw in a few first editions, and North American Aviation—advised that their Duke was blitzing Mayfair and Belgravia—brought my father home and fired him.

When he came home in disgrace, with a steamer trunk filled with booty and no end of entertaining routines about life under the bombs, he tried at once to enlist in the Air Corps. Everything went against him: his eyes were weak, he stammered, he had a bad back, his teeth were unsatisfactory. The Navy wouldn't have him either, but the Army said his teeth made the worst case against him, so he had all his uppers pulled, and after he got a plate Mother and I drove him to Fort Ord, where he tried one last time to enlist, and was turned away. I remember his blank silence, and for the first time he frightened me. He drove us home to Hermosa Beach and disappeared into Mexico. Mother bailed him out of jail three days later in Tijuana. The charge was drunk and disorderly.

He got a job soon enough with Rohr Aircraft. Jobs were easy then, and no one took time to meditate on the character of prospective employees; if men were sane, American, and exempt from military service, they were just fine.

My parents bought a new-built tract house in Chula Vista as soon as Rohr signed Duke on. The house hadn't been painted, the front lawn hadn't been seeded, when he was offered a better job as chief engineer of a B-24 and B-29 modification center in Birmingham, Alabama. We had owned and lived in that little house less than three weeks when my father sold it, and our last night there my mother read me the fable of Pandora's box, and I lay awake staring at my father's locked steamer trunk.

My father was paid more than a thousand a month in Birmingham, a lot of money then. The plant where he worked was run by an engineering firm called Bechtel, McCone and Parsons, and my father's principal superiors were Ralph Parsons and John McCone, neither of whom approved of Duke's character, both of whom recognized his energy and resourcefulness.

The plant Duke supervised was a huge network of hangars beside the airport to which bombers fresh off assembly lines were flown by ferry pilots to Birmingham for changes or additions to their bombsights, armaments, navigational gear, or interiors. As soon as they were modified, other ferry pilots flew them to Guam or England or India. The pace of work was hectic, the pressure to perform extreme, the cost of error mortal.

It was among Duke's inspirations in Birmingham to hire midgets to work the tight places inside wings and fuselages, to rivet joints and lead wires through places inaccessible to grosser persons. To round them up, my father sent hiring scouts with contracts and pockets filled with money to cities across America, where they hung around race tracks and booking agencies and penny arcades and carnivals, and within a few weeks a new labor force was on the case. (Later, when the war was winding down, just before my father was fired, his midgets were laid off, and I saw them protesting, milling in their city clothes with signs and sandwich boards outside the locked chain-link gate of the dismal plant, protesting how things were with a single word: UNFAIR!)

At the beginning in Birmingham my father rode high, and so did Rosemary: "I was drunk with all that money." We spent a few weeks in a suite at the Tutweiler Hotel, looking for suitable quarters for a chief engineer, and then moved into a showplace on Beechwood Road, directly across the street from the entrance to the Mountain Brook Club.

The house was white, with a columned slate terrace surrounded by lilac and magnolia trees. Live oaks grew from an acre and more of lawn that sloped down to a boxwood hedge, and there was a formal garden out back, with a Victory Garden for vegetables, and to tend these growing things a gardener was employed, an old black man with one arm who ingratiated himself to Duke by holding open the Packard's door when my father left for work, saying "Mornin', Cunnel Woof." The rest of the day the gardener napped under a shadetree, with a Mason jar of my mother's lemonade beside him, watching the grass grow, and sometimes shooing away flies with his good arm.

I remembered this house as about the size of Mount Vernon, with race horses gamboling along a mile-long split-rail fence. When I saw it recently it had shrunk, in beauty as well as scale, but it drove my mother and father into the poorhouse. Although the rent was only two hundred per month (my parents had never before paid half as much) and the gardener and fulltime maid together cost fifteen dollars a week, the house was unfurnished, and its many rooms were a challenge to the Wolffs' extravagance.

My mother and father had fun. There were many friends, a rootless assortment such as war and natural calamity can throw together: artists who drew the modifications my father required, pilots, inventors, mechanics, gunsmiths, mathematicians. These people came together without histories, and were peculiarly alive to the present. The house on Beechwood Road was open to anyone passing through Birmingham who had anything to do with airplanes.

A pilot stayed with us. He had been shot down over Rabal, and was horribly burned. Natives brought him back to life and hid him from the Japanese, and he escaped on a raft. The pilot gave me a Japanese bayonet, and told me never to call Japanese people Japs. He also told me my dad was "one hell of a man." He set up his dozen or so electric trains in our basement, with an insane network of HO gauge tracks, Gordian crossovers and model alpine villages and engines that whistled and blew steam. Where this pilot went his trains went, and when he prepared to fly his Dukefied B-29 to Guam, I saw the trains, packed in wooden crates, loaded into the plane's bomb bay. He wore dark glasses and a flight hat with sheepskin earmuffs, and gave me the thumbs-up just before he revved his engines and rolled away.

The gardener let me draw a puff from his cigar, but my neighborhood chums wouldn't believe this. While two of them sat listening, I telephoned the Mountain Brook Drug Store.

"My father wants to know if you sell cigars."

(They did.)

"My father wants me to get him three cigars."

(What kind?)

"Cheap cigars. Can I get three for a nickel? I only have a nickel."

We took them to a stream beside our house, and smoked them down to the butts, fast. My friends puked into the stream; we were five and six. They went home to take their lickings. I didn't feel all that bad, considering, and came to the dining room for supper. Mother frowned. Father was hearty:

"How are you, old sport, hungry?"

Not very hungry, I admitted.

"Have a cigar. Something to whet the appetite?"

My father offered me something longer and finer than the thing I had just smoked, and I said I thought I would rather not, no cigar, thanks anyway.

"Oh," my father said. "I think so. Here. Take it."

I shook my head, but he stuck it in my mouth, and lit it, and made me smoke it to the stump, even though he and

Mother hated the smell of the things. He wasn't angry, not the least bit.

When I was recently in Birmingham a white-haired retired judge spoke of a lady recently married into an "old Buminham family" as being of "unsuttun or-i-gin," by which he meant, I think, that she was a Jew. I'm not sure what kind of society Birmingham claims; the city was infertile cotton land when the Civil War ended, and any place proud to call itself The Pittsburgh of the South might govern its pretensions. The city's landmark, atop a hump of red clay called Red Mountain, is a statue of Vulcan, not as the god of war but in his subsidiary role as god of iron; he is advertised to be "the largest iron man in the world"—iron and coal make Birmingham go. Vulcan holds aloft what looks like a popsicle, but this is in fact a torch, lit red if there has been a traffic fatality within the previous twenty-four hours, green if not.

Whatever passed for "society" in Birmingham neglected my father, but it was at a rare and now inexplicable visit to the Mountain Brook Club that three extraordinary events converged. Driving to the club my father told me our bulldog had died, and at the club my father learned that his mother had also died, and as he walked toward me with this news I jumped from the diving board into the pool, and in that way, before my anguished father or mother could reach me, learned to swim. This achievement interested me more than the death of my grandmother.

When Duke's mother fell sick at seventy-eight with pneumonia, a complication of heart disease, he insisted that she be treated at St. Francis rather than Mt. Sinai Hospital. He laid it on thick with the staff: Hattie was to have the biggest room, best treatment, no expense spared, here was the widow of The Doctor.

But he stayed in Birmingham till she died on the last day of January, 1944, three days after she entered the hospital, and left Ruth Atkins and Bill Haas to keep the vigil at her bedside. The funeral was at Bill's house, and Duke came home for it—too late some people said, too soon by half most said. When the bills were presented by St. Francis my father said screw 'em; as the nuns and priests did unto The Doctor, so The Duke would do unto them.

There were harsh words at the funeral. My grandmother had left her most cherished things to Ruth and to Bill and to other cousins, and nothing to her son. At The Doctor's funeral Duke was pugnacious. He considered himself a man of attainments, and was insulted that his own mother had not trusted him to administer the measly two thousand, all the cash she left, placed in trust for my education. His mother willed Ruth Atkins her furniture and jewelry, Bill Haas her bull's-eye mirror, and Bill's mother the grandfather clock. What remained after the two thousand was put aside for me, beyond Duke's reach, was to go to him four years later, when he reached forty. But nothing remained. My father didn't know exactly whom never to forgive, so he chose never to forgive all of Hartford.

After his return from the funeral, the financial pressure built quickly to an intolerable level, and my parents moved to 2800 Hastings Place in Mountain Brook, a large corner house giving, in contrast to the Beechwood Road establishment, the illusion of modesty.

During the move I went with my mother to gather the last of her clothes. The front door was open, and this alarmed her, and as we crept along the hallway to the circular stairs she paused, and held her fingers to her lips, and I held my breath. We heard nothing, climbed the stairs to my parents' bedroom, and I saw something brown and wet on the banister, but was too terrified to say anything. We looked into the bedroom and saw Mother's clothes heaped on the floor, and blood on the quilt, blood on the pale-blue curtains, on the doorknob three inches from my mother's hand; she squeezed my arm and pulled me with her down the stairs.

She telephoned my father before she called the police; after all she knew about him she still trusted him to know what things meant, what to do. Duke came to the house carrying the Air Corps Colt .45 he had been issued in London and had never returned. He found a broken window back of the house, and went through the front door and down the basement stairs and emptied a clip of big medicine into four dark and deserted corners of the cellar. That was where the police found him, maddened by the outrage to his wife and son, shouting for some phantom son of a bitch to show himself and have it out. But the intruder was gone with a few unpaid-for goods and his story.

Father had the jitters for a long time after the break-in. A couple of months later he came home from work to find me sitting cross-legged on the front lawn at Hastings Place, working with a hammer, a nail and an unexploded .50 caliber machine-gun bullet a neighborhood kid had swapped me for a boat in a bottle. I had been trying, with increasing determination, to hit the firing pin hard enough to make something happen. My father saw me from his car, ten yards away, and spoke to me just loud enough to be understood clearly:

"Put down the hammer and nail, put them down now. Put down the bullet, come over here. Good, that's good."

Then he came out of the car fast, and ran toward me so violently I thought he would run me down, and took me in his arms and held me so tightly I thought he meant to hurt me.

After dinner that night I sat on the bottom step of the back porch. I picked up a stone and idly pegged it at a robin tugging at a worm, just as I had hundreds of times before. This robin I hit, and he beat his wings once or twice, and then he died. I buried him, and began to have a care.

The Doctor, after the death of his daughter, had been attentive to his son's health, but my father was obsessive about mine. Like a lot of kids I had been born with a heart murmur, nothing that much worried doctors, but it tormented my old man. The merest earache or fever or sore throat would bring a medic with his bag, generally past midnight; perhaps to ease his own discomfort our family doctor suggested that my tonsils and adenoids be removed at the close of my first-grade year.

They wheeled me in for ether with my mother beside me promising ice cream when it was over, and my father promising a new bike, and when I awoke there was the ice cream, and there was the bike; I was used to good care and kept promises.

In the next room was a kid about my age, who had been there almost a year. He had accidentally set fire to himself, and his face was grotesquely disfigured, like the face of the pilot shot down over Rabal. My father would stop to talk with the burned kid, and while I was too young to understand all the intricate twists of courage, I knew that boy was special, like the pilot with the trains, and when my father talked with the boy I sometimes caught my father looking at me, measuring himself, I guess, or maybe me, wondering how we'd do.

Sometimes that summer my parents would take me with them to wrestling matches. My father knew the wrestling impresario, a woman who smoked cigars and could tease him. There was a trick to teasing Duke. It was okay, quite merry, up to a point. If the line was crossed into what he perceived as presumption or malice, he'd blow.

Once only as a kid was I humiliated for him, and that time he wasn't humiliated at all, just confused. It was at a factory softball game, engineers versus grease monkeys. They had asked my old man to be plate umpire. I sat in the bleachers behind home with two friends and my mother, and at first I was proud. Then the game heated up, and some calls were disputed, and it was clear now that my father didn't know much about baseball, and thought of the event as better-humored than it was. Some people in the stands shouted at him, wisecracking about his eyesight and his attention span. Then someone yelled "kill the umpire" and I turned to the general source of the noise and screamed at no one in particular to shut up, and my mother shushed me, but my anger amused the crowd, which began to chant in unison KILL THE UMPIRE KILL THE UMPIRE KILL THE UMPIRE. Then my father called what was probably a ball a third strike, and the batter wheeled on him and shook his fist at my father's face which I couldn't see behind his mask. I began to cry, and my mother took me away. My friends were afraid to speak all the way home, and none of us mentioned that softball game again.

8

My mother, married to Duke more than eight years, had never loved him. And yet: "I never thought of leaving him." In Birmingham Rosemary changed her attitude toward status quo. Two circumstances converged: Duke met a woman who fell in love with him, and Rosemary met a man who fell in love with her. The story comes from my mother.

Duke's lover was young and pretty, a talented painter from Mississippi who worked in the design department of Bechtel, McCone and Parsons. Rosemary learned about her in 1944 at a friend's Thanksgiving party. She was asked where Duke was, and said he was shooting wild turkeys upstate, and a couple of married men laughed, and so the last to hear heard. A few weeks later she came face to face with Betty, after Duke had promised never to see her again. My mother had come by bus to prowl through downtown department stores; it was the middle of Duke's workday, and my mother was surprised to see the Packard parked at a store entrance, and just as she saw my father, he saw her. He was alarmed, but beckoned her to join him in the car.

"Why should I? I'm shopping. Why are you here?"

My mother knew why he was there, and just then saw Betty, a pale redhead, leave the store my mother had been about to enter. Rosemary climbed into the Packard, and my father began to drive away when a woman's voice followed them:

"Duke! Where are you going? Wait!"

To his marginal credit my father stepped on the brake instead of the gas. My mother remembers the rest:

"She opened the door of the Packard before she noticed me. She recognized me from the plant, and clapped her hand over her mouth and said, 'Oh, my God!' It was funny, like something at a play. Duke recovered fast. He climbed out of the car, and came to my side to help me out, and introduced us quite properly, without even stammering. Then he said to me, 'Let's go home.' But I said no, I wasn't finished shopping. And then I walked away. I felt smug; I knew I'd handled myself well. When I arrived home I found him in the library. You were on his lap, bathed, fed, and in your trap-door Doctor Dentons. Duke was reading you a poem from *Now We Are Six*, 'The Knight Whose Armour Didn't Squeak.' It was a lovely, sweet domestic portrait. When he saw me he smiled and said, 'Look, Mummy's home, give Mummy a kiss.' When I headed upstairs to my room he dumped you off his lap, without ceremony, and ran after me: 'Now wait a minute, this isn't what you think ...'"

My mother had been busy, too. She did volunteer work for the Red Cross, winding bandages, packing parachutes and driving for the motor corps, giving rides to soldiers who came into town. She met many pilots.

"I was the first human they saw when they stepped off the wing, and I guess they figured it didn't hurt to try, so most of them asked me for dates. I'd laugh and say no; it didn't bother me, gave my ego a boost. But this one, a lieutenant, young and handsome, struck a responsive chord in me, and I gave him my name and phone number. That was the first time."

My mother and father were at a movie, and when they

came home they found a note from the maid beside the telephone, Lieutenant Sullivan had called Rosemary.

"Duke was outraged that I would give my number to a pilot, of all people! I laughed in his face: 'Come off it! Do you really want to get into all that with me?'"

They fought. Then Mother went to a lawyer, and he served papers on my father. Rosemary saw all she wished of Lieutenant Sullivan, and Betty tried to see Duke, and gave him an ultimatum: someone had asked to marry her, she would rather marry my father, what did he want to do? He wanted to heal things with my mother, who couldn't understand why.

"Betty was pretty, and bright and very refined. There would have been financial considerations, of course, but I wouldn't have made trouble for them."

My father advised Betty to marry her admirer, and begged my mother to reconsider, but she was adamant, and maybe in love, maybe not in love. In any case, they were dead-ended, and the time had come to tell me what was what.

We sat on the steps of the back porch at Hastings Place about dusk of a breezy evening in early summer. My mother and father spoke gently and precisely. There were no storms, and they led to the hard news slowly, but I saw it coming from miles off. Any kid can see it coming. Maybe I tried to argue with them, and probably I cried, but mostly I remember trying to swallow. I remember too my father saying, truly, that he didn't want this. So I knew my mother did, and there opened between us a separation, not her fault, certainly, but there.

They left me alone finally, sitting on the bottom step. I threw a stone, hard, at a bird hopping across the backyard. I missed it, and didn't throw another.

Father and Mother agreed that she'd take me to Martha's Vineyard for a couple of months, to visit friends. We went to Oak Bluffs, and I spent hours every day walking the beach alone, or haunting the penny arcade and missing my father. Twenty years later I drove through that gingerbread town on a bright day, and my good humor vanished as though a shade had been drawn across the present.

My father wrote my mother every day, elegant pleas for her to come home, promises of reform.

Lieutenant Sullivan wrote letters, too, from Dallas, where he was now stationed at Love Field, and they had greater effect than my father's. I would lie awake in the little cottage where Rosemary and I were guests of Duke's friends, a husband and wife who had once worked for him, and I'd hear the names—*Duke . . . Sully . . .* —and sometimes laughter, and sometimes what sounded to my straining and uncomprehending senses like a plot that did not mean my father well.

Rosemary decided to join her lover in Dallas. We made a hellish late August journey on troop trains, traveling by coach from Boston to Chicago without a dining car, and my mother fueled me with cookies and Cokes, and when we reached Chicago I was failing. I threw up on the railroad platform, and while we waited for the Dallas train my mother took me to a tearoom, because it had no provocative smell of food.

"We had to wait forever, because soldiers had priority. I was wearing a brand-new green silk dress, because I wanted to knock Sully's eyes out when we reached Dallas. I ordered you tea, and it came up right away, all over the dress. I jumped away from the table, so angry and upset; I knew it wasn't your fault, but you were the one who ruined it, and began shouting at you, and you were crying. So of course this waitress charged over: 'It's not his fault!' She looked at me as though I was such a bitch. I don't know; just another low moment, I guess."

It was like hellfire going south; the windows wouldn't open, and we had to stand most of the way. The soldiers took me up as a mascot, and taught me their high school songs.

Dallas was no more gratifying than the train that brought us there. Lieutenant Sullivan was four years younger than Rosemary, who was twenty-seven. He had proposed marriage, but the first time he took her dating to the officers' club at Love Field, where they were joined by his friends and their teen-aged dates, he and my mother decided they weren't destined for each other after all, and that was that; they never met again.

My father didn't know where we were, although Rosemary was once again boarding with a couple of his friends, who worked for North American Aviation in Fort Worth. I was left with a sitter by day, and often by night, and I never lay off pestering her, *I want my daddy*. Telling me this now my mother assumes that I missed Birmingham because our life in Texas was so mean; when I suggest that I missed my father she looks puzzled.

She sought a job, without luck. "I tried Neiman-Marcus, as a salesgirl, but I guess I wasn't glamorous enough. Finally I was offered a job as a hostess in a restaurant, twenty dollars a week, but your sitter cost me that much, and I realized I was banging my head against a stone wall, and so I called Duke, and I guess I led him on, and got him to say he loved me and wanted me back, and I said I'd come back. Then a friend found me a job at North American, and I could have kicked myself, because I'd promised you we were going home, and we had to. But I always wondered what would have happened if I'd stayed. Oh, well."

My brother was born nine months after the homecoming night. Duke had arranged a party:

"We had a wingding," Mother says, "and I felt emotional, thinking I'd cut off all my chances for happiness, forever, and I got loaded, and that night Toby was conceived."

Another "mistake," another "accident." The fragility of life, the bleak hazard and blind luck! My brother came as I came, an unwelcome surprise, and we were told this offhandedly, as though coming here or not coming here were all one, two simple facts.

The names are absurd. *Arthur* for a legendary English king, pattern of honor. *Geoffrey* (with its awful monosyllabic abbreviation), an olde monniker to seal the Duke's connection with that scepter'd isle, blessèd plot, other Eden, homeland of Purdey, Garrard, Harrod's and The Connaught. Then *Toby*, not, God knows, the Tobias of the Old Testament and not even Tristram Shandy's Uncle Toby, but Toby as in Toby jugs, those ghastly ceramic knickknacks that my father collected, favoring Dickensian "characters." These curios, so very British, he held in as high esteem as his hunting prints, so Toby was lovingly titled.

"Bud Bowser put the skids to your dad."

He worked for my father, who had brought him to Birmingham from California. Mother and I returned to Hastings Place to find him living in the guest room. He was a little guy, with overhanging teeth and a pencil-line mustache, and he developed an unpleasant affection for my mother, who didn't return it.

"He wouldn't stop making passes, and finally I told your father, who tossed him out on his ear. He didn't hit Bowser—I asked him not to—but he frightened the weasel half to death."

So Bowser wrote Yale, requesting a copy of my father's transcript, and the blank sheet he got back he took to Duke's superiors. They didn't fire him just then; there was a war to be won. But my father was rubbing their fur the wrong way: the affair with Betty had violated office proprieties, and every week someone telephoned trying to put a lien on my father's salary, and when he drank too much he became abusive, and he had no respect for paperwork. All he could do was modify airplanes.

One day Joe Freedman received a call from Birmingham. Freedman had been a friend and attorney to The Doctor: he was the first mayor of West Hartford, a stage Jew who smoked cigars, told risqué (which he called "risky") jokes in Pullman cars, wore a pinky ring, and knew his way around. His brother Max was a counsel to the Marx Brothers, and the Freedman Brothers played spectacular poker, and called all women "broads." Joe was on retainer, for life and no pay, to my father, who loved him. The call to my father's Hartford attorney came from a high executive officer of Bechtel, McCone and Parsons. Look, the man said, Mr. Wolff has huge debts in Birmingham, and has drawn thousands of dollars against his salary.

Joe Freedman whistled.

Well, said Duke's superior, the matter is awkward, of course, but he tells us not to fret, that his trust fund will come available in six months.

Freedman laughed. "What trust fund?"

There was an uncomfortable silence at the other end of the telephone.

"Hey, what you have here is a man stiffed you. You guys are in business, haven't you ever met a deadbeat?"

The silent one on the other end spoke to confess that he had heard of such a creature.

"Now you know one close up, Duke Wolff. Why don't you can him?"

"Because he's a genius," said the man on the other end.

But when V-E Day came, that executive fired The Duke, gave him an hour to clear out his desk, and assured him he was washed up in aviation. Seventeen years later, a week after the Bay of Pigs invasion, my old man, Saunders Ansell-Wolff III, applied for a position as an investment consultant. He gave as a professional and character reference the man who fired him that day, John McCone, Director of the CIA.

9

Duke took what he could get, a job way down the greasy pole with Bell Helicopter in Marietta, Georgia. It came with a sixty percent pay cut and a warning: his record was known, he'd be watched closely, he'd better mind his step. My father didn't complain about his demotion; he was confident he would rise again, and installed us in a few rooms of an ante-bellum house on Peach Tree Battle in Atlanta.

Toby was often sick that pre-air-conditioned August. The heat shoved like steamed towels against our faces. My mother was anxious, and my father was tormented by back pains from an old injury when he was tossed hard by a wave body-surfing in California. Still, he read to me every night—*Robinson Crusoe, Aesop's Fables, The Arabian Nights, Tales of Uncle Remus* and my favorite, *Treasure Island*—and he bought me a model airplane engine and mounted it with a brass flywheel. Then he took it apart to show me how it worked, and never got it together again.

The first time I saw him upset by an event that didn't

directly touch his family was when he heard "we" had
dropped an atomic bomb, and then a second one. A cynic
might imagine he felt peevish that he had not been put
wise to the character of his work on A-bomb-carrying-B-
29s, but I remember his simple shock when he listened to
the radio and heard what we had done to them. I recently
asked my mother what he had said when he first saw the
reports and photographs from the European death
camps.

"I don't remember anything special about his reaction," my mother said.

So what did I hope my mother would tell me about my
father's reaction to the camps? That it was "special,"
deep? I expect too much.

Bell transferred my father to its Buffalo plant. Mother
went north on the train, sitting in coach with Toby on her
lap, and Duke and I drove. The Packard was gone, too
swell for our means, replaced by a black sedan, an old and
cranky Pontiac. The car's tires were bad, and the clutch
was shaky, and my father's back hurt. We tried to sleep
one night high in the Blue Ridge Mountains, my father
shaking with cold in the back seat while I trembled and
complained in the front.

It was my father's delusion that once we got north Bell
would pay our living expenses while he sought a house,
and he decided a suitable resting place under these terms
would be the Hotel General Brock, the best on the
Canadian side of Niagara Falls. The four of us checked
into a honeymoon suite, and because we had no cash we
used room service for all our needs, and ate with
newlyweds in the Rainbow Room. Duke calmed the
management with frequent assurances that Bell would
soon and happily pay, and in this way stretched our
welcome to six weeks.

It was an awful time for my parents. Toby had
dysentery, and Rosemary soaked his diapers in the
bathtub while Duke lay abed, rocking from side to side
and crying aloud from pain, till finally he could bear no

more, and went to a quack in Buffalo, who shot his spine full of Novocaine.

"Maybe I was too harsh," my mother remembers, "but I thought much of his trouble was psychosomatic. When things went really to hell his back always seemed to go on the blink."

I had a lovely time wandering the hotel alone, running the elevators, chatting up the staff. I went afield, learned the lore of the Falls by following tour guides, memorizing their pitch till I could reel off the dates and names and fabulous events, the circumstances of this successful tight-wire walk and that failed barrel plunge. The town was full of soldiers, and some let me show them around. I trusted people who wore uniforms.

One asked if I'd like to take a little trip with him across Rainbow Ridge to the New York falls, and I said sure, why not? He said his life had been unhappy; when I asked why, he seemed irritated. We passed out of Canada, walking across the Niagara River, and when we reached the American frontier he instructed me to say I was his son. I said I couldn't do that, that he wasn't my father, and my father told me never to lie. He said I'd better say I was his son, and I did, and the border man in the uniform let us pass through.

The soldier was young, almost too young to shave, and seemed sad, but sometimes he broke into weird laughter. I thought I'd better not ask questions, just do what he told me. He asked if I trusted him, and I said yes, but I didn't know what his question meant. He said trust was the most important thing there was, and that he was unhappy because no one trusted him. We were standing at the tip of a promontory, looking at Horseshoe Falls, and at *The Maid of the Mist* steaming close to the eddies, way below. Across the gorge I could see the General Brock, and I wanted to go home. I said I wanted to go home, it was late. The soldier said I could leave after I passed a little test. I asked what he wanted me to do. He didn't reply, just bent down and grabbed my ankles and picked me up, and lifted me across the chain-link fence, and held me head-down

over the misty brink of Rainbow Falls. Not for long. I
didn't even scream, I think, though no one would have
heard with the racket of falling water. Then he jerked me
back to earth, right-side-up, and said *there*, now you can
trust me, good-bye. The man at Rainbow Bridge let me
back across; he must have been a sucker for kids.

I wasn't spanked, or even rebuked. Maybe I wasn't
believed. The next day, though, I was spanked. My
mother gave me money to buy drugs for my brother and
father, and I spent it instead on a carriage ride around
Victoria Park, admission to the Houdini Museum of
Great Escapes, and passage on *The Maid of the Mist*. My
mother spanked me, because my father was too weak
from drugs to do it.

He never even saw the Bell plant in Buffalo till after he
was fired, and he tried in vain to collect some expense
money. He explained, with patient eloquence, that the
management of the General Brock depended upon the
good will of Bell, and then he explained to the
management of the General Brock that he was *sure* the
bill would soon be paid, once some red tape was
unknotted, but the management had lost confidence in
my father's assurances, so Duke sent my mother and
Toby away by bus, and he and I checked out late at night,
without much luggage, and without saying goodbye or
thank-you to our hosts.

Our destination was New York City, sanctuary with
Duke's friends Hubert and Caroline. He was a Dane, an
affable layabout refugee from the war who cared almost
as much about progressive jazz as about reefer. His wife
had been another of Duke's Hartford ladies, but she was
long reformed from the gentle influence of her finishing
school. She wrote for the *The Daily Worker*, and her
avocation was labor agitation. The Hanishes lived in a
cold-water walk-up on East Fifty-seventh near the Third
Avenue El; in addition to us there was another rent-free
comrade, an Indian with lids always half-hooding his
black eyes, and a turban I was privileged to help him
wind, and an inscrutable grin that my mother now tells me

had much to do with the quality of Hubie Hanish's weed, which he and his guests called tea; the Indian smoked joint after joint after joint, while he had, seriatim, private epiphanies.

"I did the cleaning," my mother remembers, "and Caroline cooked. After dinner everyone would go to the front room—it was a railroad flat—and sit on the floor. They'd pass around the dope, but your father wouldn't touch it. He thought it was goofy, for pansies. He'd drink a quart of Black Horse ale from the bottle, and they'd all listen to records, Fats Navarro, Lester Young, Benny Carter, Charlie Parker, Art Tatum. I tried some dope once: we went to a loft party on the subway, and it was like traveling in a golden chariot. We weren't, though. We were at absolute bedrock, ground zero. Duke sold the car, and then he hocked his watch."

I was almost eight. My father didn't want me to wander New York, but I did. I stayed on Fifty-seventh Street usually, walking east to the river to watch the tugs work against the current, or hanging out at Fifty-seventh and Third, in front of a deli, listening to hard street talk. I believed that all slang, and especially the word *bucks*, alluded to violent crime.

One night I was in the bedroom I shared with Toby, who was crying; my mother and father were quarreling in the kitchen next door. I was playing with blocks, and my tower fell against the kitchen door. My father came boiling through the doorway in fury; he thought I had been eavesdropping. He hit me across the ear with his open hand, and I went rigid with fear and confusion, and couldn't even stammer. When Duke was angry past control his face contorted: his cheeks danced, their muscles bouncing spastically, and he touched the tip of his tongue to the front of his upper teeth. He hit my head and arms and legs, never with his fists, shouting from incomprehensible frustration, and finally I found words to beg him to stop, what had I done? He hated eavesdroppers, he said, and I told him I was innocent of eavesdropping, whatever it was, and hated *him*. And that stopped him. His hands fell to his sides, and his shoulders sagged. He didn't say he was sorry. Toby was screaming, and so was my mother. The Hanishes were improbably giggling in the hall outside, where the Indian stood lost in thought. My father turned his back on me, and left, and shut the door gently behind him. I undressed, and lay under the covers weeping. And five minutes later my father came to the edge of my bed and sat beside me and said we had nothing but each other, just us, nothing else. I said I didn't care, I still hated him, and I did. And he kissed me gently, on my cheek and then my mouth; I didn't pull away from him. And then he stood, ran his hand through my hair, and left the room again. I lay there for half an hour after my mother tended my brother, and tucked me in. Then I left my bed and crept down the hall toward the light and broke through the circle of dopeheads to my father, enthroned on the room's only chair; he was staring ahead, at nothing.

"I don't hate you! I love you!"

"Of course you do."

The next day I turned eight, and my father took me up Fifth Avenue on top of a double-decker bus to 125th Street, and back down to F.A.O. Schwarz, where he let me pick a wind-up submarine from the tank filled with toy warships, steamers, and sloops. Then he took me to lunch at the Edwardian Room of the Plaza, and told me to take good care of my brother and mother. He had that morning taken a job with Pan American Airways to try to find out why the tails fell off some of their airplanes. A couple of days later he left for Lima, Peru, alone.

With Duke's first paycheck we moved from East Fifty-seventh to the Park Lane, a nod to Duke's swell London address. We soon ran the well dry again, and so two weeks before Thanksgiving became paid lodgers at a fieldstone farmhouse restored by Doak and Julie Kimball in Essex, Connecticut. Doak was my father's Hartford friend, and a drunk; his wife had a short and sour temper. They took us in because they needed money. Doak was unlikely to notice we were around, and Julie wished we weren't.

Toby had dysentery again; many babies died of it after the war, catching it from soldiers returning from Europe. Toby gave it first to me and then to Julie and then to her son Buster. Buster wore Coke-bottle glasses, was as fat as a Norway seal and a year older than I was, and it was his single life-skill and pleasure to beat the bejesus out of me whenever he caught me alone, usually when we walked to and from school every day.

The plan was to stay with the Kimballs till Duke settled in Lima and sent for us, a month or two at most, and Rosemary knew after a couple of days that something less than a month would be her limit. Doak was generally comatose, but at least he smiled a lot; Julie was always angry, and when her son sprained a finger beating his fist against the side of my head, she raised our room and board fee, to defray the cost of her son's splint.

To earn enough to keep Doak in whiskey she had decided to raise turkeys for the Thanksgiving slaughter, and my earliest memory of Essex is being chased into the living room by one of those disagreeable yardbirds. She butchered them in a barn and made me witness this bloodletting, to learn at first hand the iron realities of life. My mother didn't dispute with Julie about my education, or much of anything; she was spooked by Toby's continuing illnesses, and while I was indisputably unhappy I was also whole and robust, and learning to roll with a punch.

Our bathtub was once again put to a use for which it had not been designed. After Julie slaughtered her turkeys she hung them wrong end up, and their blood did not drain from their bodies; it pooled in their bodies, and turned them lavender, and they weren't fit to be sold. My mother recalls the situation:

"My God! She plucked them in the kitchen, and every time air slipped through a crack in the walls or floorboards a turkey feather blew into our food. A butcher told her she could rescue the damned things for sale if she soaked them in a bathtub, and guess whose bathtub she soaked them in? I thought I'd never eat another turkey as long as I lived, but I guess you can get used to anything. Still, I never got used to the Kimballs."

As the winter got colder, Doak got drunker, Julie less satisfied, and Buster bigger and meaner. His mother told my mother that Buster was insecure, and my mother told his mother the boy was merely awful. He'd eat half a dozen eggs and a stack of hotcakes for breakfast, a trencherman's portion at school, and then my school lunch; then he'd take on fuel before dinner.

Snow fell, silence thickened, and I taught myself to read. I was staring at a comic book, *Plastic Man*, and suddenly the balloons above the art were as palpable as thunderheads, and the words spoke to me.

Christmas came, and was not festive. My mother was restless; we got our passports, had had our shots, which made us suffer; we had done our parts, were owed Peru. The two waking Kimballs often asked when we might be moving along. Rosemary pressed Pan American for a departure date. Pan American told her to sit tight, certain complications had developed. And then in early January my mother got a collect call from Duke. He was in New York, would be at the Saybrook station in a few hours. He had resigned. Okay, so he had been fired. He was *not* drunk. Well, so what if he was?

We moved to Saybrook's Pease House, a summer hotel beside the Connecticut River that had long ago gone fleabag. One night Duke woke from drunkenness and heard what he thought was a prowler and was probably a cat, and he filled the beaverboard walls with .45 slugs, and the next morning we packed our bags again.

We moved a few blocks to a rooming house on Main Street. We all slept in one room and shared a bathroom and kitchen and dining room with other lodgers, old women. One ate at the table from her rocker, lurching forward to her mashed food, forking it at the still point of her swing, rocking back. She was a victim of fits, and frequently fell from her chair entirely, provoking shouts of consternation. My father would carry her to her room. Another old lady liked to lift her skirt above her waist whenever I came near her.

I would sit after school by the river, watching the ice break and flow toward Cornfield Point and Long Island Sound. When the ice finally melted I tried to fish from the end of a condemned ferry dock. Duke used me to test a fishing device he and a local barfly had designed in our bedroom over teacups of dark rum. The contraption had an elaborately springed red flag that was hoisted when a fish took a line hanging from a float. It was going to make my father and his friend rich, and they had drawn plans for the patent. It didn't work on the river. Duke was also the second-in-command on a two-man assembly line for a lampshade manufacturer who was in and out of business in less than three weeks. We were poor. Finally my father found work at Pratt & Whitney, his first employer, at a job not unlike his first job.

"I was resigned to Duke," my mother remembers. "I saw no alternative to life with him; I was dragging my feet." But one night she unloaded on him, detailed her opinion of her life. He commuted in an ancient sixteen-cylinder Cadillac, rose at five to punch in at eight in Hartford, returned after dark and after dinner. This day, payday, he came home cold and tired and dirty and drunk. It was March. My mother was waiting:

"I was sitting at the foot of the bed, and he was sitting in a chair, taking off his shoes. We were close together, about as close as I am to you now. I said terrible things to him, and he hauled off and slapped me, very hard. He had never done anything like that before, and it stunned me, and I hit my head against the side of the bed. It raised a lump, and when I showed him what he had done he was miserable, and he promised . . . well, you know how he was."

Soon after this battle my mother complained to the owner of the rooming house about bedbugs, and she said there weren't any bedbugs in her house, and my mother said there were, and the woman said there weren't either, and my father warned the old lady not to call his wife a liar, and she said who are you to talk about respect, you don't pay your rent and you beat your wife and your little boy uses the most *awful* language in front of the other lodgers and if there are bedbugs here I know who brought them. We were out on our ears again.

Duke decided it was time to trade up, there being no place to fall from the rooming house. He drove to Hartford, and huddled with his counsel. Joe Freedman, for an absolute first claim on everything we would ever own or earn, plus rights to our souls and whatever chemicals and spare parts could be taken from our bodies, advanced a down payment on a two-floor frame house on Mile Creek Road in Old Lyme, across the Connecticut River from Saybrook. Freedman's generosity testifies either to my father's persuasive powers or to... Freedman's generosity. This was understood to be my father's final call on his attorney's indulgence.

The place was a pleasant, brown-shingled farmhouse previously owned by a German pathologist obsessed with things Japanese. He had imported Japanese bamboo, which had fructified insanely, and had turned his property into a Japanese beetle ranch. This we did not know in April, before the bamboo and beetle season were fully upon Connecticut. My parents instead saw twelve pretty acres, a large red barn, a disused tennis court, and a house free of turkeys and lodgers and bedbugs, with wide floorboards. It was a wonderful house, and there I lived, from eight to eleven, what I thought was a commonplace childhood.

10

A few days after we moved into our house my father furnished it. At W & J Sloane in New York he came upon a model house, a full-scale furnished replica of a salt-box. A salesman asked if he could be of help, and my father said yes indeed, he'd like to take it.

"Take what?" asked the puzzled fellow.

"The whole ball of wax," my father said.

"The whole *house?*"

No, my father patiently explained, just the furniture. And so upon the fixture of Duke's signature to a document making many improbable promises, we were Early-Americanized, with pewter mugs, a pine corner cupboard, many pieces made of maple, hooked rugs and Currier & Ives winterscapes. (Above my parents' bed my father hung two watercolors painted by his lover Betty during the Thanksgiving weekend she spent with Duke in Mississippi. My mother didn't protest: they were pretty watercolors, nicely framed.)

That summer my father found a job in nearby New London, designing plant layout for a moribund manufacturer of printing presses. On weekends my mother and Duke would picnic or dine with some Hartford friends,

Jack Lester, who lived in Essex with his wife Connie, and Warren and Georgiana Rice, a bit up Mile Creek Road from our place. Duke was comfortable with these old friends, who never challenged his version of himself; though he was broke and they were not, he didn't borrow money from them, or at least they never loaned him any.

My father's friend Gifford Pinchot was a sailor; he kept a Dragon—a venerable racing sloop of thirty feet with huge overhang, narrow beam and low freeboard—at the Essex Yacht Club. I had been pestering my father to take me boating, and Pinchot suggested that Duke charter a powerboat for a weekend to give me a taste of salt water. My father said he despised "stinkpots."

"Boating is sailing, period," my father said.

"I didn't know you sailed," Pinchot said.

"Of course I sail."

"Then take the Dragon."

Affixed to the transom of this delicate, impeccably varnished mahogany boat was a five-horsepower outboard, used to navigate the Connecticut River against unfavorable winds or currents. The motor did indeed stink when it ran, and it was noisy and it vibrated. During three days of clear weather and twelve-knot winds it was our only means of locomotion, up the coast to Stonington, past McCook Point, which my father warned me was treacherous, but seemed nothing much to think about as we left it to port. I asked my father why we didn't sail, and he explained that the halyard was broken. When we returned the boat to Pinchot he asked how everything had gone, and my father said "aces." Later, in the car, I asked my father why he hadn't mentioned Pinchot's broken halyard, and he said he had fixed it.

"Why didn't we sail, after you fixed it?"

My father said nothing, and I understood that I had asked the wrong question. I searched this experience to unriddle what I said wrong, but couldn't puzzle it out. It never occurred to me that my father lied.

I spent the summer with Albert Payson Terhune's books. Reading about his noble collies Bruce, Lad, Treve, and

Wolf I was gripped by a fixation; I had to have a collie, and not just any collie, but one who looked like Buff, with a white mane, broad head, golden body, alert ears, and sad eyes.

I got the dog in August, for twenty dollars, the value of an immature war bond my grandmother gave me on my first birthday. The pup was six weeks old. My father drove us home from Norwich, where we found him, with the dog in my lap, sleeping, pissing, crying and licking my face. I named him Shep, of course. We slept together the first night home on a second-floor screened porch, my favorite place in the house. I didn't really sleep, at first. Thunder was booming far off, and lightning broke on the horizon, somewhere over Long Island Sound. Lying in my damp sheets, with the apple tree scratching against the screen, I tried to comfort my dog, and at length he fell asleep, and then I could.

To have something small and loved within my power was bracing and frightening, and still is. During the first few days after I got my pup I would carry him to the side of the house, where he explored the lawn I mowed, and a gravel path, and the edge of the overgrown garden. In the garden was a well, girdled by a decrepit bench. The well was no longer in use; it was said to be very deep, at least five hundred feet, and it was covered by a heavy wagon wheel. No child could fall or squeeze between the wheel's spokes, but stones could be dropped through, and I liked to listen to them bang against the side of the well as they fell, rattling dully till somewhere near China they'd splash, a hollow, final thud.

My dog could fit through the interstices between the spokes, and I sat with him in my lap while he licked my hands; my hands trembled to thrust him through, and hold him above the mouth of the well. My hands were to blame, not my head. My hands were curious. I had no wish to hear my puppy fall like a stone against the side of the well, to hear him cry and splash. I did not long to mourn him. It was not pleasant to overcome the will of my hands with my head, but it seemed necessary. Once I held Shep above the wagon wheel, thought I would put him through the wheel's open wedges and hold him, as I had been held above Niagara Falls, and return him to safety, as I had been returned. But I did not put him through the wheel, and after a few days my hands settled down, and the temptation to test my life with another life never returned. Years later I tried to talk with some college friends about this experience. We were drunk, with a confessional fit upon us, and we had all recently read Camus, *The Rebel* and *The Stranger*. I told my story about Shep at the well, and waited to hear their stories, but they had none. They had had nothing in the way of such a temptation, or nothing they wished to share with me, and so I never again mentioned the experience, till now.

When my dog was a year old I did hurt him, badly. I threw a cherry bomb into our meadow when I thought he was safe in the house, and he tried to bring it back to me, and it blew up in his mouth. He recovered, but from then on he was spooked by loud noises, but he never thought to distrust me.

I recently drove through Old Lyme, and stopped at the grade school, a pretty tree-shaded stone building with a graceful slate roof, on Main Street of a pretty tree-shaded town with a famously graceful Congregational Church. The school's exterior proportions corresponded with my recollection. It surprised me to see that things aren't always evanescent and diminished; Old Lyme was where I had left it a quarter century ago.

The classrooms did seem reduced, with lower ceilings and water fountains and much smaller desks, and there was no ink in the inkwells. But the fourth grade sat learning where my fourth grade sat, past the principal's office, left down the hall, second door on the right. The school had me in its records, beginning with my first day, a notation by Miss Mueller: "Jeff's father brought him to school. They seem unusually close. Both stutter."

My father told me we were lucky to stammer, that it gave us more time to think between words, that people paid close attention to us because we stammered. Attention was what I wanted least my first day of school in Old Lyme.

"Now, children, some of you are new to us. So that we all know one another's names, I would like each of you to stand, beginning with Marilyn and moving from right to left across each row of desks, and say your name. My name is Miss Mueller, and I'm certain we'll have a good year and all be friends."

Marilyn Mather stood, and said her name, followed by Carl Gerr and Skippy Sheffield, then Eliot and Norman and Lionel and Dorothy and Margaret Dean and it was my turn, and I stood, blushing. I stood that day gasping, laboring to pry out two syllables, *Jeff Wolff*, not much of a trick, except for a stammerer. That first day, like the first day at every new school, they wouldn't come. I squirmed, forced gutturals, gulped air and grunted it out, and nothing would come.

"Just say your name," Miss Mueller said, not unkindly.

"Juh-juh-juh I can't."

There was laughter. I would have been happier with less laughter, or more. Miss Mueller asked how it was that I could not say my name, but could so simply say *I can't*. It seemed even then like a reasonable question, but it was not a question I could answer, any more than I could tell those children my name. So I was marked special, perhaps dangerous, maybe dumb. I resolved to by God disabuse them of dumb.

Miss Mueller told them my name, and welcomed me to Old Lyme. She was a good woman. From her I learned where copra grew (but not what it was), the crucial importance of sisal to the peoples of several faraway lands, and that places where zinc and tungsten are mined are colored dark blue and maroon on some maps. I learned that we Americans were the most wonderful things that ever were, and the sight of Margaret Dean, an eight-year-old American girl one row ahead and two desks to the left, confirmed this judgment.

Miss Mueller was the niece or grand-niece or third

cousin of a President of the United States. She confessed this shyly during a rest period, and not in the least boastfully. I think the ancestor was Millard Fillmore, but he may have been Chester Alan Arthur. Miss Mueller also had a proprietary interest in a political Tyler, I think, because the first patriotic exclamation we learned was *Tippecanoe and Tyler Too!*

When I returned to my old school to ask what had become of my classmates and teachers I sat talking in the principal's office with his secretary; she had worked at the school when I was a student there, and didn't agree with me that a very long time had passed since then. She knew almost all my classmates by name, but she didn't remember Marion. Marion entered Miss Champion's fifth-grade a month late. We gave him a rough time, because of his name, because he was a new boy, and because his father drove a Studebaker, which our fathers said looked like it was going when it was coming. Marion came to our class Halloween party got up as Superboy. What a costume his mother had put together, and hang the cost! Blue velvet tights under crimson shorts cinched with a sun-gold belt. The cape was silk, he said, probably rayon, and in place of a regulation chest insignia—red *S* on a velvet field—Marion showed a lightning bolt.

This gear raised Marion in our esteem, and he must have enjoyed the sensation, for he wore the costume to school the following day, and the day after that. Miss Champion suggested that he might retire it for a year, but he said he couldn't, that this was what he wore, it was what Superboy son of Superman wore, that he was Superboy and it was what he wore.

Even Miss Champion laughed at the idea, Superman in a Studebaker. But Marion held to his claim, even placing in evidence his dad's thick glasses, a point of similarity with Clark Kent's. We were not persuaded, and it went hard with Marion. And then he offered to demonstrate his powers. He would fly. He would not, he said, fly far, because he wished only to prove a small point. He would fly the following afternoon, while his mother was elsewhere playing bridge. He would launch himself from the roof of his house, beside the public library.

The next afternoon we assembled in his front yard. From the refuge of his attic Marion watched us gather, like a lynch mob. We felt foolish and put-upon, and I was surprised to see Marion crawl through a dormer window and climb to the peak of his roof, almost three stories above us. He inched along the roof to its edge. The wind tugged his wonderful cape, and the sun hit its violent colors—royal blue, crimson, gold—and it was almost possible to believe. Marion, patient but condescending, looked down and asked *us:* "Are you ready?" The girls especially seemed to stir and blush, and one of them called out, "Fly, Marion," and he did. Off the roof, and the cape spread, and he hit the frozen lawn, and gasped and rolled to his stomach. Someone fetched the librarian, and she sent for Dr. Von Glaun, and he shooed us all home and set Marion's leg.

The next week Superboy came to school in civvies and on crutches, and until his father and mother took him away in a new Hudson Hornet to another school in another town, no one teased him. He had said he would fly, and to our satisfaction he had flown.

My father heard about Marion, of course, and admired the boy's spunk. But he used the experience as an occasion for proscription: Don't boast, don't lie, don't be bullied into dares, "use the old bean, use the noodle."

I was too young then to know that my father told me many things about himself that were not so, but I sensed that he might have once been the kind of boy who would tell his friends that he could fly, and that he might have been the kind who would crawl out a high window and go to the edge of the roof. But now I knew he would not jump off that roof.

My father instructed me. He taught me to catch and to throw a football, and didn't tire of our games of toss before I did. He taught me to swim properly, but never with the easy grace he showed in the water, everything moving with power and certainty, his long arms entering the water with his elbows bent just so. It was satisfying to watch him swim straight out from the water's edge, and notice people on the beach notice him. He wasn't showing off. What he did well he took for granted. What he could not do, or had not done, he held in esteem.

He was particular about teaching me to shoot, and to clean my rifle after every use, and to carry it empty, on "safe," with the bolt open, in the crook of my arm. One Sunday he was sitting on a log high up the beach below McCook Point, reading *The New York Times*. I was between him and the water, where I was meant to be. I had built a sand castle and was shooting at this rather than at the tin cans my father had set by the water's edge. As I destroyed the castle from its front, I began to shoot at it from other angles. My father didn't notice as I moved around till my back was to the water. I took aim at a high turret, and my eyes were indifferent to the background of my target till I pulled the trigger, and saw what I had just done. The bullet dusted away the sand turret, and thucked into the log six inches from my father's thigh.

He didn't confiscate my rifle. He didn't beat me. He didn't shout at me. He comforted me, but he also let me know something consequential had just happened; this did not upset the balance between us, but affirmed it. For several years after I pulled that trigger I did not argue with my father's judgments.

He spanked me twice in Old Lyme, both times for showing my mother insufficient respect. Once Rosemary told me to clean my room, and I stuck up my middle finger, shot her the bird. Her back was to me, I had noticed. That she was standing in front of a mirror, I had not noticed. My father next spanked me the night before a Cub Scout meeting. Rosemary, then inclining toward good works of civic-mindedness, was our den mother and had set us Cubs a project to complete with pipe cleaners and paper. We were to build teepees and populate them with Indians. At bedtime I showed her a small copy of human figures, standing like tripods.

"They're cute, Jeffie, but why do they have three legs?"

I laughed, was proud of myself, called for my father. I sometimes misjudged him, and in just such a way, thinking he would wish to be my accomplice in an act of wiseacre mischief, a pornographic tableau for his wife's den of Cubs. My father was beside himself with disappointment at my disrespect for my mother, for something she did only to help me take pride in her. He hit me hard that night, with his shaving strop. I had committed a slight offense, a bit of dumb salaciousness, but now I know he was wise in his fury. I was inclining toward a belief that I was apart from other people; I had begun to sneer a little, and Duke despised the sneer above all facial gestures, all expressions of character.

We began life in Old Lyme with a 1937 Ford station wagon, a woodie with cream metal and a dark-brown leather interior. Then Duke "bought" an MG. It was the first sports car Old Lyme had ever seen, and it embarrassed me and made everyone else in town laugh. It was necessary that we have two cars because every month or so one or the other was towed away by the sheriff. The Ford was the more frequently attached: the dealer in Saybrook had serially repaired all its moving parts, and sometimes liked to be paid. The Essex Boat Yard replaced the body's wood with ash and cherry and teak; the car was such a beauty I imagine the yard owner thought he might as well keep it while he waited for my father to make some small deposit on account. Somehow or other Duke always found a way to bail out his cars, which meant more to him than anything, except us, and my mother sometimes wondered aloud whether they didn't matter more to him than we did.

My father found his work in New London beneath him. During my fifth-grade year he commuted to Coatesville, Pennsylvania, where he designed a maintenance program for Lukens Steel. He did well, and minded his manners on weekdays while he lived with a genteel English couple on a horse farm in Paoli. He came home weekends, bearing gifts. When he finished his work for Lukens he helped design and supervise the construction of a supersonic wind tunnel at M.I.T., and then he stayed on in Boston, working for Stone and Webster. No one fired him during those years; he worked hard. I don't think he was paid very much, or was high up the organizational charts of his companies, but this helped keep his profile low. He lived in Boston at the Engineers' Club, and sometimes I'd take the train up to see him, and he would take me to dinner at Locke-Ober's or the Ritz-Carlton after a Red Sox game.

While my father lived well in Boston, and I mourned his absence, my mother fended off druggists, grocers, snowplowers, heating oil dealers, phone and electric companies, everyone who sold something locally that my father needed or wanted. Usually she pleaded ignorance ("My husband does the finances"), sometimes she lied ("Check's in the mail"), and sometimes she begged ("We'll freeze...starve...be snowed in...get sick..."). She never wept, though. I cannot remember having seen my mother weep. This must be a failure of memory. I'm sure my mother must have wept in front of me. I can imagine why, but can't remember when.

It was a hard time for her. I was increasingly difficult to manage, and my father's presence in Old Lyme on weekends was as unpleasant for Rosemary as his absence weekdays was inconvenient. He'd lie abed of a Saturday or Sunday morning, reading and resting. He liked to be waited upon, was always courteous in his requests ("While you're up could you get me a beer...the paper...a sandwich...my glasses...my lighter...a small screwdriver..."), but he expected his courtesy to be answered with immediate action. One rainy afternoon, soaking in a hot tub, he called downstairs to my mother, asked her to move the electric heater a bit closer to the tub, he was feeling a slight chill. She climbed the stairs, stood above him, held the heater over the brimming bath water.

"Perhaps you'd be more comfortable," she said, "if I put the heater right in there with you."

My father stared at her. "You wouldn't." My mother smiled, feinted with the glowing heater. "Jesus," he said, "you wouldn't do *that!*" She didn't.

"He'd arrive on Friday night with a present for you, a present for Toby, and a bag of dirty laundry for me," my mother remembers, smiling now.

He took no interest in the house after furnishing it and watching W & J Sloane unfurnish it a few pieces at a time. He lavished energy on his gadgets. Like his father, he cherished small, expensive, precise things. He never just sat, with his hands at rest. He tinkered with a shotgun, clock, collapsible this or inflatable that. He always cleaned his possessions—polished his boots or oiled a rifle—but never the mess he made cleaning them.

He was generous on my behalf with his weekends. Autumn Saturdays he'd take me to Yale football games, and in the spring to the circus: we'd go early to New London to see the tent raised and wander the Ringling Brothers menagerie and freak show before the main events. Every third Saturday I was taken to New London to be scalped at the barber shop of the Mohecan Hotel, getting my crew cut according to my father's instructions. This ordeal was usually followed by lunch downtown, an occasion for talk about manners and codes, and then a hunt for something that had attracted my father's interest. I noticed him change when he raided the shops. There was bluster in his voice, a forward, aggressive lean to him that disarmed the obsequious merchants who urged my father on even as they must have suspected he would never pay them. Salesmen like to sell; Duke understood this, perfectly.

When we returned from his sprees my mother sometimes tried to talk with him about the bills, what were they to do about them? Duke would flush with anger, pout, refuse to have his weekend spoiled by small beer. The bills, which she stacked on his desk, and on the floor where the desk used to be after a visit from W & J Sloane, he tossed unopened in the trash.

The trash was collected once a week by Mr. Dean, a laconic, lantern-jawed, long-time Old-Lymer who drove a dying pickup with rotten wooden slats. As my father grew reckless about paying him, Mr. Dean became indifferent to our accumulations of rubbish, which made my father angry, which made Mr. Dean surly, which made my father furious, which caused me discomfort.

I loved the trashman's daughter, Margaret, and she did not love me back. I think the intensity of her lack of affection for me may have been aggravated by her father's experience with my father, but in fairness to everyone I gave her, all by myself, reason enough to avoid my company.

Margaret was tall, intelligent, dignified, reserved. She was *Margaret* always, never *Maggie*. Her dark hair was braided in fastidious pigtails, and she wore long gingham dresses made by a mother or sister or herself to pinch a bit at the waist and flair at the skirt. When she smiled she blushed, and at ten her face had a woman's structure. During a few warm days in early spring, I dreamt of walking with her and Shep in our woods, and saving her from something. I dreamt of having her in our house for dinner, and keeping her there, forever.

These stirrings were not I think sensual, but they were grave. My mother laughed them off, from the perspective of someone for whom love had temporarily lost its definition. I'm not sure my mother could remember, staked as she was to my father, what first love felt like. My father could, because he had not loved deeply till he loved my mother, or perhaps because his imagination was more lively than my mother's. Or perhaps he was simply a better actor.

Anyway, Duke listened to me tell about Margaret Dean, and advised me well. Everyone advises everyone well at these times, and the advice doesn't vary: be gentle, not thrusting; give time, room, respect; have other interests. And like everyone who asks advice about love, I didn't follow my father's. I assaulted Margaret with unsigned notes, and then with signed notes declaring love. I ruined her days in school. Once she brushed past me walking to lunch and said one word: "Please." I mistook her meaning, and glowed all day. That night I telephoned to ask if she would like to meet my collie. She hung up when I stammered my name. I sent her a note:

"Yesterday you said please to me. I love you."

A note, for once, came back: "I meant please leave me alone. I don't like you."

I had so upset that lovely girl that no one teased me about her, because she couldn't bring herself even to gossip about my foolishness. But the Christmas of our fifth-grade year I developed a plan. I was given my usual twenty-five dollars to shop in Hartford with Ruth Atkins. This year I bought my mother nothing, my father and brother nothing. It seemed to me my plan could not fail to win me Margaret Dean. The plan hinged upon giving two gifts, one of them commonplace, the other a *coupe d'éclat*. The first was a gift to my belovèd of wool mittens from Harry Atkins' wholesale store. These were selected with dear care. I had stolen Margaret's own mittens from her cubby while she was at lunch, to learn her size, study her taste and leave her in need of new mittens. I chose a pair embroidered the Scandinavian way.

I was left with twenty-three dollars, and I spent it all on the top-of-the-line Gilbert *"ATOMIC"* chemistry set, powders and liquids and test tubes and scales and retorts fitted in a bright-blue metal box the size of a briefcase. This gift was not for me, nor for anyone in my class, nor for anyone with whom I had ever exchanged a word. It was for the nicest boy in the sixth grade, the best looking, best athlete, most popular—Walter "Walky" Dean.

On the last day of school before Christmas, during the class party, I gave Margaret her mittens, and without reading the card I had illustrated with broken hearts pierced with arrows and sad-eyed snowmen melting away, without opening the package I had wrapped with remnants of paisley taken from my mother's sewing basket, she dropped the gift in a rubbish bin. I was hurt, but not surprised. I walked across the hall to Mrs. Graves's sixth-grade classroom. I set the heavy, lavishly wrapped box on the desk of Walter Dean and said "Here. I love your sister. Make her love me back."

My life was no unbroken series of humiliations, only an almost unbroken series of humiliations. I don't think I knew this, any more than I understood that we lived an odd life. My mother, like other mothers, belonged to the P.T.A. and the League of Woman Voters, till being among people to whom my father owed money became too painful for her, and she retreated into the house. She hated trying to live the lie that we had standing and means, but she didn't tighten her belt. What was the use, after all? Duke was resolved to go deeper in debt; she might as well dress and feed herself and her children well.

We shared many acts and interests with regulation Americans of the time, saw the same movies, worried about the Russians and the Bomb, listened every Sunday to Jack Benny and Fred Allen. My mother laughed when others laughed at Senator Claghorn, my father at Mr. Kitzel. Like almost everyone else we celebrated Christmas, and how! The routine those three years in Old Lyme was unvarying: On Christmas Eve Duke would take me to New London to choose a tree, and we would have lunch, and he would drink an eggnog, and another. He would tell me that times were hard, which I knew, and that this year, unlike last year, the horn would pour forth no plenty. I would smile bravely. We would find a tree, always "the best tree we've ever had." Duke would stop on the way home at a roadhouse, for a few drinks to celebrate the season. I would be introduced to bartenders who would grasp my hand too firmly and tell me, shaking their heads, "your dad's a hell of a good sport, one hell of a guy, you're a lucky kid, your pop's the best, tops, believe me." Now it was Canadian Club, straight, no rocks, a Canadian Club chaser. I'd be sent off to play pinball or the jukebox. Snow would fall; snow fell every Christmas Eve we lived in Old Lyme. Rarely, a bartender would push-familiarity past the limit. I remember a place called The Lobster's Claw near Niantic, a roadhouse with a husky blond, about twenty-five, behind the bar. I knew enough not to like this bartender, noticed a nasty indifference in his manner. After a few rounds he looked at my father:

"What'll it be, baldy, same again?"

There was a heavy quiet in The Lobster's Claw. My father studied his empty glass, and his hands. He beckoned the smirking bartender with his index finger. The bartender, thinking he had created a successful jape, approached my father, who grabbed the young man's shirt and emptied a full ashtray down its front. Then Duke walked out, holding my hand, and the barkeep shouted after him, "Never come back, you silly-looking bastard." It was "silly-looking" that bothered me.

On the way home my father would break the rear end of the Ford loose on the slippery roads, to teach me, he said, how to handle a skid. When we hauled the tree, wet with snow, into the living room, my father swore at it. Mother tried not to show her anger. It was Christmas Eve, my night and Toby's. The roast was overdone and cold. She saw that Duke was drunk, his speech had gone British and his manners were too fastidious. He wanted not to be drunk, but he was, and this made him sad, which made him drink some more. After dinner we tried to trim the tree; one Christmas my father knocked over the tree, and broke ornaments. My mother was always brave on Christmas Eve. She lit a fire, put out the lights, plugged in the tree. Beautiful! My mother managed to smile. I was sent to bed, and did not sleep. I heard voices downstairs, rising, my mother angry now, "please, Duke, *please!*" And then my mother would run upstairs, and my father would stumble after her and bang against the walls heading toward their room, and he would look in on Toby in his crib, and talk heavily at him while he slept. I would lie awake with Shep beside me on the floor, and not once all that one night think of Margaret Dean.

My mother was bone tired Christmas morning, and my father hungover, but they let me at the stuff before dawn, and watched me. It was grotesque, I think. I loved it, tearing at a sixth package before I had finished unwrapping a fifth. The things with cards written by my mother and father I opened first. The year of my presentation to Walky Dean I got just what I had given him; my father was trying to tell me something, or make me feel better. I also got a Flexible Flyer, and that morning, riding it down icy Braggart's Hill I set my tongue against the metal steering bar, and it stuck: when I tore my tongue away it bled so badly that I had to be taken to Dr. Von Glaun.

Dr. Von Glaun was good to us. I thought I wanted to be a doctor, because that's what my father told me I wanted to be, and because I wanted such a set of instruments as his father and grandfather had owned. Dr. Von Glaun told me about the rigors of his profession, and let me look into his microscope.

He saved my brother's life. Toby had a stomach ache, together with a couple of symptoms not by themselves alarming. Dr. Von Glaun managed an inspired diagnosis by telephone of a rare disorder, the small intestine slipping into the large, a process that leads to awful pain and to death when the patient commences to eliminate his own organs. Dr. Von Glaun arranged the operation in New London, had someone come down from Boston with my father, who even paid the specialist.

Toby was a long time recovering. He turned fussy and spoiled during his recuperation and after, and I began to feud with him. He learned to take advantage of an absolute injunction against hitting or pushing him, and my mother took his side in our disputes: he was endangered in a way I was not, he was littler, and he resembled her in appearance and temperament as I resembled my father. Greater distance opened between us. I would swear that Duke did nothing to divide my mother from me, that he never suggested that she wasn't brilliant or that her taste wasn't flawless. Yet my mother felt his judgment on her like a weight, and if memory is false, perhaps she and I were nudged, and did not merely drift, apart.

She was dutiful, patient, never harsh. I was scrubbed, dressed, fed, maintained, given music lessons, brought up better than our means allowed. She was always good for a game of baseball, and could outslug and outrun me and my friends till we reached the sixth grade. Still, something was missing between us. I sometimes felt, watching her look at me, that she wished she were alone. She must have felt I wished I were with someone else.

So, with a sick brother, a pigtailed belovèd who would have liked to shazam me from the earth's face, a mother distracted by bills and lack of love for her husband, I spent much time alone. I read, walked with my dog, read, rode my bike, read. I angled for sunfish, alone, or walked through swarms of deerflies to the mudflats near Duck River, to sit and stare at something other than the pages of a book.

I wasn't a pariah at school, just an outsider, weird, set apart by my stammer and my father's elegant taste and manners and my morbid notion of humor and my short haircut. My schoolmates parted their hair, slicked it down like nine-year-old bank presidents.

I had one friend, a classmate. Michael was a good athlete, courteous, quiet and, like me, accustomed to solitude. His mother had left Old Lyme, leaving his father with a son and two daughters. Michael's father worked at the United Nations as a translator from Japanese into Russian, Russian into English, English into Japanese or any of about a dozen other combinations. He had helped break the Japanese military and diplomatic code just before Pearl Harbor, and his hobbies were mathematical puzzles and cryptograms. Children were for him an uninteresting mystery, and to solve the conundrum of his son's upkeep he turned to my parents, who welcomed Michael as a lodger, more or less at cost.

My life changed. Michael was respectful to my parents,

cool-tempered, a born instructor. He tried to teach me
things. He advised me how best to play Margaret Dean
(to no effect), how to do long division (to no effect), and
how to fend off my mother's irritation by volunteering
small domestic favors so that greater services were not
required. He agreed that my dog was beautiful and
intelligent beyond all other beings, and that my brother
was a pain in the ass. He agreed to these things because he
calculated by his agreement some solace to me and no
hurt to him.

Michael was a brother. So we fought sometimes; I
began the fights, but never won them. Michael was two
inches shorter, but he was a bulldog once he dug in. There
was a delicate balance between us: on the one side he lived
in my house; on the other he had higher grades, more
friends, and was better at baseball.

Baseball occasioned our meanest fight. Even before
spring began to lift the load of winter kids in our school
would put together hardball games in damp meadows,
boys and girls playing together, and in these pre-season
games I did okay. I was always reaching for the fences, my
father's son, but at bat I usually got a piece of something.
My fielding was uncertain; I threw far and sometimes
accurately.

Old Lyme Elementary School had a baseball team, and
when the season truly began it played teams from nearby
Saybrook and Westbrook and Madison and Essex and
Deep River. My mother was a driver for away games,
piling as many as eleven kids in the Ford, and to repay her
for this service, I guess, the coach sometimes played me. I
didn't like Mr. Carver: he was an ass-slapper and
arm-puncher, one for pep talks, a cave of winds.

During my sixth-grade May our team was practicing
for the season opener against Deep River, out of town. I
was trying out for shortstop, and Skippy Sheffield, a
switch-hitting catcher who looked at eleven like he'd for
sure be with the Red Sox before I could legally drive, who
in fact went nowhere at all, drove a line drive at me. From
fear I raised my glove, and the ball slapped into it, and

stayed there. Not knowing what else to do with it, I threw it to second, where it was caught, and there was a double play. Mr. Carver, looking elsewhere, did not see this. He did see me lose a pop fly in the sun, and saw the ball hit my forehead.

The next day, Saturday, Mr. Carver was to stop at our house to pick up Michael and me. The Ford had been towed away again, and my father had not yet devised the sweet-talk to get it back. Mr. Carver arrived with a car full of kids and told Michael to get in back and me to go home, he wouldn't need me today, maybe some other time. Michael didn't want to leave without me, but he did. I went to the side of the house and stood watching Japanese beetles, piled six deep, perpetuate themselves with tender leisure. My father was fiddling with an altimeter he needed for his dashboard, and heard what he suspected were tears. He came outside and asked me what was wrong.

"Nothing."

My father did not care for "nothing" as an answer to his question, and he asked again, sharply. I slapped a ball into the pocket of my Rawlings "Phil Rizutto" glove, and sobbed out the story, without neglecting a reference to yesterday's double play. My father grew very angry, and he dragged me, against my mother's protest and my own, to his MG. Along the way he jammed on his head a silly tweed cap, the kind that heel-and-toe downshifters of advanced years still wear. The MG driver's cockpit was on the wrong side. This was going to be unpleasant. I tried to talk my father into leaving it be, but this made him even angrier: a dumb injustice had been done me, and Duke would set it right.

The teams were at play when we arrived, and Old Lyme was at bat, with Michael taking a lead off third. He looked at me as though he wanted not to know me. The game stopped while my father parked the MG, the *red* MG, six feet from home plate, nowhere near the other parents' cars, black sedans, maybe a gray coupe for a sport. My father approached Mr. Carver, shouting. My father's voice rose, and began to stammer. Mr. Carver made the mistake of touching my father's arm to calm him, and my father cocked his fist so fast Skippy Sheffield ran from the batter's box. Then my father noticed me, and he didn't throw the punch. He lowered his voice.

"Put my boy up."

Mr. Carver explained that there was a batter at the plate.

"I want my boy to bat now."

I was pushed to the plate. The pitcher was rattled, and walked me. I tried to steal second, was thrown out standing up, and "our" side retired. My father drove me home then, and couldn't speak to me. I wouldn't speak to him.

That night Michael and I fought. I began it, picking on him, working him over while we brushed our teeth and got into our pajamas. I made cracks about his height, his haircut, his clothes, his sisters, his father.

"Your old man's a fanatic ascetic," I said quoting Duke, knowing the meaning of neither polysyllabic in the accusation.

"What's that mean?" Michael said.

"Don't you know *anything?*"

Then I said my father thought his father was a cheapskate, and that he didn't pay my father a fair share of Michael's costs. So finally I got what I wanted, and we tumbled on the floor, punching and kicking, trying to hurt each other. I swore; Michael was silent when we fought; he meant business. My mother stopped us. She came upstairs because my dog was howling, and when she pried us apart neither of us would say what caused the fight, because for once we both understood exactly what had caused it.

That night we lay silent for a long time on the sleeping porch. Other nights we talked as soon as our lights were out, about sex, about seeing the world together, about school, cars, the stuff Ripley printed in *Believe It Or Not*. That night neither would speak first. Then Shep began to whimper. He was so confused and miserable, and Michael laughed, and called the dog up on his bed. I didn't say "Shep's my dog, you can't have him," because I didn't even think to say it. So we were past it, and then we began to talk, and I told Michael he shouldn't have gone to the game without me, and Michael said he thought I was probably right about that. I didn't know what else to say, except that I had lied about what my father said about his father.

Michael said, "Jesus! Did you *see* old man Carver's face when the Duke was about to pop him? It was great, he near peed his pants. Skippy moved pretty quick too."

Good friend. My father had called his father a cheapskate, though. And not long after he called him a cheapskate Duke rode home from New York in the army surplus jeep Michael's strange father drove, summer and winter, without a top. This was winter, and it was snowing, and the cockpit was a chaos of noise. Duke chose that time to make his pitch, a labyrinthine hard-luck story with allusions to temporary setbacks in oil shale and uranium investments. Michael's father pulled to the side of the Merritt Parkway and opened his glove compartment and peeled three hundred off a bankroll, three times what my father had asked to borrow.

"Here."

"I'll pay you back in sixty days, maybe less."

"No, you won't. You'll never pay me back."

And then Michael's father drove on into the storm. My father didn't throw the money in the man's face, or so I heard from Michael, years later in a letter, and by then I had no reason to doubt him.

Finally, all credit exhausted, we had to leave Old Lyme. "I couldn't go to a grocery store within twenty miles," my mother remembers. "Every week someone came to take something away, the furniture, a record player, the stove, even firewood." Joe Freedman wanted the house itself, and that was that, an escape was planned.

Duke got a job with a New York engineering firm as a

consultant to Averell Harriman's European Co-Operation Administration. He was bound for Turkey, to organize an airline. My mother and Toby and I would go south, to Florida. I was not told these things, but overheard them, and was instructed not to speak of them lest people "misunderstand," lest tradespeople lynch my mother and father. I wanted to say goodbye to Dr. Von Glaun, but this was not possible; we owed him money; he was not understanding.

I wanted to say goodbye to Michael, whose father had removed him from our house after quarreling with my father about something having no evident bearing on money, a question of politics or child psychology. Later Michael went to Alaska to earn money for college, earned it and was driving home (in a jeep), fell asleep on the Pennsylvania Turnpike (in a blizzard), went off the road and was paralyzed. Much later he fell in his shower, and was terribly burned by hot water while he lay helpless. I heard this a couple of years ago, when I stopped by my old school. I drove to the house where Michael lived when he left us, where he lives now. I parked outside for half an hour, saw curtains move, a face, perhaps, at the window. I couldn't open my car door. I drove away, entered the Connecticut Turnpike. I was terrified of my fear, and returned to his house, ran to the front door, rang the bell, waited not nearly long enough for a paralyzed friend to wheel himself to his door, and drove away again. I never said goodbye to Michael when I was eleven, either.

We stole away, my father in the MG to a garage near Hartford where he hid it, my mother and Toby and I in the Ford. A few days later Eaglebrook, trying to put the arm on its alumni and would-be alumni for gifts, tracked Duke to Old Lyme, wrote the postmaster, and got back its letter stamped "moved, left no address." The dogged school then wrote a town officer, and he wrote back:

> The above mentioned person left this town of Old Lyme some time ago, and as I understand it leaving many large

and small accounts unsatisfied. These creditors would like to know of his whereabouts also. This is the third such inquiry which this office has answered, perhaps less bluntly heretofore; in any event, we are unaware of this person's whereabouts, and know no person who is, but many who wish they did. Further inquiry is not desired.

11

Our Ford, like the Joad's truck in *The Grapes of Wrath*, was burdened by every possession we didn't leave behind to be picked over by creditors. Nothing stored except the MG and Shep, stuff tied to the roof and fenders like dead deer. By the time we hit southern New Jersey, mid-August, with the temperature in triple figures, the overloaded wagon began to boil over, and the oil pressure began to fall, and there seemed no way the money would stretch as far as Florida.

By Delaware Mother looked crazy. She drove sitting on a pillow to see out the high windshield, and pressed so hard against the door she seemed to want to break through it. Her knuckles were white on the wheel; she stuck her head out the window to dry the sweat from her face and escape the battles raging between Toby and me. I wonder what she promised herself during that damned trip, how close I came to being left in a Myrtle Beach motel room with a note tied around my neck: *Hi! My name is Jeff. All I'll eat is Stuckey's pecan stuff. I want a pair of beaded Seminole moccasins and to see a snake ranch. My mother left, looking for a better way to live.*

I nagged my mother for a boat and motor. Excepting Toby, always indifferent to material things, we were a family of material lusts, fixations that came down like fevers, and hung on. My father's wants were the most varied and capricious: anything of quality, a novel car, a blackthorn walking stick, folding scissors, a tattersall vest. Mother, with sand between her toes, wanted always to be somewhere warmer and sunnier, and she studied out-of-town newspapers, travel folders and shipping schedules the way Father studied Abercrombie & Fitch catalogues. My desires were fewer than my father's, but as severe: an outboard-powered dinghy, an outboard-powered runabout, an outboard-powered racing runabout, an outboard-powered racing hydroplane.

A couple of months before we left Old Lyme I had sent away to Evinrude for a catalogue, and would spend an hour and more every night studying it, and especially a picture of a smiling boy and his dad being pushed at dawn along the misty shore of a verdant lake by a three-horsepower Fastwin, with Weedless Drive. I wanted one. My father knew I wanted it, and my mother knew I wanted it. My mother found my wish not at all novel, but beyond possibility. To satisfy my ardor for boating Duke sometimes chartered a leaky gray rowboat, with a Johnson Seahorse on the transom, and let me drive him about in it. This didn't entirely satisfy my dream, which was to be free not only of land but landsmen, to go somewhere under my own power, alone. Still, my pleasure at the tiller of any outboard was so extreme that Duke yielded to me, and in effect robbed a boat dealer near New Haven of a one-horsepower Evinrude and a Penn Yan dinghy, a gorgeous eight-footer with spruce ribs, mahogany seats and trim, and white canvas topsides. He promised to pay for this after a check cleared, stock was transferred, when his accountant returned from holiday abroad . . . presently.

Two months later the boat, which I was allowed to drive in the bay at Point o' Woods while one of my parents watched from the beach, was repossessed. The motor too. I did not witness this. All I knew was that as soon as my father left for Turkey, my boat and motor were gone. My mother spared me the particulars, told me only that there was no room in the car to take the boating gear with us to Florida, but that she would replace it when we got there. This she knew she could not do; I knew she would not do it, and from the moment I no longer had the boat I had once had, I gave her no peace.

"You beat on me all the way south," Mother says.

What kind of boat can I get? Another Penn Yan? Cross your heart? Father gave it to me. I miss him. You won't break your promise? When will I see Shep? Are they feeding him what he likes? Tell Toby to move over, he's on my half of the seat. I'm hungry. Can we see the Spanish moss place? What's Spanish moss? I miss Dad. Why did we have to move? Can we buy the boat as soon as we get there? The first day? Promise?

We pulled in lame and broke, and found temporary refuge with a couple who had lived near us in Old Lyme. Melinda had been Duke's childhood friend in Hartford and had encouraged our move to Mile Creek Road with an uneducated eagerness she did not display upon our arrival in Florida. She was stocky, foulmouthed, tanned butternut, and thought kids were a pestilence.

She ran a development on Treasure Island called "Pieces of Eight" or "The Black Dog" or somesuch, a residential resort whose houses had names like "Ben Gunn's" or "Bill Bones'" or "Dead Man's Chest." The main house was "Long John Silver's," and there was a power launch called the *Hispaniola*, and it was enough to gutter forever my enthusiasm for my favorite book.

I didn't like Melinda, her taste in proper nouns, or Florida. The water tasted of sulphur, it was hot, strange things crawled across the sand, mangroves looked ridiculous. Melinda's kin were Nature's avant-garde, and walked Treasure Island naked, which I would not do, and I was embarrassed to reveal my priggishness. My mother wore a bathing suit, but to accommodate the spirit of the place where we were guests obliged Toby to go bare-assed. He sat on beach cactus, and cried.

After a week of this we found a cottage for fifty a month on Siesta Key, near Sarasota. It was only a quarter mile from the Gulf of Mexico but that poorhouse was the meanest place I ever lived. It was tiny, with beaverboard partitions soft as mold from the dampness that penetrated everything always, chilling us and mildewing our clothes. The bare wood floors, painted gray, were slick and cold and loosely joined; they bristled with splinters. The stink of sulphur hung like perpetual fog, sand stuck to bedclothes and vinyl upholstery, the rooms were dark, and I was ashamed to live there.

Shame encouraged fantasy. I imagined myself else-where and otherwise, wished myself into other people's skins. I had come upon a book called *Big Red*, about a trapper who worked the Maine woods with his boy and his boy's red setter. The book attracted me because it was set in a place so unlike Florida, and about a boy alone with his father. I missed my father, and I let my mother know this every half hour or so.

Duke sent checks, almost adequate for our care, and letters telling about Turkey and his adventures, begging us to be cautious, reminding my mother not to let Toby or me come down with polio. Mother was more interested in his checks than his prose, as I knew. I would study those letters, with his black, thick characters, so grotesquely outsized that he filled a sheet with only sixty or eighty words. They invariably closed with some expression of affectionate longing that caused me to run to my room, slam my door and fall upon my bed. I have never broken myself of the morning jitters for incoming mail—the good news, big break, grand slam—and it began then, waiting for those blue, tissue-thin envelopes (not so many of them, either), covered like a fanatic's bumper with gummed instructions, warnings, expostulations: FRAG-ILE ... DO NOT BEND ... RUSH! ... SPECIAL HANDLING ... URGENT COPY ... EXPEDITE! My father actually believed that special requests received special treatment. In fact, many of his letters never arrived. That is, some checks never arrived. That is, my mother had my father's assurance that he had sent—PRIORITY—some checks that never arrived. Perhaps they drew too much attention to themselves.

I wandered a lot, and liked people to strike up talk with me. Most of them were nice, carefree tourists or retired old-timers who missed their grandchildren in Michigan. Sometimes they asked questions:

"Where are your parents?"

"My mom's here in Sarasota."

Some would ask then where my father was. Whether they asked or didn't I told them:

"My dad's a trapper in the Maine woods. Next year I'm taking my collie Shep up there to run the traplines with him. We'll live in a log cabin."

People who had asked my father's whereabouts said *really, how curious, how nice for you all, what fascinating work*. Other people just stared at me. Later these stories drifted back to my mother, and she asked me with gentle amusement to be truthful, said that I sometimes puzzled people. After my mother spoke with me about this I continued to tell the same story, except to confirm the suspicion, yes, my parents were divorced, and I'd be leaving soon for Maine, my dad and I preferred a cold climate.

I entered seventh grade in a Quonset hut set behind Sarasota High School. There were no black kids in my class of thirty, but plenty of kids of a kind I had never before seen, boys with torn clothes and sores on their skin, classmates with breasts as big as my mother's. Ringling Brothers wintered in Sarasota, and midget-sized children of midgets came to my school with regular-sized children of The Tall Man, olive-skinned children of acrobats and animal trainers, and the boastful, tetchy get of wire-walkers. I couldn't quite catch the drift of the teacher's

Georgia accent. Besides, she was pretty. I was aroused when I stared at her. She blushed when she caught me staring at her, or felt me staring at her back. I blushed too. I asked to be switched to another class; she wanted this too, but neither of us could make our reasons understood to ourselves, let alone the principal, so we were stuck with each other.

I had stomach cramps every school morning, pains that doubled me over. My mother believed in them, and didn't believe in them. An internist performed a fluoroscopic examination, and suggested it might be good medicine to bring Shep to Florida.

I played a lot, hung around the Sarasota municipal pier feeding Old Pete, a broken-winged pelican, and making up stories for the old codgers on the beaches. Sometimes I'd hitch-hike back home, and if my mother wasn't around, and she usually wasn't, I'd take the key from where she'd hidden it and unlock the cabinet where my pellet rifle was kept and pick my way through the palmettos to Sarasota Bay off the eastern shore of Siesta Key. I'd hide in the mangroves and shoot at cabin cruisers passing by, or at trees, or straight up in the air, to see if I could make a lead pellet fall straight down, on me. When Shep arrived in a crate at the Railway Express depot I put my days to better use, watching him run the Gulf beach, chasing the gulls that teased him till he was almost out of sight, then back the other way, till he was almost out of sight, back and forth till we used up an entire day, an ambition realized.

I had a friend. Ernie lived in a trailer park just off the Tamiami Trail. Our derelict Schwinns brought us together. He'd ride to my house, or I'd ride to his trailer. I liked his trailer better, and so did he. His father tucked a pack of dirty playing cards, held by a rubber band, beneath some unused handkerchiefs. Ernie's father was never home, and we always had an extra rubber band, just in case we broke his. The cards were kept in a cigar box with an eight-page Tijuana bible that spelled tit *tut*, and a thing whose use we couldn't guess at, what I knew the following year was a French tickler. Ernie was the grungiest kid in class, and it upset my mother that I chose him for my friend. I didn't choose, he didn't choose, we were all that was left after the others chose. Ernie told me his father did it every night to his mother, and I told Ernie he was full of it, and told my mother the story to illustrate what dumb people will try to put over on people as smart as I was.

My mother said I was twelve now, it was time to talk. I said I knew what there was to know. She asked me if I understood that people sometimes made love because it was pleasant, and not merely to have babies. I said I had heard this, and believed it, that dirty people did these things. She told me that many kinds of people did such things, why she herself sometimes did such a thing, just for the hell of it.

I was stunned. I would have been more stunned had I understood that my mother was speaking not principally, or perhaps at all, about intimacies with my father, that my mother was trying, with good will, to tell me something she thought I should know. I was stunned.

My mother had met an ex-policeman from Michigan. This man, like Ernie's father, lived in a trailer, but his was north rather than south of Sarasota on the Tamiami Trail. He was thick-necked and coarse; he had appeared at our cottage once or twice, and on "our" beach, where he let Mother oil his hairy back and belly. I didn't like him, and he didn't like me, though he pretended he did. Mother knew he was pretending, but didn't much care.

These memories are painful for my mother, I know. I think they bear down too heavily for their specific gravity; my mother made mistakes of taste and judgment, but I was a hanging judge.

"I know my shortcomings as a mother in Florida. I was self-centered, trying to have a good time, regain my youth, be desirable again. Your father had been so imperious about people, who was okay and who was a jerk, and once I was away from him, free to pick people

myself, I picked people for friends he wouldn't have.
Maybe he was right. I certainly made dumb choices."

I think of Sarasota and I think of sex, and the memories
depress rather than excite me. The girl who sat in front of
me in class we called Pear-Shape, and I bullied her so
relentlessly about her breasts, was so cruel to her for
having them at all, was so obviously "troubled" and "in
trouble" that Mother was called to the school for a
consultation. An inventory was run of my offenses, the
principal ticking them off on his fingers. Mother
explained that our home life was difficult, money was
tight, that father was away on business, we would all try
harder, she couldn't manage me really, she had just begun
a job, what could she do? What, damn it, did they *suggest?*
    It was agreed I was bright. Good intelligence quotient,
blah-blah-blah. Alarmingly mature about some things,
irregular, even backward, about others. Poor citizenship,
bad attitude. Perhaps a hobby would help.
    My mother asked me after the meeting if I would like to
try a hobby. I told her I would like to take up boating as a
hobby, to drive a Penn Yan dinghy powered by an
Evinrude Fastwin with Weedless Drive.
    In fact I had "interests." After October my chief
preoccupation was Christmas, not what I would get but
what I would give. I wanted only one thing other than my
boat, an electric train, and I knew my mother would not
buy me an electric train. She had taken a job as a
salesclerk in a swank downtown store for ladies, and I
would run her to ground there to beg small change for a
movie at the Ritz, or a soda at Rexall's. She found it
awkward to deny me when she was among customers or
her employers; she was embarrassed by me and eager to
be rid of me, and I knew to the penny the price of being got
rid of.
    The purpose of these raids on my mother's petty cash
was in fact devious, perhaps even selfless. Reading by
flashlight one autumn night I cast about for something to
lose sleep looking at, and found the 1949 Sears Christmas

catalogue. I put check marks beside gifts I would buy my mother, beginning with a redwood chest which I set about filling with stuff: a sun hat, beach sandals, a garment called a "halter," jewelry after the fashion of the Aztecs, a blanket. To pay for these things I accumulated my allowance, plus what I could cadge from my mother at work, plus what I stole from her purse at night. I also baby-sat for the sons of a dentist and his wife, children and parents so exotic in their regular habits and uncomplicated affections that I would sometimes stand mute in their presence, studying them as a naturalist might study unnatural phenomena.

The coins piled up, and then the gifts. I don't know what I meant them to mean to her, what I thought I was saying. Maybe I didn't think at all. I know there was about this something aggressive, and that my zeal for generosity led me to new delinquencies.

Downtown Sarasota was seedy, and never worse than near Christmas. That was the first year of "Rudolph the Red-nosed Reindeer" and it played ceaselessly on a p.a. system strung with chrome stars and gaudy rubber angels from the aboveground power lines. People took their beneficial rays with ten shopping days left. People with sunburns bought plastic snow for the plastic tree.

I cased the gift shops and souvenir stores for something special to steal for my mother. I chose a card. It had snow stuck to it, and a message in raised letters, and a silk puffed lavender heart smelling of lavender. I stashed it under my Red Sox jacket, but the envelope fell out near the door and the owner nabbed me. I cried, but this cut no ice with him, and he sent for a cop. The policeman made as though to arrest me, and promised to send me where I could never do harm again. He walked me out of sight down the block, cuffed me behind the ear and told me to go home and be a good boy. I went home.

We decorated a starveling jack pine. Christmas was cold and damp, and my mother was astonished by her gifts. Where had they come from? Who paid? Why so many? I smiled, was an enigma, knew what I knew. There was an electric train, after all. It wouldn't run. My mother worked over the wires and connections like someone with one last chance, twenty seconds to unriddle The Meaning of Life. She remembers I was "not a little man" about the silent, motionless train. I remember I couldn't for the life of me figure out why she had bought it for me.

From Turkey my father had sent me a ceremonial sword, a fez, harem slippers and a chronometer, my first grown-up watch. This told things bearing on tides, dates, and time zones. It divided time into units as large as months and as small as milliseconds, and had three different buttons to be pushed. It had luminous numerals and hands (with two sweep second hands). Its face was black, with three silver sub-faces. It said it was made in Switzerland, had seventeen jewels, and was shock- and water-resistant.

I wore it to school the day Christmas vacation ended. A wise guy across the aisle, Jimbo, the son of a furniture dealer who hadn't given my mother a job, also had a new watch, some American thing, a Hamilton, maybe a Bulova. It too claimed to move on jeweled bearings, and to be shock and waterproof.

"Your watch isn't worth shit," Jimbo told me. "Shocks and water'll bust it."

"Read it. It's water-resistant, shock too."

"Resistant isn't proof."

"Bullshit."

Jimbo proposed a lunch-hour watch drop, followed by total immersion. I agreed, unhappily. There were witnesses. Pear-Shape was pulling for Jimbo, and only my pal Ernie for me. We held our watches by the ends of their straps, and *one . . . two . . . three . . .* dropped them to the floor. Or I did. Jimbo didn't drop his. Mine broke, and he laughed. My watch never ran again.

The next day I brought my ceremonial sword to school, and offered to put it in one of his ears and out the other—magic, maybe—if he didn't drop his watch into a basin filled with water. He did this. His watch was made to be dropped into a basin filled with water.

Paula Wilson, the prettiest girl in class, who sat behind me where I couldn't see her, told me after school she was sorry I had broken my watch. So I was sorry that all year I had dropped pencils on the floor so I could wheel my head around at ground level to look up her skirt at her clean white cotton underpants. Paula became my "nice" friend. Her parents lived in a large white mission house, with a red tile roof, near the Ringling Museum. They inexplicably liked me, and let me take Paula to the movies. At the movies we even held hands, but the experience was a little like a week in the country on the arm of the Fresh Air Fund.

Everything was falling apart. I fought every day after school, and Ernie's old man decided I was a bad influence on his boy. I was. Ernie and I sometimes took our air rifles to an abandoned construction site to have shootouts like we saw in the Westerns Saturday morning at the Ritz, or the gangster movies we saw weekdays when I could get him to skip school with me. In the beginning we shot at each other from hiding places, potting in the other guy's general direction and shouting "varmint" or "yellow rat" at each other. But the stakes went up, and finally I got him in the back of the neck when he broke cover to run to another hiding place. He collapsed, I thought I had killed him. When I reached Ernie he was thrashing around in the sand, screaming. Nothing would calm him till I let him shoot me in the back at a hundred paces. It hurt like hell, and we never played together again.

Duke had been hired and sent to Turkey with his employer's knowledge that he didn't like to pay bills, and with the warning that here was a final chance for a gifted, careless man. My father began work in August 1949 with a year's contract, on a year's probation. In April, nine months later, he arrived unannounced in Sarasota, in the MG. (He had stashed it in Harry Atkins' garage, confiding that it was "hot." Ruth's husband Harry, bless him, was a sucker for Duke's intrigues.)

My father had been fired. He didn't explain why. It

didn't matter; we were broke, so my father's first act was to move us to a more comfortable house, a small, tight, clean cottage down Siesta Key near Midnight Pass. This had better access to a beach, and Toby had a backyard where he could play without being cut by cactus and nettles.

I cared only that my father was home. He brought with him a trunk filled with toys and curiosities, things for Rosemary from the Istanbul bazaar, for Toby a mechanical monkey that twirled a stick and then climbed it, postcards of bearded horsemen waving swords and antique rifles, a pair of Zeiss field glasses for me. A boat was promised.

Weeks passed, and my mother wondered aloud how we would eat. Duke grinned; piece of cake, Pan Am had lost his luggage en route from Vienna to Paris. They couldn't find it, conceded failure, and would buy him off for fifteen hundred dollars, plenty till another job came along.

I changed when my father came home. My stomach cramps disappeared, I had someone to mediate the bitter disputes between Toby and me. My father came with me sometimes to watch the Red Sox in spring training.

The Red Sox had been playing exhibition games several weeks when Duke returned, and I had cut school many days to watch them. Walt Dropo was shaping up to be 1950 Rookie of the Year, Billy Goodman was hitting well, but I went to watch Ted Williams, distant and slope-shouldered, alone with himself. I wanted to get Ted Williams' name on a baseball, an almost unattainable ambition. The team was vulnerable when it crossed an open lot to reach the field from a shower and equipment building. There I tugged sleeves, called names. I had two Spaulding balls, one to be signed by every member of the starting line up except Williams, the other wrapped in tissue paper, virgin, for Him alone. Day after day he shrugged me off, ran beside me without looking at me, once ran *over* me when I tried to block him. Everyone else smiled and signed.

One day Williams was coming off the field after a

powerhouse afternoon against the Tigers in an exhibition game, and there I was again, looking whipped.

"Don't stand there like a mutt, kid, you'll never get anything you want."

What a voice! It said words! To me. I held out the ball, for Williams had stopped beside me, looking down quizzically, as though I might be for sale, something to eat.

"Pen? Haven't you even got a pen?"

I thrust him a ballpoint. He had to scrape it a few times against the horsehide to get it flowing, putting two runic legends on the ball. But he was signing.

"Ted, would you put *To Jeff from Ted Williams, The Splendid Splinter?*"

"Jesus, what a bozo."

And then he was gone, tossing the ball back over his shoulder. The ball said *Ted Williams*. And the damned pen had skipped, so most of the characters were broken. At home I studied the ball. It didn't satisfy me. I closed the breaks in the letters of his signature, making it bold and perfect. Then I practiced his script till I had it better than he had it. And then I wrote on my ball what he would have written had he had time: *For Jeff, A Great Kid, Ted Williams, The Splendid Splinter, Batter Up!*

I took my ball to school. Everyone agreed it was a fake. Everyone agreed the *Ted Williams* part was a forgery, too. A few days later Toby took this ball into the backyard and lost it. He admitted this to me, but not to my parents. He told them he had seen me foul it into a mangrove swamp, that I blamed him for everything. I hit him in the stomach, where I was never to hit him. My mother cuffed me, and I ran away from home for an hour or two.

Things got worse all the time at school, and by May Miss Bartlett couldn't bear me anymore. I played hooky, was scrappy, profane and never left Pear-Shape in peace. In my campaign against this girl I had followers, and one day, testing the waters, I proposed a class debate on the question of Pear-Shape's misery. Incredibly, Miss Bartlet agreed. I led the affirmative. Resolved: something like *Gail's Chest Is Provocative So It Is Okay To Call Her Pear-Shape*. The negative won walking away, but not before my team drove Gail sobbing from the Quonset hut. Miss Bartlett dismissed the class three hours early, and the next day her boyfriend, an alligator-wrestler at Sarasota Jungle Gardens, came to school with her, and took me aside:

"Watch it, bub, I'll be keeping tabs on you."

This I found droll, and repeated it several dozen times that morning at Miss Bartlett's back, with what I took to be an accurate swamp-gas accent. Some of my classmates laughed, fewer each time.

That afternoon my father met me at school in the MG. He had just had a call from my teacher, she wanted to talk with me. I warned him how unfair she was, not to listen to her. My father, in a pleasant humor, said he would judge her fairness for himself. I was to wait for him in the car. The top was down, the sun was vicious, the leather seats stoked up; I had been instructed to sit tight, not even to open the car door. I watched the high school team, the Sarasota Sailors, practice baseball for an hour, and then another hour, and I wondered why I couldn't be like them, just nice. I was afraid. I saw my father walking toward the car, slowly. He didn't look angry, merely determined.

"Miss Bartlett told me all about you," my father said, as we drove away.

"Let me explain," I said, and then said nothing.

"There's nothing to it, really. You're a dime a dozen, just a wiseguy."

We drove awhile, and I said, "I'll be better, I won't be like that anymore."

"Maybe," my father said. "I hope so. Because that's why I'm going to beat you when we get home, so you won't be like that anymore."

I was hysterical, my father was calm. I pressed him for specific torts and he shrugged. All he said was one thing:

"I've mailed three hundred résumés, and no one has answered."

He showed anger only once, when I resisted going into my bedroom. Then he grabbed my arm so hard I knew he would break it if I didn't move, and his tongue did that awful curling thing it sometimes did, and I let him put me where he wanted me, on my belly, facing the wall, with my pants and underpants pulled down. Then he began to beat me with his razor strop as hard as he could, whistling strokes that emptied my lungs from the first hit, so I never caught my breath to scream while I lay staring pop-eyed at a wall poster, big fish eating little fish, while my mother on the other side of the locked door did scream: *Let me in! What are you doing, you goddamned awful man, what are you doing to him!*

Then it stopped, so my mother didn't drive off to get the police but to make an appointment with a lawyer, she had had enough, that was all she would take. When it was over my father hugged me, and said only this: "Be good. Try, at least. Don't be like that. Try."

And then I wept, so ashamed of it all. knowing better what I had done than he knew. Miss Bartlett knew, my mother knew. anyone would know. And when my mother returned, ready to unload on him for the last time, dying to be rid of him forever, wanting to protect me from him, she found him in the bathroom, preparing to shave. Mother saw us through the open door. I was sitting on the edge of the bathtub, looking up. My eyes were still red from weeping, but I looked at my father's thick, muscular legs and broad back, the sweep of his throat, with full admiration and wonder. Peach fuzz had begun to grow on my cheeks. My father was wearing only the baggy Sea Island cotton Brooks Brothers boxer shorts he favored, always pale blue. He had lathered his face with a brush, bone handle and badger bristles, a heavy instrument I sometimes rubbed dry against my own face. It was as soft as my mother's fur coat. He swirled the bristles in shaving soap packed in a teak bowl, and lathered his cheeks and then his upper lip, and then his chin, and finally his neck and throat. He stropped his straight razor against the long tongue of dark leather he had just beaten so powerfully against my ass, and he began to shave, sure, daring, straight strokes, first his cheeks, and then his upper lip, and then his chin, talking to me.

"That strop was my father's, the razor too. His father's before that . . . Good blade . . . Surgical steel . . . Very sharp blade."

My father was shaving the side of his neck.

"The Doctor used this every day till he was seventy . . ."

My father was shaving the other side of his neck.

"One day he was shaving his Adam's apple . . ."

My father was shaving his Adam's apple, stretching back his throat like a hanged man, choking off his words, pulling me forward off the cold edge of the tub to make them out.

". . . and he suddenly realized he wanted to pull the damned razor right across his throat, be done with it. He never used it again, gave it to me."

My father stood still, stared in the mirror, saw me there, grinned and pulled the razor across his throat. Blood bubbled up slowly from the white foam at my father's throat. My mouth opened, a choked noise came out of me, and my father turned and looked down and smiled and said gently, "It's nothing, look." And it wasn't much, just a tease, a slight cut, but that wasn't what he meant by *it's nothing*. I knew then that if it got too bad for him, he could do it, *it's nothing*.

It got bad for him. He tried to get work everywhere and no one wanted him. Word was out, I guess. His résumés turned more and more desperate, trying to do the magic they'd done before. I have one from those days, mailed about the time the fifteen hundred for the lost luggage had run out, and the Ford was in the garage for another valve job. Now he spoke, read, and wrote—"fluently"—French, Spanish, Italian, German, Turkish, Persian and, in one of those bravura gestures he could never resist, Burmese. The Sorbonne degree now came from "*Lá*

Univèrsité de Sorbónne, Ecóle Aeronautìque," his italics and accents. His employment in Birmingham was described, in part, like this:

> ... Integrated a survey of entire aviation industry for War Department which resulted in Bechtel-McCone Corporation being detailed to construct and operate the Air Force's largest modification center, at Birmingham, Alabama. Accomplished entire plant planning and layout as well as engineering and general construction supervision on above. Organized and administered Engineering Department of 350 as well as 3,200 persons in Production Division, including material control, scheduling. planning. and production control. Designed all modifications installed in B-24 and most installed in B-29. Responsible charge of all the above.

He said in his résumé that he had been well paid for such one-man-band play, never less than eighteen thousand a year since 1940, half again as much for the job from which he had just been sacked, from which he did not say he had just been sacked. However: "I am eager to return to aviation work, and will consider any salary above $8,000 per year." This gambit of generosity was declined, my mother believes, by as many as two hundred companies, most of which were hiring in those days of Red Scare and cost-plus contracts.

My father was drinking a lot, usually whiskey but sometimes his Big Trouble drink, hundred and fifty-one proof Hudson Bay rum. He argued at night with Rosemary, and one morning she appeared at breakfast with a bruise on her cheek. She wouldn't speak to my father, and this caused me to pity him rather than her, she was so intractable and he was so eager to be forgiven.

Sometimes they had fun. At the Ringling Hotel they met a young piano and organ player named Rip. He was an odd bird, short and wiry, a pocket-sized Rory Calhoun with dark curls, an awful temper, and a gentle wife. After Rip finished playing, the two couples went to the Tropicana, a Siesta Key roadhouse, where a drunk for no clear reason called Duke a "Hebe sonofabitch." My father beat the man badly, and Rip wanted to shoot him dead in the parking lot, but didn't, and the next day Rip took me to the lockup where my father proudly confessed to assault, and was released with a pat on the back by the genial Sarasota police.

Rip's mother owned a huge establishment three hours away on Lake Wales, and one night after work he and Duke and I drove up there in his van. Rip would slam on his brakes every time he saw a rabbit, park wherever the van came to rest, grab a snubnosed .32 from his glove compartment and chase the animal into the brush, shouting and shooting at it. Like many things this puzzled me, but I assumed I was puzzled because I was inexperienced in the ways of the world, so I did not ask Rip or my father why our host was so angry at rabbits.

To reach the lakefront estate we passed through a gate, with a gatehouse guarded by a sullen fellow who might once have played tackle if he could remember whether to go right or left. The house was surrounded by a stone wall, with broken bottles imbedded along its top. My father asked why all the caution, and Rip laid his index finger ninety degrees to his lips.

We arrived at dawn, and mist was coming off the lake. Rip asked me at breakfast if it would interest me to see the boathouse, and I said it would. There, ready to be launched by a geared lift, was an outboard hydroplane, a class-B Jacoby, canvas and varnished mahogany ply-wood, with a ten-horse Mercury hurricane hung on the transom.

"Keep it under forty, and wear the lifejacket," Rip told me.

I drove till they made me stop, after sundown. Rip's mother took us to a simple riverside restaurant where we ate catfish, and everyone made a great fuss over her. This was the happiest day I had ever had till my father began to drink rum, and fell silent, and stared at Rip's mother hard, and told Rip his mother bullied him.

"Don't spoil it, Duke," Rip said. "Careful now."

He was looking hard at my father, who suddenly laughed and said, "What the hell!"

"That's right," Rip said, and did not laugh. "What the hell."

When I turned twelve my mother had urged me to join the Boy Scouts, hoping I would be reformed by their decent program. After my father beat me for uselessness and bad manners I became a paradigm Scout, shooting up through the ranks, almost to the top. I was obsessed. I was a wonder. I had never before been a wonder, and I liked it. I beat the system, found the accessible angle. The only merit badge required for Eagle not on my full drape was Pioneering, the fundamental badge demanding forest lore, the felling of trees and construction of fires, competence in the woods.

My certificates of merit were concentrated elsewhere, in the sedentary, domestic, and commercial arts, nursing (First Aid), communications (Morse Code and Journalism), home economics (Cooking and Dog Care). While my fellow Scouts came relaxed to monthly ceremonies, where they got a badge or maybe two with a handshake, I came flushed and eager, taking them five at a clip: Personal Management (which required my father's supervision while I drew up a budget, and explained to him why it was better that one live within one's means, and why a hundred dollars was put to better use working for America in a savings bond than hid under a mattress. "Talk over with parents or guardian how family funds are spent to meet day-to-day and long-term needs. Tell how you can help with the family budget." Another requirement my father happily helped me fulfill was to prepare myself to tell my Scoutmaster "how important credit and installment buying are to our economy. Find out and tell what you must do to establish a good 'credit rating.'")

I got Leatherwork and Law, Traffic Safety and Salesmanship, but Pioneering was beyond me. Still, all this didn't come to nothing. Under the rubric *Awards and Honors* I kept "Life Scout, one badge short of Eagle" on my résumé till after I left college. And I learned in cold type that masturbation caused neither madness nor warts, but merely revealed mental distress, wasted time, and made a boy unfit for games or the company of his fellow Scouts.

A hundred days after my father came home from Turkey, Boeing, in Seattle, bit at his résumé. The pay was six-fifty a month, less than he wanted, but it was another chance, and he prepared to leave the day the letter came. We were to follow when he found a house in a good school district.

Duke loaded the MG and told Toby and me to care for our mother, just as he always did when he went away, which seemed to be every time I thought we were safely together again. I begged to go with him, promised I wouldn't get in his way, would keep him awake on the road, would be his navigator. I thought if I asked this carefully, using just the right words, he'd take me, so I asked every which way, but he didn't relent. Finally he let me ride with him as far as downtown Sarasota, and let me take him to the Rexall for a sandwich. I said he needed fuel for the long drive.

There were no tourists in August. The town was stifling, empty sidewalks and melting blacktop, just another tropical backwater. The drugstore was air-conditioned to arctic temperature. I felt the frosted leatherette booth through my shorts and T-shirt, and looked at my father across the table from me, relaxed, not at all eager to get moving. I wanted us to stay where we were forever. I ordered my way through the menu, canned pea soup, hot turkey sandwich with stuffing and mashed potatoes scooped out like a volcano and filled with thick tan gravy. My father gave advice:

"Turkey in these places is lousy. It's turkey roll. Next time order hot roast beef, rare, and if it isn't rare, send it back."

I guess I have been unhappier, more frightened, but I don't know when. My father saw this. He said it would be all right, we'd all be together in six weeks, life would be better, I'd like Seattle, hell, you couldn't get more than half a mile from the water in Seattle even if you wanted to. I asked if Mother would like Seattle and Duke said sure, she'd love it, just so we were all together. He squeezed my hand, and then I began to bawl, tried to shove mashed potatoes and stuffing in there to shut myself up, but it was no good. My father stood up, and I thought that was it, there he went, here I was, this was all there was going to be. But he came around the table and sat beside me, put an arm around me and hugged me, kissed the side of my face, didn't let me go while he talked.

"Christ, a lot of it's been bad, a real bitch. A little while, be brave, it will get better. I don't like this, either. I won't let it happen again."

I asked again if I could go west with him. He shook his head and I tried to dry my eyes. I saw then that our waitress and another were looking at us, giggling at my old man with his arm around a big kid like me, kissing me, wearing his rimless specs and a tweed hat, looking nothing at all like a regular at the Rexall, or any place.

"You can pick up the tab," my father said, mock-punching my arm. "Here's a tenner, you figure the tip. Spend what's left on a flick."

And then so fast I couldn't even say goodbye he was gone, out the door, and I sat there, staring at the waitresses. They turned their backs, and I picked up the ten and left without paying. The full August heat blasted my face and dried my eyes. I could hear the high whine of the MG's little engine as my father changed gears. I looked down the street toward the noise, but he was gone.

I walked up the street to the gift shop where I had been caught shoplifting. I stole a wooden alligator for my brother and a postcard for my old man. The postcard showed a kid and his father fishing in the Gulf, pulling in some huge goddamned thing, a marlin or tarpon or something. I didn't hide the card, just walked out with it.

The rest was squalor. Mother made friends with a German whose G.I. husband beat up the woman and shot into their bedroom window when she locked him out of their cabin, a mile from us. The woman was forlorn and hysterical, with wild hair and astonished eyes. She hid with her nine-year-old daughter in our house a week after my father left. The daughter played doctor with Toby, and I played doctor with her. I was rather old to play doctor with her. Then the woman and her little girl moved to the cottage next door. The G.I. came every night after the bars closed, cursing and threatening, revving the engine of his pickup, honking its horn. A policeman answered my mother's call, but this was an old movie for him. He told Mother the woman could have had the guy locked up long ago, but she wouldn't press charges against him.

"She hates him and she loves him," the cop told my mother, winking. "He must have something she likes, whaddya think?"

A few days after my father drove away, my mother took a job at a Dairy Queen on the Tamiami Trail, dealing cones for fifty dollars a week, wearing a paper cap. I asked when we would leave for Seattle.

"Never. We're not leaving here. I'm going to divorce your father."

This was not Birmingham now, where a little boy was led gently to the realities. My mother described her wishes, but didn't justify them. She had thirteen years to think about leaving her husband. She was thirty-two, and it must have seemed like a now-or-never option. I guess I asked her why she had misled my father, who had left Sarasota believing his wife would follow him west. If I asked her she didn't tell me, she was too busy to answer my questions. My mother worked ten hours a day, six days a week at the Dairy Queen, and at night she took typing lessons, to better herself. I wanted to telephone my father, but Mother said she couldn't afford long distance calls; besides, she didn't know his number.

I hitch-hiked downtown a lot, and haunted travel agents. They were indulgent to a twelve-year-old kid, business was slow. They told me the fare to Seattle, train and bus, one way. I kept the fares in my head. One agent asked why didn't I fly, so I got the dope on planes too.

I told my mother I'd find the money to go west to my father. Somehow. She'd stare at me then, and I'd ride my bike to Midnight Pass, and fish in the swift current between the tail of Siesta Key and the head of Casey Key. I'd walk the beach with Shep. It was deserted except for jelly fish left by the ebbing tide, and the gnawed hulks of horseshoe crabs, buzzing with sandflies.

School would begin in two weeks. Next door the man in the pickup wheedled his wife into opening the door. They laughed for a while, played the radio loud. Then he beat her up. The little girl must have slept through it; I never heard her voice. So the days and nights went.

The last night I lay in bed sweating, listening to frogs croak out back. There had been much rain that summer, and this had brought a red tide and a plague of frogs. There were so many frogs near our house that cars speeding to Midnight Pass at night sometimes skidded on them. Midnight Pass was a makeout spot. I lay awake thinking about girls. My mother was supposed to be at typing class, and I was minding Toby. I left my bed. I wanted to lie in the living room. I had lit a lamp for my mother in there, and light leaked beneath the crack of the door shut between the living room and the hall outside my bedroom. I opened the door, but they didn't see me. I didn't see everything, just my mother and a cop's gun hanging holstered from a rocking chair in front of the door I had opened. I shut the door, returned to bed, fell asleep. It was all over.

I told my mother next morning I wanted to go to my father. She didn't argue. Okay, she said, you'd better fly, it's safer, I don't want you crossing the country alone on a bus or train. We'll have to find out what it costs, and when the planes leave. I know the cost, I said. Delta, I told my mother, left Tampa that night, stopped in Atlanta, went on to Chicago. There'd be a long layover at Midway, then

With my father and mother at a Los Angeles country club, 1940.

THE DUKE OF DECEPTION

*Cadet A.S. Wolff, St. John's Military
Academy, Manlius, New York, 1923.*

*My father at thirty-six, in a publicity photograph for
Bechtel-McCone and Parsons, Birmingham, 1944.*

With Tommy Ray (left) *and Bobby Shearin* (right), *my pit crew, preparing* Y-Knot *for a race in Tennessee, 1952.* (Shelbyville Times-Gazette)

At Choate graduation, 1955, seventeen.

Princeton suite-mates, 1959, I am to the left of the young gentleman wearing a tam-o'-shanter, a disdainful expression and a bear's claw.

My brother Toby, sixteen, guessing ages and weights at the Seattle World's Fair, 1962, the summer following our La Jolla reunion.

Left: *Skiing with friends in St. Anton, 1962.*

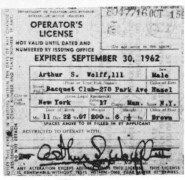

DEPARTMENT OF TAXATION AND FINANCE
BUREAU OF MOTOR VEHICLES

OPERATOR'S LICENSE

NOT VALID UNTIL DATED AND
NUMBERED BY ISSUING OFFICE

EXPIRES SEPTEMBER 30, 1962

Arthur S. Wolff, 111 — Male

Racquet Club—270 Park Ave — Hazel

New York 17 — Man. — N.Y.

Mo. 11 Day 22 Yr. 07 — 200 — 6 — Brown

*The Duke's New York driver's
license. It gives his address as The
Racquet Club (in fact at 370 Park
Avenue), a place where he had once
or twice been a guest.*

SAUNDERS ANSELL-WOLFF, III	141
2420 MANHATTAN AVENUE	
MANHATTAN BEACH, CALIFORNIA 90266	90-1352
	1211

PAY
TO THE
ORDER OF_____ $_____

_____ DOLLARS

90-1352 MANHATTAN BEACH BRANCH 90-1352

Bank of America
NATIONAL TRUST & ASSOCIATION
1200 Highland Avenue
MANHATTAN BEACH, CALIFORNIA 90266

⑆1222⑈1352⑆ 00646⑈07252⑈

*Arthur Samuels Wolff—a.k.a. Arthur "Saunders" Wolff "III,"
a.k.a. "Saunders Ansell"-Wolff "III"—had many "checking
accounts."*

My father, eighteen months before he died.

With my boys, holding Justin, photographed by John,
who told me my father was dead.

Northwest to Bismarck, Great Falls, Spokane and Seattle. Okay, she said, okay, you can go tonight.

No malice, tears, promises, yelling, apologies. I hitched to Sarasota that afternoon to buy a boat and outboard, told the dealer to put them on my account, just like Duke would say it, and send them to me air freight, care of Boeing. The dealer ran his hand through my hair before he laughed me out of the shop. The plane left on time from Tampa. Before I boarded, Mother stuffed twenty dollars in my pocket, and reminded me that we'd first driven into Sarasota a year and a day ago. I didn't hate her, and she didn't hate me. But except for three brief meetings I didn't see her again till I was twenty-six.

Not long after I left for Seattle Ruth Atkins, who had promised my grandmother on her deathbed to keep an eye on me, tracked Rosemary to the Dairy Queen, and broke in line ahead of the customers. She challenged the pretty blond lady in the paper cap:

"How could you have sent him away? To that awful father! What were you thinking of?"

And what could my mother say? That I wanted to go, which was true. What she said in fact was this: "It was just too much for me. I couldn't keep it going."

It still hurts her: "Sending you to Seattle was a dreadful business on my part, because I hadn't contacted him before you left." So the arrival was messy. I spent twenty hours at Midway, eating hot dogs and drinking root beer, and I arrived sick in Seattle. There was no one there to meet me. My father had left on a two-week vacation three weeks after he began work. He couldn't be found. Travelers' Aid took me in hand, got hold of my mother and gave me for a few days to a Boeing colleague of my father's.

It was all right, I wasn't scared. I was happy. I was where I wanted to be, it would be fine, I knew it. But for my mother it still required explanation, and she offers it: "I didn't call to tell him you were coming till after you left Chicago because I didn't know what he'd do. Maybe he'd come back to get me. Maybe he wouldn't take you."

12

It was what I longed for, but I can't reconstruct our reunion scene. I remember my father disapproved of our lie that I was eleven, to get a half-price airplane ticket, but he disapproved even more of our having paid cash for it. So unquestioning was my trust in this man that it had never occurred to me, when I landed in Seattle and he was not there, that he would not find me, soon.

Perhaps my father told me, when he came for me after a few days, where he had been. Probably he was cast down by the news that my mother was quits with him. But I remember no despair, no anger. He seemed unambiguously happy to see me. Right away he looked to my needs. I had landed in Seattle with a single gladstone, a bag my father called a "bulldog," a battered leather satchel with worn brass hardware that had belonged to his father. The day after my father picked me up at his colleague's Mercer Island house he bought me clothes and a white runabout powered by a five-horse Evinrude, just muscle enough to lift the hull on a plane. The boat was mine to use as I wanted, as long as I promised my father, honor-bright, to wear my life jacket. I kept the promise; I understood that my father would forgive me anything except a broken promise or a lie. Truth, he told me, was our most powerful bond. I knew never, never to lie to him. The truth made everything between us possible, he told me. I believed what my father said, but I had to train myself in casuistry to distinguish between the crucial truths he told me and the petty farragoes he sometimes used—necessarily?—to confound shopkeepers and clerks, people outside our lives.

It must have rained sometimes during the eighteen months I lived in Seattle; they say it never stops, except now and then in August. But I remember only sun and snow, Mt. Rainier looking down on Lake Washington and Puget Sound. I must have had trouble in school: my transcripts describe a bothersome boy with shabby grades and a terrible stammer who frequently visited the principal, the speech therapist, and the psychological counselor to account for his many Cs and Ds, his Fs in Latin and metalworking. I remember friendly school chums, teachers with pale, broad Scandinavian faces, who taught without accents at the spanking new junior high, Nathan Eckstein.

Nathan Eckstein was not only new, with electronic learning aids and a gym whose basketball hoops had nets, it was also said to be the "best" junior high in Seattle, with the "nicest" boys and girls, and to send me there Duke endured a tough commute from the University District in northeast Seattle way south to Boeing. Maybe he didn't mind; he still loved to drive the MG, especially since he had installed an exhaust cutout for a straight pipe that made a daunting noise when police weren't around to hear it.

At first we lived in a rooming house in the University District. We camped out in a clean single room, sleeping in a double-decker, my father on the bottom. Before school started I spent the few hours when I wasn't exploring Lake Union and Portage Bay in my new boat reading magazines: I became engrossed in *Sports Afield* and *True* and *Argosy* and *Field & Stream*, especially the rifle ads. I thought I wanted a lever-action deer rifle, one of the Marlin or Winchester 30-30s I studied in full-page four-color ads. My father assured me I was wrong, I didn't want to kill deer.

"Okay," I said, "can I kill a rockchuck? A smaller rifle will do it, with a scope."

My father asked me what a rockchuck was, and I explained it was a little woodchuck that lived among rocks, in the mountains. My father told me of course I couldn't shoot at a rockchuck, so I never got to be a hunter.

I read *Argosy, True, Yachting* (which paid some slight attention to motorboats) and two others, *Quick* and *Confidential*, which I hid in the foot of my sleeping bag. Offsetting these periodical revelations of an impure world was the influence of some students who roomed in our building, with whom my father was friendly. They were good to me, as entertained by my show of sophistication as by my innocence. One was Ted Holzknecht, captain of the University of Washington football team, a *Collier's* All-American center. He brought me to a couple of Husky practices, where I told Ted's teammates that I was tight with Ted Williams, the guy who played for the Red Sox. Perhaps they knew of him? I had a ball signed by him, somewhere in Florida.

If I told my father the truth, I lied to others by inadvertence, or before I could call back my words. The inadvertent lies were passed along like contagious diseases from Duke to me to someone else. My father had played football for Yale, swum for Yale, flown fighter planes for England. My own inventions were fantasies usually, sometimes evasions. When people asked about my mother I never told the plain truth, just as I never told the plain truth in Sarasota when I was asked where my father was. I told people who asked where my mother lived that she was driving west with my collie dog and older brother, would arrive any minute now.

Duke's only rival for my esteem was Elgin Gates. Weekdays, Gates worked as shop foreman for an outboard dealer on Lake Union, tuning racing motors. I kept my boat where he worked, and he let me run errands for him. On weekends in season he raced big C- and D-class hydroplanes; he was the best in the Northwest, which in 1950 meant best in the country. I saw him break a couple of world speed records, and thought that was something I would like to do.

I had never had a hero, other than my father and Ted Williams, till I found Gates. He had all the virtues: he was available, he had skills I wanted to have, people acknowledged his ascendancy, he had presence. Best of all, his respect for me came grudgingly, but it came. At first he shooed me away from his shop, then he tolerated me, then talked to me, then instructed me to fetch him coffee. One day he asked me to hand him a quarter-inch crescent wrench, without telling me what one looked like. A bit later he asked for a valve puller, then told me to remove the lower unit from one of his own motors and fix it to another. I was his pitman.

He drank beer two gulps to the bottle, and when his wife—who wore lots of lipstick and had big ones—came around to ask for money, she flirted with me. Gates would dig into his wallet while she tossed her red hair out of her eyes:

"Why didn't I wait for you, honey?" she'd say. "Why didn't I wait for *you!*"

Elgin Gates taught me about the class system:

"The bosses always screw the working stiff." He'd talk to me while he cleaned his hands with Lava soap, dug the grease from beneath his nails with a slim silver knife. "I sweat, the man upstairs drives the Caddie. I sleep in a trailer, his wife farts through silk. Get an education, kid; hand me that beer. Want a sip? I said a sip, not a whole goddamned chug."

"Shit, Elgin . . ."

"Don't cuss around me. You're still a pup, don't know shit from shine about anything but boats and motors, don't know all that much about them, either."

I learned. After a few months Duke let me trade the Evinrude for a class-A Mercury, with a Quicksilver lower unit. Now I had wheel steering on the runabout, and a dead man's throttle. I entered a race during Seattle Seafair, a hundred miles of laps around Mercer Island on Lake Washington. Eighty boats started the marathon, twenty finished. Drivers dropped out not because of the rigors of the weather or the course but because for grown-ups it must have seemed, after a few laps, a mindless way to put in hours, going in circles all day, kneeling in the wet, greasy bilges of a small boat, being shaken and screamed at by a small motor. I finished near the bottom of the survivors, but not plumb at the bottom. The first thing I said to my grinning father, who had stood four hours at the end of a dock watching my boat come into view a mile away and recede, amused him:

"I can win with a lighter hull."

Duke bought me a lighter boat. I began to win races. I tuned my own motor at Elgin Gate's shop, but my father got his Boeing pals to design and build a breakthrough refueling system for marathon races. Boeing also painted my motor cherry red, and ran various propeller configurations through its computers to find just the right prop for my boat, motor, and weight. I weighed less than a hundred pounds, so I went fast, and I was dumb enough to drive as fast as I could every second of every race. Duke took me to any race within a day's drive, and cheered me on. Whatever I wanted to do, as long as I wanted to do it badly enough, he wanted me to do.

After a month in the rooming house we moved to three rooms on the ground floor of a big lakefront house in Laurelhurst, the Lake Forest or Grosse Point of Seattle. By now I was accustomed to the gross shifts of circumstance and fortune that seemed to govern our lives. I didn't question our habitation of a room in a boarding house, or our habitation of this swank place. I knew for sure there was always food enough—always had been and would be—and just money enough. And when there wasn't money enough, Duke bought what he wanted anyway. He "bought" a Chris-Craft Riviera, a seventeen-foot varnished mahogany runabout with red leather seats. The varnish blasted the sun back in my eyes when I drove it around Lake Washington. We kept that boat tied to a dock jutting from a stone bulkhead at the foot of our front lawn, and I liked to sit just staring at it, wondering how long such a lucky streak could last.

Many of my schoolmates at Nathan Eckstein (few of whom had last names like Eckstein or Wolff) owned boats like mine, or my father's. Everyone at school was handsome or pretty: "neat" was the adverb that included all possible virtues. In Sarasota I had favored blue jeans, with wide sloppy cuffs, and plaid-dyed cotton shirts, ersatz flannel. Now I wore suntans, with blade-sharp creases, and in place of my Buster Browns oxblood loafers, buffed every night till my wrists ached. I tried to work my hair into a duckass, but not when my father was around.

After school I hung out at the Bar-Bee-Cue in the U-District, and drank cherry Cokes and fed the juke, listening to Les Paul and Mary Ford, "The World Is Waiting for the Sunrise." I knew enough not to pay to hear Vaughn Monroe's "Ghost Riders in the Sky." At home, after I folded my "neat" maroon V-neck Lord Jeff sweater, hung up my rayon sports shirt, and combed the duckass out of my hair, I set the table and made our beds. When my father came home we cooked something taken from a can. After dinner my father read, while I pretended to do homework.

My homeroom teacher taught me both Latin and Washington history, and for her the fall of Rome and the War of Charles Griffin's Pig—a one-shot war on Washington territory, without bloodshed, that lasted from 1859 to 1871—were events of equivalent magnitude. Even I knew better than this; my father didn't pretend that Washington history mattered all that much to my future, so I was by inference licensed to neglect my studies, and to act according to the assumption that all I needed ever to know, I knew. This must have troubled my homeroom teacher, but she didn't show it, and I remember her as gentle and patient, featureless, unprovocative, the lady who called the roll and gave me three *D*s and an *F*.

I was a serious student of jazz, however, my father's pupil. I listened to him play blues changes on a four-string guitar, and Bix's key of C piano thing, "In a Mist," on a rented upright. For at least an hour every night we were home we listened to records—Jack Teagarden, Art Tatum, Joe Venuti, and Eddie Lang. The first record Duke gave me was by these last-named two, who called themselves the Mound City Blue Blowers; the record had "Kickin' the Dog" on one side, "Beatin' the Cat" on the flip. My father told me what to listen for, and I loved those sessions with him, listening to the record spin, staring down at the label (Blue Note, Commodore, Jazz Victor) and then, when someone began really to drive, looking at each other, shaking our heads from the wonder of it: Jesus, wasn't that chorus *something!*

Dixie Thompson was blond and clean, wore glasses, had wonderful grades and the school's best smile. Her father, a doctor, drove a Packard. Because he drove a Packard, an automobile my father respected, he became our doctor. I spent a lot of time with Dixie, always with other people around. I wished it otherwise, but Dixie was sociable. In her freshman year at the University of Washington, where she called herself Dixie Jo, she was runner-up Queen of Frosh Day, losing—incredibly—to Twink Goss. Senior year she was president of the Husky YWCA and a member of an honorary sorority that "raised funds for a scholarship by selling candy canes at Christmas."

Dixie may be remembered by others for her good heart, good will, and good works, but I remember her face. I carried its picture in my mind seventeen years, and once in New York, after a long night at *Newsweek* and three hours boozing at the Lion's Head, I returned to my hotel room dead beat and drunk; at four in the morning there was nowhere to get another drink, and I was resigned to calling it a night when I felt a presence in my room. It was Dixie. I even switched on the television, to see if she was there. I found her in the telephone book, listed just like this: *Thompson, Dixie*. I dialed, got a sleepy roommate, said "wake her up, it's Geoffrey Wolff from Seattle, Nathan Eckstein, tell her Jeff, she'll remember Jeff Wolff." After an argument the woman woke her friend, and I spilled memories on Dixie, who finally spoke:

"It's almost five o'clock in the morning. Some people work."

Then she hung up. I still think she should have talked a couple of minutes. I wrote her next morning, told her all about myself, my kids, my wife. She wasn't all that interested, I guess, because I haven't heard back, and it's been almost ten years.

My father didn't fret about my mother's decision to stay in Sarasota. He simply didn't believe she meant to leave him. Oh, she'd try it for a while on her own, just as she had tried to leave him in Birmingham, but she'd come to her senses. There was condescension in his lack of doubt: my father didn't believe my mother could survive without his help. He thought she'd sink, and then he'd save her. He was a sentimental man, and I think he believed that because he loved my mother, he could make her love him back. He believed too in The Family, that we all belonged together.

So he telephoned her often, to no end at all, and I always talked with her and Toby. My mother tells me that during one of these calls I asked to return to her and she said no, I couldn't travel back and forth across country at my pleasure. I can't believe I asked to return to Sarasota, but my mother has lied to me seldom, except about being the son of a Jew, and perhaps my father had been drunk and frightened me. Anything is possible, but I just don't believe that I wanted to leave Seattle for Sarasota.

I wasn't fair; I always took my father's side. When he returned from Turkey my mother begged me not to tell him about the ex-policeman from Michigan, about what she called her "indiscretions," and for a while I didn't. But then I did. I couldn't keep secrets from my father. I hope that was the only reason I told him, and not to watch what happened once he knew.

I didn't think of my father as sensual, like my mother. My father had "an eye for a leg," as he said, and liked to talk with pretty girls; but I thought of him then as true to my mother from marriage till death. Now I wonder what it was like for him to take me to the movies with a thirteen-year-old girl squeezed between us in the MG, the girl giggling and flirting with my father. She sat beside me in the dark, beside him too, and he smelled the same hair I smelled. He was always a father, always correct, just like any father.

One afternoon I got a glimpse of something different, what could happen if my father decided not to be like everyone's dad, if I pushed us closer together as accomplices and violated the natural order of things. It was a summer Sunday, a few months before I turned fourteen, and my father and I were sitting on our lawn watching sailboats. A Lightning capsized nearby, knocked down by a gust. Its mast broke, and my father towed the boat and two girls sailing it to our dock. They were eighteen, maybe twenty, and shivering from cold and fright. Duke gave them dry clothes, and made them tea while they used our phone. Soon they were laughing indiscriminately, and especially at the sight of each other rattling around in my father's poplin Burma shorts and extra-large polo shirts.

Duke asked if they'd like rum in their tea, and they looked at each other, and said yes, giggling. My father played them records, and soon they were drinking rum without tea. They made a fuss over me, one of them especially, and it came to me suddenly, when her friend made another call and said to someone in a whisper not to worry, "we'll get a ride home when our clothes are dry," that something was about to happen to me. Two boys, two girls; that was how the girls seemed to see it. Maybe I had it all wrong; maybe the girl who was so sweet to me was just sweet, fond of kids, with a little brother of her own. But it seemed to me that what I had been dreaming about nights was about to be done to me.

I began to search for details that would verify this miracle to my friends. That I was to be done rather than doer nagged slightly, so to add a few years to my age, pronto, I asked my father if I could have a beer. He stared at me hard and said okay, he didn't see that a beer could do much harm. The girls giggled at this, and I sat silent and sullen for a few minutes while Duke played "In a Mist" for them. Then I took another liberty, walked to the piano and opened my father's silver cigarette case, lit a cigarette with his silver Dunhill, took a practiced drag, inhaled it. My father was beginning the final eight bars, his best section, but when I lit the cigarette he came off the piano bench fast, and slapped the cigarette out of my mouth.

"That's too much. I'd spank you if we didn't have guests. The party's over, ladies, my little boy has forgotten his manners, and his age."

The girls dressed and straggled away in their damp clothes, and waited at the end of the driveway for their friend. I went to bed. I know my father was too hard on me. Something might have triggered his jealousy, but I think probably I had enraged him by my material liberty with his cigarette case. That night I lay awake wondering why I couldn't ever seem to learn where my father's edge was; one step on terra firma, the next off and tumbling into space.

My father never had dates while we lived alone together in Seattle, or he had none that I knew about. I didn't wonder why. He was saving himself for my mother. But once he surprised me. It was the day before Christmas, and he hired a cleaning lady to scrub our rooms. Before she arrived from the referral service he sent

me away to a double feature downtown. I arrived home
before I was expected. The cleaning lady's instruments of
work were leaning against the back porch railing, and the
house was just as I had left it. The cleaning lady, maybe
sixty, was as skinny as a broom, and drunk. She pinched
me on the cheek. I wasn't friendly. She joshed my father.
There was a smudge of lipstick on his cheek, and his
necktie was loose. He looked to me like a clown, but he
couldn't know why, couldn't see the lipstick on him. He
could see the cleaning lady's smudged lips, though, and
right away he opened great distance between her and
himself.

"You can leave now," he said.

"I haven't cleaned up yet, honey," she said. She was
saucy, unmindful of my father's short temper.

"That's all right," he said. "Some other time." He was
surprisingly courtly.

The cleaning lady stood up stiffly, as if on her dignity.
"It's not as easy as that, honey, *some other time* ..." She
was mocking my father, on Christmas Eve.

"Here, take this," he said. He gave her a twenty. She
blew him a kiss, and left laughing.

I asked my father if he had kissed her.

"Of course not. Jesus, how could you think that?"

"There's lipstick on your cheek."

"Oh, that," he said, touching his cheek, blushing.
"Well, yes, there was an office party, pretty girl there, red
hair, nice popsie, about twenty-five, just a friendly kiss,
very pretty..."

As though "pretty" made a difference. It made a
difference.

My father's work at Boeing was as liaison between design,
engineering, and production, just what he had done at
Lockheed for the XP-38 and at North American for the
XP-51. Now the project was the XB-52, and this was the
Atomic Age; aviation had changed, was all business. My
father had not changed, was not all business, and if his
easy way with regulations won him admirers who worked

under his charge on the mockup and prototype of the bomber, it also drew the attention of people without much sense of humor.

It drew the attention of the FBI. My father was careless with papers and blueprints, and didn't always lock his desk at night. This was a nuisance, but nothing to cause the heavy trouble about to come down on him after his security check. My father required a "Q" clearance—virtually an atomic clearance—for his work, and the FBI had just accumulated a meticulous record of his life.

It was late August, 1951. I remember because it happened the day after the unlimited hydroplane race near the Floating Bridge. Our Chris-Craft Riviera had just been "repo'd" (my father's word for "repossessed," a word he had such frequent occasion to use he abbreviated its three syllables to two), and we were watching the big inboard hydroplanes thunder around the markers from my own little racing runabout, *Y-Knot*. The boats were powered by airplane engines, Allisons and Rolls-Royces, sometimes two engines, and they could surpass two hundred miles per hour. One of the boats back in the pack was a gray, ungainly thing with two supercharged in-line engines, and on a straightaway it began to move up. The engines were winding high, the superchargers screaming, and my father touched my arm.

"Look away," he said. "That guy's about to blow."

I looked sharp, saw the boat hobbyhorsing a little. "What?" I asked my father. "What did you say?"

"He's pushed those Allisons too far. They won't take that much. There. He's gone."

And I looked where the boat had been, and there wasn't any boat anymore.

"Let's go," my father said. "That's all she wrote."

The next day the FBI came to visit. It was Sunday. They identified themselves and my father told me to leave the room. Two of them talked to him. I tried to hear what they said. They were polite, serious. My father didn't raise his voice. When he said something, which wasn't often, they didn't interrupt him. When they left they shook

hands with him, and with me. One of them reminded him
not to leave town, they'd be in touch. My father said of
course, he'd be at home.

A few hours later he packed the MG and we drove to
Port Angeles and took the ferry to Canada: Victoria, on
Vancouver Island. My father checked us into the
Empress, and I heard him use the name Saunders Ansell.
The Empress was huge, and my father knew his way
around it. He said that was where he'd been, "with a
friend," when I flew to Seattle from Florida. We had tea
with cakes and cookies and crustless sandwiches cut into
thirds and quarters. My father looked at me across the tea
table in the fancy lobby and said I needed a decent jacket.
We went to the best haberdasher in Victoria, where he
bought me a Black Watch tartan jacket. It came with
brass buttons with a crest stamped on them, and my
father insisted that these be removed, and replaced with
solid, heavy, plain brass buttons. I was proud of my
picture in the mirror. I reminded me of someone who had
been raised to eat cucumber sandwiches in the lobby of
the Empress.

My father was distracted. The next day we drove out
the island to a place called Wilcooma Lodge, perched on
the side of a fjord. We ate smoked salmon and looked at
the water. My father drank whiskey with Lon Chaney,
Jr., a guest, and when he came to bed he woke me up. He
sat on the edge of my bed, rocking back and forth, holding
his head in his hands, He was drunk, but he wasn't angry
this time. He was sad.

"I've done awful things," he said.

"What things?" I asked him, afraid he might tell me.

"I don't know." His hands were in front of his face, held
there like a mask. "Jesus, a man like me, power to waste
life, engines of destruction...Sometimes, old man, it
weighs heavy, believe me. Very, very, very heavy indeed."

Then he gave me specifics. He had drawn the line with
the XB-52, had argued against its development as an
atomic bomber. He couldn't allow another Hiroshima,
Nagasaki, he already had "enough blood on his hands."

He was in trouble because of his anti-atomic position, "deep trouble." The FBI wasn't finished with him.

We stayed a week. I was proud of my father's courage, the risk he was running. We rowed up the fjord, talking about old times. My father put his arm around me a lot, said he wanted me to be anything at all I wanted to be, as long as it served other people. He told me again how important it was that we tell the truth to each other, hang the cost. He told me I was okay, and that was all that mattered to him. He said he thought maybe Rosemary wouldn't come to Seattle, but that was all right, maybe we'd travel south, see how she and Toby were doing.

He taught me to drive. I got three miles down the gravel driveway of Wilcooma Lodge, shifting pretty well, and then I lost it on an easy right-hander. The left fender and door were goners, but my old man managed to laugh about it, told our English hosts I had "pranged her into a ditch." He told me "never mind, you'll get the hang of it."

That day he made a long call to Seattle, and when he hung up he got a tow truck for his car. We followed in a taxi to the Seattle ferry, and boarded early, after the MG was put in the hold. We watched people come up the gangplank, slowly at first, then more frantically as the ferry prepared to shove off.

"Tell you what," my father said. "I'll bet you a buck someone misses the boat."

"If the boat's gone, how can we tell?"

"We have to see him miss it."

"I don't know..."

"I'll do you better. Someone has to miss the boat, and be so goddamned mad that he shakes his fist at us, jumps up and down, and throws his hat on the ground."

"I'll take it. A buck."

"If he throws his hat on the ground, and jumps up and down on it, you'll owe me two bucks, okay?"

"Deal."

We had the hawsers aboard, were slipping into the channel. "Look," my father said, pointing. I owed him two bucks, and fifteen years later I paid him.

We stood out on the windward railing all the way to Seattle. It was a clear night, dry and cold, and we saw the sun go down toward Asia and for an instant, like a flashbulb, light up the Olympic range. My father laid his arm over my shoulder. I wanted to comfort him.

"Is it going to be okay?" I asked him.

"Yes," he said.

And this was so, for the time being. Much later I learned what happened. The FBI had traced him back, stumbling over debts and a few scrapes with the police, some heavy drinking, the kinds of things the FBI finds when it looks. All the way back to his first job at Northrup. Here was a careless man, a good engineer, a patriotic American. Then, abruptly, in 1936, he disappeared. Groton hadn't heard of him, except to tell someone in Birmingham it hadn't heard of him. Yale hadn't heard of him. The Sorbonne didn't know what the hell it was being asked to verify, *what* school of *aeronautiques?* My father hadn't, as he claimed, been born in New York, at Columbia Presbyterian Hospital. Who was he? Where had he come from? Here was a man in close proximity to atomic bombers who seemed to have been dropped into this country, a few years before a world war, from nowhere. Here was a man obliged to answer some questions.

He answered them, somehow. Boeing kept him on. I can't imagine why. Probably cost-plus saved him. Cost-plus government contracts have saved many another. Boeing's profit was a fixed percentage of its costs; the higher its payroll, the more the company earned. My father was of some use to Boeing, imperfect as he was. And perhaps the FBI decided that even a man with bad character can be a patriot.

A few weeks after our flight to Canada and my father's return to Boeing, Alice, "Tootie," my stepmother, arrived.

13

Alice came in with the century. When I met her in a high corner room of the Olympic Hotel she was fifty-one, and looked older. My father, forty-three, looked her age. She had been twice married, widowed, and then divorced. Her first husband was a chemical magnate (his firm, Sandoz, developed LSD) and a prig. Alice cherished his memory, and was proud that he had considered himself undressed without his spats. He wore pince-nez, and was by all accounts a very serious gentleman.

Her second husband was different. He stroked a Harvard eight that won Henley, was a member of Porcellian and a class marshal. That was about it for him, though. He liked Mexico—the sun, the hours and the spirits—and he spent Alice's money fast, capital as well as interest. Like my father, he was younger than she.

I liked Alice. She had a musical voice, trained to its vibrato precision by singing coaches and finishing schools. I liked the pretty white hair she wore piled on top of her head, and her formality. She was fastidious, but didn't seem cold. She was big, I guess "Rubenesque" is the

159

euphemism, and she put on airs, but they were the airs of a schoolmarm, and I found them comfortable, at first. Later, when she pronounced the *is* in "isolate" to rhyme with the *is* in "sis," I'd straighten her out, and still later I'd mock her. But then, just thirteen, I reckoned she must know something I didn't know.

My father introduced us with pride; he "knew we'd love each other." I'd had no warning about Alice, had never heard of her, before he took me to her room. She and my father kissed when she opened the door, but this was friendly, not at all carnal. I don't know what I thought my father and this woman were to each other, but I didn't think of their association as a betrayal of my mother.

I was wrong. Later I learned that Duke had known Alice since we lived in Old Lyme. He had met her in Boston, and they had spent much time there together, hobnobbing with her ex-husband's Harvard friends. They had rendezvoused in Paris while we lived in Sarasota, and my father had been with this nice lady at the Empress in Victoria when I left Sarasota, and at Wilcooma Lodge when I landed in Seattle.

Rosemary was outraged when Duke told her about Alice. I, of course, applied a double standard to my parents, but it was easy to rationalize: There was always between Alice and my father the sense of an arrangement rather than a passion. They liked each other, and then they didn't, but I never felt ardor ebb or flow between them. But I was a kid, and saw what I wished to see.

I didn't know, or even sense, that my appearance repelled Alice. I was wearing pale-green gabardine trousers when she met me, and these were held in place by a quarter-inch white patent leather belt. Over a shiny shirt with representations of brown-skinned islanders at play beneath palm trees I wore the tartan jacket my father had so recently bought me, and this jacket she especially despised. She was also disappointed in my table manners. We ate that first night at Canlis's, a fancy restaurant high on a hill overlooking Lake Union, and I worked through the courses pretty fast. She finally said, "Please don't wolf your food," and I said, "I'm a Wolff, why not?" Duke laughed, and told me to slow down. I noticed Alice's neck go blotchy red, but I didn't know yet that this was a danger signal, *We Are Not Amused*.

The next morning she took me to the Prep Shop at Frederick & Nelson. The clothes were laughably uncool but I indulged the nice lady, let her trick me out cap-a-pie. I stood firm on the question of my hair, so the boys at St. Bernard's and Collegiate, where Alice's son had been schooled, would not have recognized me as one of their own. That second night we ate in the Cloud Room of the Camlin, and I watched my father's measured moves with his eating equipment while he talked to me and Alice listened, now and then touching the corner of her linen napkin to the corner of her mouth.

"I spoke with Rosemary this morning." My father had never called her *Rosemary* to me before, always *your mother*. "We've decided that a divorce makes sense, better for her and for me." He didn't wait for me to say anything, but there was nothing I wanted to say. "You'll stay with me, of course." I nodded, took a bite of roast sirloin. "Toby'll stay with his mother. He needs her, and it's fair." I nodded. "I guess there's not much more to say about this. You know how she feels?" I nodded. "Well. How would you feel about Alice staying here in Seattle?"

"Duke," Alice said, motioning him to quit now.

"Living with us, I mean," my father said.

"Oh, Duke! Give the child time!"

I tried to get a whole asparagus into my mouth without dripping hollandaise on my new flannels. "Okay with me," I said. "Fine," I said, smiling at the nice lady across the table.

We moved to a big house on Lake Washington, northeast of the Sand Point Naval Air Station. I got a new, faster boat, specially made for me. I had the whole top floor of the house and could play whatever music pleased me, as loud as I wanted. I didn't see much of my school friends, and Duke didn't see much of his Boeing friends. Alice wasn't comfortable around them. I began to hear how differently they talked, the gaffes they committed. My father wouldn't wear a tie every night to dinner but I had to, and at first I liked this.

The MG went up on blocks when the cold weather came, and Duke and Alice bought a brand-new Buick Roadmaster Estate Wagon, with Brewster green metal, wood trim and Dyna-Flo transmission. They were married in a civil ceremony at home the day his divorce came through, and some of his pals from MG rallies teased him about the Buick, its automatic transmission and four air holes ("Ventaports") in the hood. Alice let me sample the fish house punch while I helped her make it, and I enjoyed the lightheaded sensation. Some of Duke's friends whistled when they saw the house and the spread: smoked salmon, caviar, oysters, a Smithfield ham. I liked the impression we seemed to make, but I saw that my father did not, and that when people told him he "must've struck gold" Alice's neck went red. By now I knew what that meant.

My father got drunk and went to the garage with some friends from the MG club. They ran the engine, talked about old times, bragged about their cars. My father made me sit behind the wheel while he told again how I had "pranged" the car, and I blushed. Then he told his friends that he was keeping the MG for me till my sixteenth birthday, and I was so excited I honked the horn.

After the men and their wives left I was sent to bed. I heard an argument, much worse than anything between Duke and Rosemary, a shouting match. Alice didn't seem to fear him. He came upstairs, sat on my bed. He was breathing heavily, and I was afraid.

"Did this whole goddamned thing for you."

"What, Dad?"

"Don't *what, Dad* me! D'you think I wanted this?"

"I don't know."

"You know all right. Just don't have the guts to take responsibility."

He sounded as though he hated me. "Tell me what I've done," I asked. I was being a lawyer.

"Jesus," he said. Then he mimicked me: *"Tell me what I've done!* Nothing, kiddo, and you'll never do anything, either."

Then he left, slowly negotiating the narrow stairs, swearing. I heard one last thing before he pitched out the front door, and drove away in the Buick:

"That's all she wrote, Arthur."

A few weeks later I overheard a discussion between my father and stepmother about money, a temperate discussion about stocks and shares, annual yield, "the tax picture." I asked my father who paid for what these days. He didn't react to the question as though it were delicate. He told me his salary at Boeing was high, he had had a promotion. Moreover, he said, he had finally come into his father's estate, half a million dollars. I said that was wonderful, we were rich, right? It wasn't polite to speak of these things, my father explained to me. Gentlemen did not discuss money. Besides, while his was tied up in investments Alice would carry many of the petty household expenses. She was sensitive about these matters, my father explained, so I was never, never, never to speak to my stepmother about money, his or hers. I was to rest assured that there was plenty.

To believe the fable of the inheritance required great will, an appetite for credulity I can now credit only by assuming that I preferred this fabulous notion to the transparent reality that my father was a grifter, living off a woman who didn't seem inclined to give anything away free. I think I *couldn't* have believed in the half million. Maybe I didn't care. I was safe; as my father said, there was plenty now, wherever it came from.

Seattle couldn't hold them. On the last day of January, two months after they were married, Duke quit his job. Alice had wearied of the provincialism of the "jumping-off-place for Alaska," and of having water pour on her head every time she stepped outside. My father had been offered a job in Tennessee, with a jet-engine test center. He would have a raise in pay to twelve hundred a month and great responsibility. Incredibly, he had managed to push through the same résumé that had so recently provoked the FBI.

It was decided that we would make a proper trip of it, ship our household things and the MG and my boat and motor (this time, for sure, they went where I went), and drive southeast in the Buick. Alice and I would come to know each other, my father thought, if we traveled three thousand miles together in an automobile. We got to know each other.

There were pleasant moments. We drove south along the coast to Los Angeles, putting into the Benson in Portland, the Palace in San Francisco and the Bel Air in Los Angeles. I took on a patina of sophistication, and when Alice treated me to dancing at the Coconut Grove in the Ambassador, where we listened to Gordon MacRae and I drank crème de menthe frappé, I decided that here was a life to suit me. I saved menus (Chasen's, Romanoff's—where my father, for a sawbuck, seemed to be known by the owner—The Brown Derby and the Polo Lounge). I went alone to *Mister Roberts*, my first live play, and expressed opinions about it. My father took me to hear Billie Holiday at a simple club near Watts, and then Jack Teagarden, whose bass player called out to him when the set ended, "Duke, you old scoundrel." This was the musician who had shipped out to Europe with my father after he got the boot from the University of Pennsylvania, "after your dad left college." He let Duke buy him drinks. Alice—who wanted me to call her "Tootie," which I couldn't—went back to the Bel Air. The bass player said my dad could have been okay on guitar if he'd stuck with it. I kept a matchbook from that place.

The next morning my father and stepmother drove me to the coast somewhere near Venice, where Elgin Gates now had his own boat and motor dealership and his own Caddy. Gates offered to let me drive his D-class hydro, good for sixty and more, a marvel of a boat, if I came back the next day. Duke and Alice were happy to take me back, but I was more interested in the city now. I thought I'd like to be a night owl, studied the way my father dressed, bought *Confidential* to read about scandals in places like the Coconut Grove and not just to study pictures of Abbe Lane's cleavage.

I learned to eat salad with a salad fork. To order oil and vinegar rather than Thousand Island. To accept cheese, and to order meat rare rather than well done. I was almost ready for an artichoke.

They showed me Carlsbad Caverns and the Grand Canyon, but I wasn't much interested. New Orleans lay ahead, jazz and Brennan's. My father was amused, for a while, and then not so amused. My wisdom was gaining too fast on his own. Somewhere in Texas we passed a car in a ditch, with an ambulance and state troopers at hand. Two miles down the road my father said, as though to himself:

"That was a Roadmaster, just like this one."

"No," I said a mile later, "it was a Super. It only had three holes."

We traveled another ten miles. "You argue too much; it's getting to be a habit, and you're wrong most of the time."

Alice was asleep in the back seat. We were trying to make Dallas before dark.

"I'm not arguing, just telling you it was a Super. It had three holes. Roadmaster has four. Like ours."

My father pulled to the side of the road. Sighed. "We've come about twenty miles past that car," he said. "If I go back it'll cost us forty miles, an hour out of our day, our lives. It's not necessary. It's not even interesting. The car was a Roadmaster, that's all."

"I'll bet you ten bucks it was a Super. I looked right at it, three holes."

My father didn't take my bet. He turned us around and headed us west, into the sun. The sun woke up Alice. She asked questions; I answered them. My father was silent.

She said she couldn't believe a grown man would let his child run him all over the map this way. I thought I didn't like her. I had begun to think this earlier, hearing my stepmother make notional pronouncements about me when she knew I was well within earshot. My father drove on. He was silent. Alice was disgusted. I was happy, couldn't wait to make them count those three damned Ventaports, and get this sorted out. I almost mentioned my father's glasses to him, but something made me think this was a bad idea. When we reached the place where the Buick Super had gone into the ditch it was gone. A Texas highway patrolman was measuring a skid mark. My father asked where they had taken the wreck. The patrolman told him: the town was off the highway, five miles down yonder dirt road.

"Just ask him what kind of car it was," Alice said.

"Yeah," I said, "ask him, he'll tell you."

My father said nothing. He drove five miles to a crossroads gas station and let me sit for a minute looking out my window at the wrecked Buick Roadmaster. I figured that Alice had switched cars on me. It was just like her, and by then I knew that money could get any job done.

14

Duke's work brought us to central Tennessee, about sixty miles south of Nashville. This was Walking Horse and bluegrass country, pacific and Baptist. Now Tullahoma is booming, but when we arrived in the early spring of 1952 it had nothing but a whiskey distillery, some farms, a modest place in Civil War history as the winter camp of General Braxton Bragg following the Battle of Stones River and, still under construction, the Arnold Engineering Development Center, a jet engine and rocket test facility with ultrasonic wind tunnels where my father was plant manager.

Shelbyville, about eighteen miles away, was the town of choice. I was sent there to Bedford County Central High School, a segregated congregation of hospitable boys and girls who quickly accepted me as a novelty item whose accent and clothes were wonders. I signed up for spring football practice, and to my surprise held up, didn't cry or run the first time I was hit hard. I played end, had fair hands, no speed or judgment. I played just well enough to get dates with almost any girl I asked.

You could drive at fourteen in Shelbyville, and I was fourteen, but I couldn't drive. Duke and Alice wouldn't let me. I was sure Alice wouldn't let Duke let me. My stepmother and I argued a lot; it was a stern, bloody war, hard looks and sneers, unexplained jokes and whispers. My father let me get away with too much of this, and sometimes he was my accomplice in disrespect. I had Alice down for a phony.

She did put on false airs, overvalued "breeding" and convention, the correct sentiment, the expected. When we moved into a three-bedroom white clapboard ranch house on Lynchburg Boulevard in the "nice" part of Shelbyville, Alice brought her treasures out of New York storage, and jammed every square foot of the place with heavy pieces of mahogany upholstered with brocade and velvet. There was a huge, complicated clock from Tiffany, that told time by putative magic, that told no time at all, because the movers had broken it. There was a Sheraton dining table, and around this we ate a roast every Sunday, and delicate things other nights. I missed the meat loaf and croquettes and tuna casseroles of childhood, but Alice, if she was in fact a phony, was not the only phony in the house.

I had turned my bedroom into a shrine to café society. I pinned matchbooks from San Francisco nightclubs and menus from New Orleans restaurants to my walls, and dropped to my trusting friends the names of people I had just met in *The New Yorker* and *Quick*. I read John O'Hara and J.P. Marquand. I amplified Duke's airs and Tootie's (I called her "Toots," enraging her), and when my father traded in the MG (*my* MG!) on a gray Jaguar XK-120 roadster with red leather seats, I explained his extravagance by telling Tommy Ray, who let me drive his little Morris Minor when the police and my parents weren't looking, that Duke held controlling shares in General Electric, and worked merely to have a "hobby."

My father gave this very impression to his colleagues. Gaylord Newton, who had hired him away from Boeing, wrote me that my father was talented and energetic, at first, but "I soon found he was taking quite a bit of time off for travel around Tennessee with Alice. However, he had good ideas and built up quite a bit of enthusiasm in the men who worked for him. His only fault at that time was the impression he gave that he really did not need the job, from a financial standpoint."

Apart from my feuds with Alice, whose principal vice was the elemental vice of not being my mother, life in Shelbyville was soft: soft air, nights, voices, the soft back seat of Tommy's Mamma's Caddy sedan at the drive-in movie or burger joint, with a soft girl in my arms.

When *Y-Knot* arrived I ran her up and down the narrow Duck River, drawing complaints from people who lived nearby and winning some useful notoriety. The local paper ran my picture with a couple of friends I let drive my boat. They were my pit crew at races on TVA lakes near Knoxville. Duke drove us, towing the boat behind the Jag even though the Buick made more sense. He told Alice he preferred the Jag because it "got better mileage."

He loved that car, and drove it flat out, a hundred and twenty, between Shelbyville and Tullahoma. A policeman came to our house one night during dinner and told my father "fair's fair, I won't run you in if I can't ketch you, but look out now, you might come 'round a corner one mornin' find a 'dozer middle of the road, slow down now, drive safe, evenin', ma'am."

One night I stole it. It was late April, hot enough for my parents' new Carrier air conditioner, a conversation piece in 1952. I lay awake planning how to do it, just as I had night after night the past few weeks. Coast it down the gravel drive to the street, start it, drive it a block and park awhile, see if lights came on. I never thought I'd actually do it, but there I was, sitting in the driveway in the damned thing, my hand on the wheel. It was a still night, except for the noise of crickets. A dark night, except for the fireflies. I heard the air conditioner humming in their bedroom, bringing the temperature down into the low sixties before its solenoid tripped and it shushed to quiet fanning, then cut into a loud hum again. That was the moment, and I released the emergency brake and let the car roll, crunching. Jesus, it was a long way, fifty yards, and then I was there, blocking the road under a streetlamp. Moths beat against the yellow light so hard I thought they would wake my father. I twisted the key and the engine turned over, caught. No lights. I managed not to stall it when I popped the clutch out, but my knees were trembling so I barely made it down the block. Cut it. The house was dark. I figured I could come just this far, and still tell the truth. It would go hard for me, but I could tell my father what I had done. He'd done this much himself. He told me. Not quite this much: he had driven the Rolls only to the end of his father's driveway, but that driveway was longer. The house was still dark. I drove away, got it up to one hundred twenty on a straight country road, slowing to ten for the curves, lugging away from them in fourth. I played the radio loud, got some jazz from Atlanta, my old man's taste. Parked in front of the pool hall, where my tough school buddies hung out. I waited with the engine running till one of them came out. I cadged a smoke from him.

"Your Pa let you take her?"

"Nope. Stole her."

"Figures. Them's pretty pj's."

I drove the Jag home, and right up the driveway. Wasn't scared at all. Went to bed happy, slept like a baby. The next morning I realized the car was facing the wrong way. My father always backed it up the drive. He didn't notice, I guess, or only scratched his head when he found it after breakfast. Nine years later I confessed, and he fell into a great rage. He must have wondered in what other ways I had betrayed his trust all those years he had believed me.

Not so many ways. Finally, though, I lied to him for the first time. Alice caught me, but I bluffed it through, making an awful mess for a few days. On my way out for an evening's cruise around Shelbyville in Tommy's mother's Caddy (which we were allowed to use in return for worshiping at the First Baptist Church every Sunday, and singing in the choir, and passing time shooting the bird with what we took to be exquisite subtlety at other indentured worshipers) I removed my father's hip-shaped cigarette case from his bureau drawer. I was not meant to smoke, but my father, who smoked, did not grill me on this matter. When I returned from my night on the town's streets, my father was in a frenzy, searching for his missing case.

"Have you seen it?" Alice asked me. My father assumed that she had lost it.

"No," I said. There was still time to amend this, without penalty, to add *not exactly*, but the wrong person had asked me; I didn't mind lying to Alice.

"He says he hasn't seen it," my stepmother told my father.

"If he says he hasn't seen it, then he hasn't seen it," my father said.

Now I was frightened. I put the case in the drawer of a living-room table, and immediately found it there.

"Here it is," I happily told Alice, "right here, see? Good news, Dad, I found it!"

"I just looked there," Alice said. "I think you put it there."

"I don't lie," I lied.

"Geoffrey never lies," my father said.

"He lied just now," my stepmother said.

I went to my room, slammed my door. My father followed me but I lay dressed on my bed with my back to him.

"She's too cocksure," my father said. "Hates to admit she's wrong. She's okay. You'll forgive her tomorrow, you're too hard on each other."

I said nothing, listened to my heart whack away at my chest, didn't know what to say, now I'd done it, crossed the line. I wondered why I was the way I was. I fell asleep, finally, to the sound of them fighting about me. Alice's voice lost its finish when she shouted, and my father lost his stammer when anger controlled him, as it did that night.

A former Boeing colleague, Joel Ferrell, worked with my father in Tennessee at the propulsion laboratory. "Because of his physical size, his stammer, and his outgoing personality, your father commanded attention and discussion" in Tullahoma and Shelbyville. "He was generous and loving to a fault."

Ferrell's letter to me about my father was a good letter to get: "I felt enriched through knowing Duke because he brought humor and spice to our lives, and he was a very intelligent and capable man." Ferrell remembered that in Tullahoma's sleepy days the only place nearby to eat lunch was Archie's, and that he and Duke were finishing their main course there when a motorcade passed. Ferrell realized it was General Jimmy Doolittle, come to inspect the facility on behalf of the Air Force. He and my father were expected to greet the general, they'd better leave at once. "Let's finish our dessert," Duke said, "we'll make it." Ferrell recollects:

> Duke drove about a hundred and ten the eight or ten miles to AEDC. Just prior to reaching the gate we passed the convoy carrying General Doolittle. We prepared for his arrival. Duke had mentioned earlier that he knew the general. However, at times Duke tended to exaggerate, and most of us felt this was an exaggeration. But when Doolittle arrived, and saw your father, his immediate response was, "Well, by God, Duke Wolff! What are you doing here? Was that you who passed me on the highway back there? Of course it was!"

Ferrell also remembers that my father traveled to Birmingham to hire engineers away from Hayes Aircraft, what used to be Bechtel-McCone when Duke worked there. An old employee of my father's, and chief engineer after my father was fired, said he hoped his old boss wasn't in town to proselytize employees. "Hell," my father said, "I can't even say p-proselytize, let alone do it."

"He used to send flowers to Alice every day," Ferrell recalls. "As a consequence, the florist bills were quite high. There were discussions concerning those bills when Duke left this area."

My father didn't bend to his work with the gravity that was expected of him, and the less hard he worked the less respect he showed his superior. He decided that Gaylord Newton was self-important and incompetent, and he said so one night when he was drunk. The next day Newton fired him. "I am sorry all of this happened," Newton wrote me recently. "Duke was courteous in accepting the situation and realized there was no other recourse. About two years later I met him in New York, by accident, on Park Avenue, and we had a friendly conversation, which surprised me in light of what had happened. He said he was making out okay."

He thought he was. In fact he was on the backside of the peak. He thought his roller coaster wasn't like the others, that it would just keep climbing.

15

Duke didn't tell me they fired him. He said he had quit, to begin a business, its nature unspecified, for himself. At the time, August of 1952, I was at Choate summer school, trying to make verbs agree in tense and number, training my flat-top to lie down like a Yale man's, scruffing my new white bucks, learning tennis. This was to be a major rehab, and could have only one of two outcomes: a quick study was a *casual*, a slow study was *weenie*. I did not wish to be a weenie.

During the previous May my father had taken one of his frequent breaks from AEDC to drive me north to look at New England schools. He now agreed with Alice that it would "do me worlds of good" to leave home. My stepmother met us at the Plaza, where we stayed, and took me dancing at the hotel's Rendezvous Room and the Stork Club. After lunch next day at "21", we all scrunched in the Jaguar and drove to Deerfield. There were pleasantries with Dr. Boyden, who affected remembering my father, placing him: *how did this one turn out?* My father's hands shook as we sat at Boyden's desk beneath

174

the stairs of the main building where the headmaster could watch his boys climb and descend every day, all year, with clumsiness or grace, preparing for later, for *life*. My father abruptly left us, and Boyden asked how I spent my summers. I said I raced motorboats. I don't think he flinched, he'd heard it all by then.

I found Alice and Duke outside after my meeting with Dr. Boyden. We were meant to lie over at the Deerfield Inn and meet next morning with masters and administrators, but my father said, "You're not going to Deerfield. Let's get out of here."

He climbed the hill smartly to Eaglebrook, showing me a four-wheel drift through one of the tight bends. Alice was annoyed. The people at Eaglebrook were nice to my father, begged him to keep in touch, fussed over me. I said I'd like to go there, but the headmaster said I was too old, alas, and smiled politely.

We looked at Andover, but the school frightened me, all business. The director of admissions took no interest in my summer pastimes, but asked me why I'd failed Latin, and how I felt about plane geometry.

Choate was the place. We arrived on a beautiful green day; I saw a class being taught beneath an elm tree. Everyone looked clean in white linen jackets and seersucker suits and white shirts with frayed collars. The admissions officer was like a kind uncle; his face was ruddy, and he remembered Alice, whose son Bill had gone there and played football well. Ruth Atkins's son had recently graduated too, but the alumni whose names I heard that first day were Andrew and Paul Mellon, Chester Bowles, Adlai Stevenson, John Kennedy.

The director of admissions sent a memo after we left to his brother Seymour St. John, the headmaster:

> Mr. Wolff impressed me as a happy, grown-up boy who seemed to be as thrilled with his little Jaguar auto as though he had just received it as a graduation present. However, Mr. W. is, I gather, in charge of one of our large atomic energy projects with all its attendant responsibili-

ties. Because of his qualifications for high-powered organization, I gather Mr. W. was called in by the government for this important job. All this came out gradually in the course of the entire day which the family spent here.

During our interview Wardell St. John asked me what sports I enjoyed. I said "football, boats . . ." Before I could inventory my motorboating trophies my father interrupted: "He loves to row, wants to try crew in the spring." Mr. St. John nodded approvingly: "We can always use a good oar." "Well," I said, "I'd like to be one."

On the application form Duke explained that I was, like himself, Episcopalian and would probably follow him to Yale. There was some confusion on this latter point for I had told Mr. St. John that I would go to Johns Hopkins, and be a surgeon, but my father explained that I was referring to graduate school, after Yale.

I told Mr. St. John that I wanted to be a Choatie. My father counterfeited good-natured anger that I had chosen Choate over its arch-rival Deerfield, "my own school," but he resigned himself to my choice. Mr. St. John sent me to the Mellon Library for some tests. His memo recovers the episode:

> After the Otis Test there was just one hour remaining, so I left Jeff with the English and Algebra examinations. He chose to take the Algebra first because he thought it would be the harder. When I returned an hour later he had finished both tests and was reading a book! I had not seen the results of those tests but according to Jeff there are gaps.

And how! I couldn't punctuate or do accurate sums and take-aways. Here is the opening paragraph of my first letter to Choate: "A belated note of thanks for my jacquet" (which I had left behind). "Indeed it arrived in tyme for the 'warm' weather!" My idiosyncratic spelling of jacket came either from Society's French airs, or from my fondness for the saxophone work of a tenor man, Illinois Jacquet.

Never mind, verbal and mathematical skills weren't everything in 1952. There was a place on the application form to list relatives and close friends who had been at Choate and my father, making no reference to his cousin Buzzy Atkins, let my stepmother pile name upon name. Under the rubric *Financial Reference* he gave The Bank of New York, which returned to the school's inquiry a most artfully discreet reply:

> It so happens that the account is carried in Mrs. Wolff's name. I am writing this, therefore, fearing that an inquiry regarding Arthur S. Wolff might not be properly identified.
>
> I have known Mrs. Wolff for a number of years and have high regard for her. Your inquiry to the Bank will undoubtedly concern her financial status and I can say with confidence that I do not believe that she or Mr. Wolff will undertake any commitment that they are not fully prepared to fulfill.

A few days after Choate got this letter, I was in. I returned for six weeks to Shelbyville, strutted, swam in the pools of a couple of the town's rich kids (son of a pencil manufacturer, son of a corrugated box manufacturer), and promised two girls (daughter of the Chrysler dealer, daughter of the Mercury dealer) that if either would let me reach under her sweater she could dance with me at Choate Festivities. They couldn't imagine what I was trying to say, and instructed me to keep my hands in my lap.

Before I left for summer school my father offered advice. Choose friends with care, don't boast or lie. Study hard, listen, be polite, don't neglect the fingernails. Be brave. Dress with care but without ostentation. Neither a borrower nor a lender be . . .

I flew north to New York in early July, and boarded for

a day and night with a school classmate of Alice's who lived—just as I once had!—on East Fifty-seventh. She, though, lived between Park and Madison, in a duplex. She had a daughter my age. The woman talked like Alice, like Tallulah Bankhead in the movies but an octave higher, trilling her notes, punctuating her observations with parentheticals, *but don't you see, dear boy, what an absolute desert Alice has had to wander in, Seattle and now (where is she again, my sweet?)... Ah, of course, Shelbyville! Well, wherever...*

The lady gave a cocktail party the evening I arrived. I was meant to go to a musical comedy with her daughter, but I didn't wish to. Her daughter was as fancy as her mother but with braces which caused her to lisp. Nor was the daughter attracted to me, whose hair, growing long in training for a part, stuck up straight, as though I'd been plugged into a high-voltage socket. The daughter went to the musical with another boy, and I stayed with the grown-ups. The lady drank a great amount, and instructed me to sit beside her on a sofa. She smelled wonderful; her skin was white as milk. She took my hand, and I blushed. The guests thinned out, and then left, except for a gentleman with thick white hair and a white brigadier's mustache. He also blushed. The woman instructed him to mix her a drink, and when he turned his back to us she put my hand against her soft small breast and then between her skinny thighs, against her black silk dress. She said to me, no whisper, a statement:

"You're darling. I'm going to let you make me happy."

Then the white-haired man, whose red face was now very red, took the woman away to dinner, but before they left she kissed me ("Open your mouth, dear, don't pinch it shut") and said she'd be back soon. I lay in bed waiting for her. The daughter came home, argued with her date, a door was slammed. Her mother returned about four, and thirty minutes later I went to the bathroom, brushed my teeth, tried to make my hair lie down and stood outside her bedroom door listening to my heart pound. The door was open a crack, or carelessly shut. I opened it. I stood beside her, above her. A pillow covered her head. The room smelled of gin, tonic, lime, flowers. It smelled too of the woman. I touched the pillow, said nothing, touched it again. She rolled over. She was my stepmother's age, fifty-two. She wore a black mask over her eyes. I had never seen such a sight. She raised the mask, stared at me, blinked, lowered it. Said into her pillow:

"Oh, it's you. Go to bed."

Sometimes I smell her perfume on the street and I turn this way and that, looking for her. Now she's almost eighty, or dead.

When Duke was fired he and Tootie lit out for The Colony Club on Barbados to recover from the trauma of having to leave Bedford County, Tennessee. They traveled around the Caribbean while I tried to translate myself from a Lothario of the drive-ins to an ivy-draped lounge lizard. I made friends easily enough, the kinds my father had warned me against making too easily, boys who liked to tell dirty jokes, sneak a coffin nail or a hit off a pint of Four Roses after lights-out, laugh a lot, figure the angles.

A young English teacher taught me to parse a sentence, break it down like a machine rather than by magic, the way a boot-camper learns to strip his M-16 in the dark. All summer I charted sentences, fifty a day; the work was either perfect or it was wrong, flunk, your weapon won't work, you're dead. The teacher wasn't friendly, didn't charm. He didn't seem much to care whether I got the sentences diagramed right or didn't. But he did care; I eventually learned sentences.

A rich kid invited me to Greenwich for a weekend at his house while his parents were away. I told the dean, George Steele, "The Penguin," that my grandmother had asked me to spend the weekend with her in New York, where she lived at Hampshire House, might I go? she was enfeebled, needed me. Mr. Steele said I could not go; he neither smiled nor explained.

My record at summer's end was mixed. One master called me "a nuisance in the house." Another noticed I had "walked out of exam early." Another said that I was "the best boy in class, good inspiration." Another: "Will need much following up. Undisciplined." Mr. Steele knew everything about all of us, and he knew me: "Jeff is a pleasant youngster, good mature ability, but very poor study habits, and he's easily distracted. My thought is that he's a bit 'old' for his years. A little too sophisticated for his own good, and ought to be held down."

After school I met my parents at the Plaza. They were deeply tanned, appeared prosperous. They looked like the parents of most of my schoolmates, except not quite so deeply tanned or prosperous, and not as finely chiseled. My stepmother's neck was not as swanlike as some I had seen around the Choate campus, and her arms were flabby. I noticed my father's bald head and heavy features. A waiter at the Plaza told me with a Spanish accent that I looked just like my papa, and for the first time this was not something I wanted to hear.

I went with a Choate friend to Jimmy Ryan's, just west of "21" (which I pointed out when we passed it as a place I sometimes lunched) on Fifty-second Street. Now I was Earl Wilson. We listened to Wilbur DeParis and drank rye and ginger ale. I kept the band's beat with a plastic swizzle stick, beating it against the ashtray I stole.

Our last night in New York I spent with my father and stepmother. The woman in the black silk dress came to our room for drinks with her friend Alice. I sat mute, staring at her. She had too much to drink. I had not told my father anything. The woman sat beside him, whispered something to him. He scowled. Maybe she had whispered something about me, maybe about him. Maybe it was nothing at all. My father had also had much to drink. He turned on the woman:

"You're a bad one, get out."

"But..." she started to say.

"But..." Alice started to say.

"OUT!" he yelled, and she left.

I studied this with my head cocked. I was impressed.

We spent the summer on the Cape, in a big drafty house at
North Chatham. I played tennis, sailed a Beetle cat,
contemplated girls. A Choate friend came to visit. We
drank a quart of my father's Canadian Club while he and
my stepmother were at a party. We'd each have a jigger
and refill the bottle with two jiggers of water. We quit
when the whiskey was as transparent as gin. Alice was
furious. My father thought our hangovers were piquant.

From North Chatham I wrote Mr. Steele:

> My conscience has been bothering me about that
> weekend which I asked for. I stated that I was going to
> stay at my Grandmothers. That statement was untrue. I
> can assure you that nothing of that nature shall ever
> occure again.
>
> I never imagined that anything could mean as much to
> me as Choate does. I sincerely hope that this weekend
> business has not narrowed my chances of getting back
> into Choate.
>
> I really am very ashamed of the lie which I told you and
> I hope you believe me when I say it will never happen
> again. I look forward to returning to Choate in the fall.

How did "Grandmothers" and "occure" get past my
father's edit?

I hadn't been back at school eight weeks when I let my
father down. He had opened an office in New York as a
management consultant, and would bring a potential
client, a retired Air Force general, to the Yale-Harvard
game. He invited me to meet them there, with a friend.

My friend was the son of a hotel owner, and at fourteen
he had discovered his father's chief bellman running
whores. He had confronted the pimp, and they had
reached an accommodation, or so my friend assured me.
He didn't tell his daddy what he knew, and he got

whatever hookers he liked, superior room service, what he called "a sweetheart deal." He told me about his sweetheart deal driving by taxi to the Yale-Harvard game. The cabby had bought us a pint of Mount Gay, which my father had learned to like in Barbados. My friend's father had gone to Yale. Like Duke. But before I'd say *what a coincidence, Dad went there too* I asked my friend's father's class, college, and fraternity. 1925, Pierson, Fence, Wolf's Head. *Oh, they wouldn't have known each other, Dad was 1930, Saybrook, Deke, Bones.*

Outside a portal to the fifty yard-line on the Yale side of the Bowl I puked on the camel's-hair topcoat of the retired Air Force general. My father didn't slap me, then. He put me to bed in a tiny room at the Taft, and when I woke up he slapped me.

His office at 270 Park, a block north of Grand Central, overlooked a restaurant in the courtyard. My father used to give me lunch at The Marguery, where I learned to enjoy vichychoisse, and pronounce it. If the captain said the Dover sole was fresh I asked how it was prepared, and, whatever the reply, ordered it. I usually finished my meal with sherbet, or perhaps Brie if it hadn't been refrigerated, wasn't overripe. My father let me use his account there and at Brooks, Abercrombie & Fitch, J. Press, Chipp and Sulka.

His office had on its door a varnished ash plaque made by a woodcarver at Minneford's yacht yard on City Island:

ARTHUR SAUNDERS WOLFF III
Management & Engineering Consultant

This was quite large for the small door of a small office. There was a single room, exquisitely furnished but overwhelmed by my father's desk, eight feet long. I once slept on the desk, with seven friends scattered on the couch and the floor, after a dance at the St. Regis Roof. We were swell.

My father had a series of secretaries. The first was gorgeous and efficient. But Duke's hours were erratic, and so were his demands. I don't mean to imply that they were in the conventional sense improper, but he spent his office hours ordering stuff, and his secretary spent her time picking up the stuff he ordered, or explaining why it hadn't yet been paid for; she soon began to suspect that my father's work was transient. After she quit another came, and another, and another, each less beguiling than the one before, less polished and pretty, till at the end there was an answering service that always said my father was at a meeting.

He had brochures printed, bound and mailed to hundreds of companies. The paper—thick, creamy, thirty-pound stock, hundred percent cotton—came from Cartier. My father's name was raised, engraved in dark gray in the typographical style of *The New Yorker*. Good address, good telephone exchange (PLAZA 5-6640), good typeface. His finishing trick was to bind the brochures in Mark Cross leather.

The résumé retailed the usual crap, but now he had added a rubric, PUBLICATIONS: "Articles in regard to management, plant site selection, plant-planning and plant layout, management and administrative procedures, and several studies of maintenance procedures published by McGraw-Hill and others." The format didn't conform to common bibliographic practice, but Duke was ever a pioneer of forms.

The pitch was divided into sections divided by titled leather tabs:

A PERSONAL APPROACH: It is obvious that a camera is no better than its lens; so, too, is the final result of a consultant's effort no better than the calibre of the man who actually performs the task to be accomplished.
AN AID TO MANAGEMENT: I exercise no organizational authority in assisting clients except as directed; the value of my services being inherent in recommendations which must be acceptable on the basis of obvious benefits, sound

facts and in the form of presentations which are graphic and self-revealing.

SCOPE OF OPERATIONS: My clients retain [the subjunctive or indefinite future would have been the better tense] my services for aid in improving operating effectiveness and reducing costs in connection with the following business activities:

Management

Organization

Manufacturing and Operations

Personnel Management and Labor Relations

Marketing Distribution and Merchandising

The client is assured of the highest standard and quality of service, regardless of the location or the scope of his business.

METHOD OF OPERATION: My work is directly with top management and retention of my service is negotiated through a principal or partner. Thus my approach is realistic in scope. I make no attempt to revolutionize. Too, I have no pat solutions or systems, my recommendations being custom-tailored for each client. Having a keen regard for the human factor in personnel relations, I work with a client's employees on the basis of understanding and cooperation. This ensures that, by actually participating in the project to be accomplished, they accept the program.

SPECIFIC SERVICES: Executive Reports, Budget Control, Cost Accounting, Financial and Operating Statements, Stockholders' and Employees' Reports.

PROFESSIONAL ARRANGEMENTS: Fees are on a per diem basis, although an annual retainer may also be arranged.

This document—which promised to straighten out any muddle, cause employees to love their work and their bosses, enhance productivity and reduce production costs, analyze markets, design aptitude tests, cure colic, goiters, and the pox, return capitalists to their golf carts and capitalism to its rightful eminence—my father sent to Ford, GM, GE, Chase, The Bank of New York,

Bethlehem Steel, Sears, Roebuck & Co., McGraw-Hill (!), International Harvester, United Fruit, North American Aviation and many lesser members of *Fortune*'s Five Hundred.

Not one replied. My father did hear from the ex-tennis champs, Frank Shields and Sidney Wood, friends from Roxbury. They were in the laundry business, and wanted to sell him their towel service.

By now I knew my father was a phony. I wasn't dead sure about Yale, but I was sure he was a phony. My father's lesson had taken: he had tried to bring me up valuing precision of language and fact. So around him I became a tyrant of exactitude, not at all what he had meant me to be. Unable to face him down with the gross facts of his case I nattered at him about details, the *actual* date of the Battle of Hastings, the world's coldest place, the distance between the moon and the sun, the number of vent-holes in a Buick Special. I became a small-print artist.

I was harder on my father after I had the goods on him than he had ever been on me. He had always had the goods on me. And he had never made cruel use of them.

After my father set up his office in New York we lived for a while at One Fifth Avenue. From there I sallied forth during vacations to jazz clubs and dances. I was levered on a list of eligibles by the mother of a Choate friend, and attended The Holidays, The Collegiate, The Get-To-gethers, and The Metropolitan, *The Hols, The Cols, The Gets, and the Mets,* as we called them. I'd stand along the edge of the dance floor, a hand resting at the hip of a dinner jacket, an elbow disdainfully projected to keep strangers at a distance, looking over the talent. Casual, I went to dances, but I didn't dance at them, because I couldn't, despite Alice's instruction, dance. Weenie.

The summer of 1953 we returned to Connecticut, first to Weston, then to a small, beautiful house in Wilton, then to a big, old house on Nob Hill Road in Wilton. When my father's lease expired at 270 Park he brought his "office" home to Wilton. He had time aplenty on his hands and used it to shop and fend off creditors. Cartier, he later told me, was especially sporting, asked him only twice to pay and then assumed that he preferred not to, and left him in peace. We still listened to jazz together when I was home from Choate, but now I knew more than my father. I explained to him (sometimes patiently) why Dave Brubeck was a better pianist than Art Tatum. He wouldn't lose his temper with me but once, when I corrected him on some trivial matter of jazz fact, he left the living room, paused at the door, turned to me:

"Geoffrey, I love you. I love you because you're my son, of course. But I love you beyond that. I want good things to come to you. I want you to be happy. I want these things for you and sometimes I would rather be with you than with anyone. But not now. Not these days. These days you know too much. You talk like a barber, and you bore me to death, and I hate to be in the same room with you most of the time. I hope this changes."

Many grown-ups at Choate shared my father's judgment of me. The Head told me, in the rhythms of the pulpit oratory he so favored, that I was "the weak link in an otherwise strong Choate chain." A housemaster reported to him that "Geoff is certainly the biggest problem in the Woodhouse." My goodness: "He can be counted on to try any shortcut around any work, to dodge responsibility and to take advantage of any privilege granted him. He seems to have a completely false set of values." Only this by way of amelioration: "He is well poised; he is fiercely loyal to family and friends." I was loyal to my father behind his back. I was a scourge to his face but I wouldn't hear a word said against him by anyone else.

During Christmas vacation of my first year at Choate I was sent to Sarasota for a few days with my mother and brother. I flew into Tampa with greater self-certitude than when I flew out to Seattle three years earlier. See how I had changed: taller, with trained hair; grander, with a

Brooks Brothers tweed jacket, Brooks Brothers blue button-down shirt, Brooks Brothers tie. True, the tweed jacket and flannel trousers weren't just the things for sunshine and eighty degrees, but I was consoled by the picture I presented to my astonished mother: a young gentleman, a buck.

On the flight down I had thought much about the impression I wished to convey. Prosperity, control, worldliness. "You seemed quite worldly," my mother admits. "You let me know that you were no longer a virgin." My mother was indifferent to the significance of that fiction. "I didn't feel I had much part in your life. You had grown up independent of me; I felt I had no responsibility for your diet, health, morals, anything. I had no right to care."

While Toby gawked at his wised-up brother on the drive from Tampa to Sarasota, I confessed my imaginary sins. I had exhausted the inventory by the time we were downtown. The place had changed. Now Sarasota was spruced up, the Athens of the Gulf Coast, with live theater! I told my mother that I rather enjoyed the theater, perhaps I would treat her to a night out, dinner at the Ringling Hotel after the curtain fell.

"Shep's gone," my mother told me.

"He got bitten by a snake," Toby said. "Maybe eaten by an alligator."

"Maybe he ran away," my mother said. "Maybe someone stole him. He was so friendly."

I stared out the window, away from my mother's face and my brother's. I didn't want them to see me now. The town was just the same, seedy.

My mother and Toby lived in a basement apartment downtown. It was tiny, damp, dark. Mother worked long hours, still at the Dairy Queen. Her ex-policeman, like the German woman's G.I., came by of an evening to scream at her, threaten to choke, shoot, or knife her. His reasons at least during my brief visit, were obscure. While my mother worked at the Dairy Queen I stayed with Toby, behind locked doors.

On Christmas Mother gave me a radio with a cream plastic case, AM and FM. No gift ever touched me deeper. It represented a huge sacrifice, thirty hours work at the Dairy Queen. I knew its price to the penny, but my mother did not show what it cost her. She just wanted me to have it. The next day at La Guardia a woman jostled me and the radio fell and broke. My father replaced it with a more expensive model. He would have been kinder to replace it exactly, or not at all.

Six months later I went to Arlington, Virginia to visit my mother and her brother Steve. Mother was on the run from the ex-policeman. She sent Toby from Washington to New York to see his father an hour before I flew in. I was to spend a night in Arlington at Uncle Steve's, and a day sightseeing in Washington. The following afternoon I would fly to Maine for a week with a girl I had met at Choate.

Steve was a bureaucrat at the Pentagon, and the very image of his father, but taller. Unlike his father and like my mother he had a ready laugh. I liked him, and knew my father liked him. My father had done things for him, the small acts of generosity and kindness that older members of a family like to do for younger members, inviting them for weekends, making introductions. So I was stunned at dinner to hear my uncle make what seemed to me cruel remarks about my father, in front of me, as though I weren't there. The remarks were factual, I think, references to Duke's debts, mendacity, dependence upon Alice, heavy drinking. But the remarks were also purposeless and unearned, and I was enraged. My uncle thought I was too young at fifteen to show rage to a grown-up. Then my mother laughed, shrugged, said "What's the fuss? Steve's right about Duke, he's a faker."

In all my life I had never heard my father speak unkindly of my mother or her brother. That night a call came to Steve, putatively from the Georgia State Police. It was a message for Rosemary. The Michigan ex-policeman had been in an accident driving north to search for her, and his last words had been of their love. Mother was troubled: "I lay in bed thinking of him, half-relieved to be done with him and half-sorry he was dead." He wasn't dead, or hurt. He had just had a bit of fun with my mother.

While my mother fretted that night, thinking the man dead, I sulked. I sulked flying to Bangor. I was met at the airport by the girl and her nice mummy and daddy in their sensible Pontiac station wagon. I had spent two hours with the girl when she came to sing at Choate with the Ethel Walker glee club. After the concert we had walked behind the chapel, and to my astonishment she asked me to kiss her. Now I held her hand in the dark back seat while her parents drove us toward Blue Hill, asking me questions. I couldn't get Steve or my mother off my mind, except when I wondered if the Ethel Walker girl would let me touch one of her wonderful breasts. She noticed my contemplativeness, knew I had just visited my divorced mother.

"Do you see your mother often?" she asked me.

"I used to," I said.

"But of course you'll see her again soon," the girl's mother said.

"No," I said. "My mother died last night."

What the hell had I done now? Silence, dead silence. I don't know whether they believed me in the front seat, but the girl squeezed my hand hard and pushed her leg against mine. So that was one of the reasons I had said it. The other was to kill my mother, a simple case of murder, real hatred now. She shouldn't have let her little brother say such awful, true things about my father.

I mooned around the girl's stately waterfront house for a week, playing the mourner for her parents, who many times asked if there was anything they could do, wouldn't I rather be with my father?

"No," I said, "this is better, to be away from all that, to sort things out."

Shouldn't I return for the funeral?

"We buried her the morning after she passed away. She wanted it that way."

They couldn't have believed me! But they were relentlessly thoughtful. The girl's father had owned a haberdashery called The English Shop in a small college town in Massachusetts. He sang the college's praises and I could think only about opening an account at his store, how easy it would have been with a good connection. I told the girl's father that he had definitely changed my mind about college: Yale was too big, New Haven too dirty and noisy, his little college was the place for me, absolutely. It was better not to try to step into my father's huge boots at Yale.

The man beamed. He trusted me with his daughter. On their catboat, in their Pontiac, and on their couch I tried to feel her up. The girl wouldn't let me. This was grim business. I put aspirin in her Coca-Cola, a known specific against frigidity, and still she wouldn't let me.

"This Coke tastes awful," she said. "It tastes like aspirin."

My mother had just died, for God's sake! I had just put my mother in the ground! I was owed! I had three hands, moving them from the girl's breasts to her thighs in a random assault, praying that she'd fumble a defensive move and let me slip in there, let me unbuckle it, touch it, squeeze. I told her she had given me "blue balls, lover's nuts." This interested her and I took advantage of her distraction to run my hand up her stocking, past her garter, inside that soft, damp thigh, against those slick pants. Wham! Her legs locked together. "Take me home!" she yelled.

Driving home, hunched over the wheel, I pouted: "I guess you don't like me."

"That isn't it," she said, "you're not fair."

"You're the one who isn't fair," I said. "Listen, let me touch you, just five minutes. Just this once and I promise I'll never feel you up again."

She began to cry. I suspected fake tears. Pulled over. Brought her head to my chest, so understandingly. She stopped sobbing, lay against my chest. I ran my hand through her hair, gently, kept it far away from *there* and *there.* She could trust me. I touched her throat, didn't reach down her blouse. She could trust me.

Dear God, I prayed, *make her fall asleep and I'll believe in You. I'll have myself confirmed. Give me just this one on the cuff.* She was asleep. Her legs were slightly apart. I unbuckled her bra one-handed, a skill I had practiced on one of my stepmother's garments, installed around a pillow. The girl breathed evenly. This was it, the point of life. Suddenly she sat up straight, refastened her armor, said "Okay, that's enough, let's go home."

That night I wrote a letter to my Choate roommate: *Had a great time with my mater in D.C. Dined at the Mayflower. Plenty of nook up here in Maine. Went the distance last night with that babe from Walker's, huge hooters, HOT! Wheeled around in her old man's car, told him I had a license, scored in the back seat.*

I sealed the envelope, addressed and stamped it. But I left it in the guest bedroom when I returned to Connecticut the next day. That night I telephoned the girl, such a sweet girl, I missed her. Her father answered the phone:

"My daughter doesn't want to hear your voice again, and neither do I. And I'd advise you to apply to Yale. Maybe they'll be dumb enough to take you."

16

Toby was eight when he flew to New York to spend the summer with us. My father met him at the airport and took him to "21" for lunch.

"He introduced me to ginger beer, and the waiter knew him and seemed to like him. I was just knocked out by it all."

Toby noticed that his father "apparently didn't work," because he had all the time in the world to spend on his son. "Still, the old man had an air, even at his most idle, of great business afoot, of busyness. There were always errands to run, gloves to be selected, an umbrella to be repaired."

They never talked together about anything personal, until at summer's end Toby said that he'd like to stay in Connecticut with Duke and Tootie. "It was so nice there, just a lot nicer." Father said no, it wouldn't be fair. Besides, Rosemary would never permit it. Toby asked if he could come back the following summer, and did. He loved his stepmother: "Tootie was aces. She was generous about Mother, made me write her, said nice things about their talks on the telephone. You seemed like an alien in the house. I thought you hated being around Duke, Tootie, me. I looked up to you, of course. But things were not good between us, our feelings were complicated."

Then, the summers of 1953 and 1954, Toby reminded me of myself at eight and nine, and for reasons I cannot even now understand those memories were painful. I wasn't ashamed of the bumpkin. On the contrary: a little brother was a nice thing to have, like a crash linen jacket. I liked to show Toby off to my Choate friends. There were always plenty of Choate friends around our Connecticut houses.

When the school year ended there was a round of dances during Tennis Week at the Manursing Island Club, American Yacht Club, Greenwich Country Club, Wee Burn Country Club . . . I was invited to some of these; most I crashed. My roommate Frank stayed with us often in Wilton; he stammered too, and could laugh with my father as I could not about their afflictions. The less I respected my father, the more my friends cherished him. He wasn't like their fathers, had different toys, a different vocabulary.

He owned the eleventh edition of the *Encyclopaedia Britannica*—just like the grandparents of my schoolmates—but he also had books of dirty limericks and could recite, first verse to last, *Eskimo Nell.* My father owned things with mother-of-pearl handles, wore pigskin gloves. There were lamps in our house made from pieces of old sailing ships. We bathed with Pear's soap. Ordinary. Extraordinary was my father's set of French caricatures, *Twenty-One Ways of Committing Suicide*, black, sardonic studies of final solutions.

I was surprised how wonderful my school friends found my father's things to be; but they did, and more and more of them, more and more often, found excuses to stay with us. They enjoyed Duke's speech. A girl was a *popsie*, and if she was comely and ardent she was *fux deluxe*. My father's glasses were *specs*, and when he was tired he was *worn to the nubbins.* When my friends and I *gussied up* to go to a dance my father begged me to lay off the *gaspers*, though I smoked them anyway, black, gold-tipped Balkan Sobranies. My father thought they were vulgar, and they were. My stepmother thought my father's diction was vulgar, but it was not.

My father's vocabulary was a schoolboy's vocabulary because among us he was among schoolboys. He was a chameleon. He gave his clients what he thought they wanted: companies got his constipated management jargon, headmasters got piety, car salesmen got bank references, car mechanics got engineering lore. He was a lie, through and through. There was nothing to him but lies, and love.

The housemaster who noted that I seemed "to have a completely false set of values" added that this sad state was "partially induced by such things as receiving a sports car for Christmas." My first nickname at Choate had been "Art," because my friends identified me entirely with my father, but soon after I turned sixteen they changed me to "Porfirio," after Porfirio Rubirosa, the playboy racing-car driver killed in the Bois de Boulogne. The week after my sixteenth birthday I got my Connecticut driver's license, traded my racing boat for a 1948 Austin sedan, and wrecked it three days later. Five weeks after my sixteenth birthday I was given a new Porsche 1300 convertible, and by then was smoking and drinking at will in my father's presence.

I drove the Porsche flat out along Nob Hill Road, just as my father drove his Ferrari, a three-liter Ghia-bodied roadster he had "bought" when he "bought" my Porsche, using the third Jaguar in his stable as a down payment for both cars and promising to make killer monthly payments, which he never made. Alice was by now resolute in her antagonism to his financial caprices, and would have no part of his toys or the debts he accumulated on behalf of his toys. She was rightly aghast when she first saw the Porsche, and this further alienated me from her.

One night, with fog drifting across Nob Hill Road, my father and I nearly hit head on. We were drunk, and just managed to nose our cars into opposite ditches. We met in the middle of the road at the sharp right-hander near the wall of a sheep pasture and hugged and laughed: wouldn't that have been something, setting the old lady free of us and our damned cars at a single swipe!

My father finally did bang his Ferrari into that stone wall and three weeks later, sixteen and a half, I rolled my Porsche over a different stone wall. The girl with me was thrown clear and got off cheap, with five stitches behind her ear. I smashed my nose, had it stitched together by a sleepy intern in South Norwalk, and tried to sleep off a concussion. My father sat by my bed slapping me awake. I laughed at him walking around in his pajamas in a public building, but he wasn't laughing anymore. I was a tinhorn "Porfirio" with a "completely false set of values."

It was decided I should work that summer before my last year at Choate. The previous summer I had been fired for indolence after three weeks cutting grass and trimming hedges as an apprentice to Raymond Massey's Wilton grounds keeper, but this was to be a serious enterprise. I was hired by Tolm Motors in Darien, where Duke had his cars and mine tuned and repaired. (He had now traded himself down from the Ferrari to a Mercedes 190SL, and me from the wreckage of the Porsche to a VW.) He owed Tolm so much that he muscled me into my summer job: they were nice to me so that if he ever paid any bills he might pay them first. My job at seventy-five cents an hour was pleasant and educational. I washed and waxed the sports cars of clients who had brought them for repair. My partner in this work was a black bachelor, George, about forty-five. In light of his superior experience he was paid two bits more an hour than I was paid. We became friendly; I talked to him about Choate and he listened, and soon knew the names of my teachers and friends, answering strophe with antistrophe:

"George, I've had it up to here with Bill Morse."

"That boy too damned big for his britches. A nice one 'longside the head bring him down to size, yessir."

I resolved to teach George about the great jazz musicians who had enriched the culture of his people, but when I got permission to bring a record player to the garage where we worked alone with hoses and brushes and chamois cloth, George said he didn't cotton to jazz, he preferred the classics, Kostelanetz and Ezio Pinza. Never mind, it was my machine, and I arbitrated a settlement, two picks for me, one for him, thus: "Rockin' Chair," "Struttin' with Some Barbeque," "Some Enchanted Evening."

One day I suggested that George come to dinner at home in Wilton and then blow it out with my father and me in Westport.

"Shit," he said, "you don't know nothin'."

For reasons beyond my understanding I was trusted by Tolm to take delivery of its new Jaguars, Triumphs, and Mercedes from distributors in New York. Once or twice a week I'd come to work dressed like a Choatie, wearing a bow tie, saddle shoes, and a seersucker jacket, and take the train to New York to fetch a car. The last car I picked up was a gray gull-winged Mercedes 300SL, still covered with dock grime and shipping grease. The seats were black glove leather. It was explained that the car's speed during break-in was governed by a restraint on the accelerator that prevented me from exceeding eighty in top gear, but this could be overridden in an emergency, breaking a lead seal and placing in peril the car's warranty. Coming down the long hill at Stamford on the Merritt Parkway there was an emergency. I wanted urgently to drive Tolm Motors' new car a hundred and fifty, and I did. Tolm Motors, finding the lead seal broken, was cross and fired me, cutting its losses and resigning itself to a place at the bottom of Duke's action pile. I said goodbye to George, promised to stay in touch.

"No, you got bigger fish to fry, won't be thinkin' 'bout old George."

"Bullshit, George."

"Yeah," George said, the last word from him the last time I saw him.

The night I wrecked my Porsche I had been drinking at Rip's Lounge. The pianist and organist from Sarasota had opened a nightclub in a shopping center in White Plains. It was as dark as Dick's hatband in there; the walls were fish tanks, bubbling greenly. Rip wore a white dinner jacket when he played. It set off his brilliantined black hair to good advantage, he thought. I went there with Duke, a Choate friend, and our dates. My date was a plain-talking blonde, Buster Crabbe's daughter, and when my father said he had been her father's friend, I didn't believe him. Her father, after all, had been somebody, Tarzan! Duke had in fact been his friend in Miami, where they swam together in an aquatic circus. Nevertheless, Susie Crabbe preferred my Choate friend, Jack, and so did Jack's date prefer Jack. I studied this injustice while a wonderful jazz guitarist, Mundell Lowe, played solo. And when he was finished, Rip, who considered himself the headliner, began to play and I talked, too loudly, to Jack.

"Where do you think we'll be ten years from now?"

"I don't know," Jack said. "Who knows?"

"Who do you think's going to do better?"

"What do you mean by better?" Jack asked.

"You know. I know. We'll know then. Listen, we'll know."

My father was annoyed. "Shut up and listen to the music."

"Tell you what," I told Jack, "let's get together in ten years and see what's happened to us."

"You're serious."

"Bet your ass I'm serious!" My voice had risen. Rip looked hard at our table. Duke looked hard at Rip.

"Okay," Jack said, "a deal. A hundred I'm happier,

better off, further ahead. Ten years from now."

Our dates giggled as we seized hands. People stared at us. Rip quit "Autumn in New York" abruptly, left the stand. As he passed our table he muttered something, probably to me. My father was drunk now, and pugnacious. Maybe Rip had said something to him, we had disrupted our friend's set, it was his club. Rip headed downstairs to the men's room, and I followed him. At the bottom of the stairs he put his arm around me like a buddy, and was about to lecture me, I think, on good manners, when we were spun around by Duke's shout from the top of the stairs.

"Take your hands off him, greaser!"

"What!" Rip shouted. "What did you say?"

"I know you in and out, pal." My father was shaking his finger.

"Come down here you fake sonofabitch," Rip said. "You're all air, always have been, just a crummy, deadbeat talker, come on down, let's get this over."

"I'm no fool," my father said. "You've got a gun."

"I don't need it for you." Rip pulled the revolver from his shoulder holster.

"Don't shoot me!" my father yelled.

Rip tried to hand it to me, but I backed away. It was the snubnose he had shot at rabbits in Florida. I begged them to stop. Rip threw his pistol on the floor.

"If I come after you," my father said, "you'll pick it up; you're a mob guy, I know all about you."

Rip picked up the gun, shook out the bullets, threw the gun in a trash basket, beckoned with his hand, said quietly: "Come down here, I don't want to fight in front of my customers."

"Fuck yourself," my father said.

Rip started upstairs fast. I followed, grabbing at his coat, and by the time I reached him he was at the front door of his club, watching my father drive away, leaving rubber. There was no point chasing him, his Ferrari was too fast.

"He's chickenshit," Rip said.

"No," I said, "he isn't." But I knew he was.

I was not good to Choate, but neither was Choate good to me. Piety, courtesy, self-importance, smugness, and a killing dose of homily characterized the Choate I knew. Choate's business was to define and enclose. Alice understood this from her son's experience, and even before I arrived for summer school she wrote Seymour St. John: "Choate will do wonders for Jeff. Learning to share and also to accept restrictions pleasantly." Then another letter: "It will help Jeff, he will become accustomed to restrictions."

Cookie-cutting has its virtues. It's worth something to be taught that neighbors have rights, that conventions are not prima facie malign, that rules are not always provocative. At Choate, though, cookie-cutting was a fixation. The boys we called "straight arrows" thrived. The rest of us—"negos," carpers, corner-cutters, and wise-apples—bucked the system, and some had fun. The happy ones knew what they were doing, but I didn't. I said *no* by reflex, wouldn't take the bit, see the point, play the game, join the team. I was ashamed of myself, and bitter that Choate didn't love me. I should have understood that boys who don't join the team cannot expect to be loved by the team.

Most of the masters at Choate and many of the boys felt I laughed too quickly and too often at things sacred to them: the score of the Deerfield game, the election of class officers, our privilege not to be permitted to smoke. Seymour St. John's farewell message to my graduating class, published in the 1955 yearbook, *The Brief*, closed with an unidentified quotation "from one of my heroes." It is vintage homily, just the kind of stuff we heard at chapel every evening after dinner, and before lunch on Sunday: "The ideals which have lighted my way, and time after time have given me new courage to face life cheerfully, have been Kindness, Beauty, and Truth."

Perhaps. There were no black students at Choate, and someone once asked the Head why. There were no black students at Choate, said the Reverend St. John, because it was unfair to elevate the aspirations of Negroes by inviting them to a school whose customs, requirements, and academic standards were beyond their reach. Yet, he said, all were equal in the eyes of the Lord. So he invited a black preacher to sermonize to us every year. This was a huge man with a musical voice, a Robeson bass; he had the most cultivated of accents, the product of education at Trinity College, Cambridge. The Head beamed to hear him speak. The last time I heard him, I deployed alarm clocks throughout the chapel, and they rang at five-minute intervals for almost an hour. *Mea culpa*, it was the weak link who did this. My father had done it too, at the Clark School. It was just dumb, easy mischief, not so much the work of an angry young man as of a temperamental brat.

The spring of my fifth-form year I visited the Head for a heart-to-heart. I was in trouble. I had run up bills. From way back, midway through my first year, this had been a problem. Here's a note from George Steele in 1952: "I have had to write your parents about your Bookshop bill. Now, ere the new year, I expect you to get yourself out of your difficulties." Then came a wire to my father, with a copy to Steele, from St. George's Inn, where we were sometimes allowed to eat dinner, and in whose basement some of us smoked, a vice punishable by immediate expulsion: THE AMOUNT OF $49.19 ACCRUED BY YOUR SON JEFFREY WOLFF HAS NOT BEEN PAID. IF IT IS NOT PAID IN FULL BY THE FIFTEENTH OF THIS MONTH WE WILL BE FORCED TO TURN THE ACCOUNT OVER TO OUR ATTORNEY FOR COLLECTION.

But the immediate cause of my trouble was a breach of school regulations, sort of. Fifth-formers were obliged to be present at a specified number of meals each week, and attendance was usually recorded by a master, seated at each round table of twelve. At Sunday supper, however, the masters were free, and we signed ourselves in. I came to the dining hall, signed in, bowed my head for the Head's appreciation of our many bounties, gulped a glass of milk and left for a proper meal at St. George's. A straight arrow, aware that I had exhausted my outside dining privileges, turned me in to Mr. Steele. The Penguin took the position that I had, in effect, lied, had breached the Honor Code, was subject to the consideration of the Honor Committee.

On the Honor Committee was a boy I knew well. He was as dumb as a shoe. Three weeks earlier he had stolen my sweater. I saw him leave my room with it and retrieved it from his drawer. I had worn it every day since, in front of him. I was wearing it now. He frisked with me, told me there was no place at Choate for liars, that I wasn't good enough for his wonderful school. Others in the room, the class of the class ahead of me, nodded. I sat silent, no defense, of course they were right, the sweater was nothing weighed against my breach of honor, I was low, a miserable thing, verily.

They were sports. I was let off with a warning. I went to see the Head, and he told me I didn't deserve to remain in his school. When I left his office I felt soiled, diminished, and beyond reach. I believed the man despised me, and was right to despise me. Now I find a generous memo in my file, a record of our talk:

> Jeff Wolff came in June 3rd to say that he had just recently had a change of heart and hoped he might have an opportunity to prove himself in the year ahead. As nearly as I could judge, Jeff was completely sincere and not motivated—primarily at least—by a fear that he would not be allowed to continue at Choate next year. He admits that he has been less than honest, sloppy, and generally useless in his approach to School life. I told him he would have to be 100% in every way in his Sixth Form year or we just could not keep him. I suggested that this might be more of a challenge than Jeff wanted to accept, but he insisted that this was just the way he wanted it to be.

*   *   *

I left the Head's office, and wanted to be alone. There was only the chapel. At Choate I was never alone, except there. I loved chapel for this, sang the hymns with gusto, even reverence. Alone in the chapel I banished resentments. I prayed to be better. I tried. My *Brief* biography is illustrated with a poorly drawn cartoon of a boy studying a book titled *Being One of the Boys*. I studied the subject diligently, to my shame. Had myself confirmed by the Head, in the Head's faith. Joined the Altar Guild and the Scholarship Committee. Sang with the choir, the glee club, and the Maiyeros (pipsqueak Whiffenpoofs). I tried to make the football team: "Fine effort," the coach said, "willing. Going to be a hard competitor to stop. Fought hard as a guard. Good development." But I wasn't good enough, and so I became a cheerleader. Good God! I'd rather confess I was a pickpocket. My friends were amused. I was perplexed.

The Maiyeros gave a concert at Miss Porter's, in Farmington. I fell in love with a girl from Philadelphia. She liked me, for a while, and visited me for a day and night in Wilton during her Christmas vacation. I had hoped she would stay longer, but she lost interest quickly. She seemed uncomfortable with my father; Duke wasn't what she knew on the Main Line. She was quiet, reserved, not pretty, handsome, with mannish shoulders. I liked her for good reasons, and as usual I liked her too well. I wanted her to love me; I boasted, labored to charm, dropped names, felt her slip away, heard her telephone the New York, New Haven and Hartford to ask about an earlier train. We drove to the Norwalk station in silence. At the station she told me there was no need to wait for her train, but I did. We waited five minutes together; she pretended to read a book.

That night I wrote her a letter, twenty or thirty pages, maybe fifty. Falsehood on falsehood. *Bon mots* from *Bartlett's* that I hoped weren't familiar, because I displayed them as my own. References to my upcoming social season, so busy with coming-out parties in Boston and New York. The summer looked full too, Pater would be off as usual doing polo at Brandywine and Myopia. I'd be playing the eastern tennis circuit, Longwood, Newport Casino, had a fair chance to advance to a ranking if I could sharpen the backstroke, but squash at the Racquet Club was playing hob with my wrist. And so on and on and on... I even quoted, as a closing epigraph, a line or two from Sophocles, in Greek: *Thus do flies to gods like little boys to men*, or something. I signed off, finally, "affectionately."

This letter was probably worse than I have represented it here. I know I wrote it on Racquet Club stationery (taken from a cache my father had cadged when Frank Shields took him to lunch to sell him the temporary use of towels), and I know I sealed the envelope with wax from a Christmas candle and stuck Duke's crest, engraved on a salt shaker he had given Alice as a wedding gift, in the wax.

That night my father found the letter, opened it, read it. He didn't bring it to me. He destroyed it first, and then came to my room and woke me. He knew the toll, to the penny; he was so gentle. He didn't quote the letter at me, or refer to it. He told me I was better than I thought, that I didn't need to add to my sum. I had warmth, he said; warmth and energy were the important things. These were a long time paying off sometimes, but they paid off. Honesty was the crucial thing, he said, knowing who I was, being who I was. What he said was so; I knew it was so. I didn't even think to turn his words against him, he was trying so hard to save me from something, to turn me back. I had this from him always: compassion, care, generosity, endurance.

I had met another girl at Farmington, Marion Rockefeller; they called her "Pebbles." Cute, sassy, friendly. She invited me to a dance not long after my father's talk about the truth. I called for her at an apartment on Fifth

Avenue. Her father wished to deliver us to the Plaza. As I descended in the elevator with Laurance Rockefeller he asked me if I was kin to the Wolffs at Loeb, Rhodes, fine people. I said I was not. Perhaps then Dr. Wolff (I brightened), a good heart man at Mt. Sinai? Certainly not, my grandfather *was* a doctor but he was dead; he had practiced at a Catholic hospital somewhere in Connecticut. Mr. Rockefeller had exhausted his interest in my ancestors. I noticed him look down at my feet. I was wearing black loafers with my dinner jacket. He looked at my cummerbund. Mr. Rockefeller also wore a dinner jacket, but with pumps on his feet and a black vest crossed by a delicate gold chain. I thought he looked better than I looked, and I thought he thought so too. I danced a few times with Pebbles, a St. Paul's boy cut in with a fierce scowl for me and a grin for the pretty girl, and I never saw her again.

My nose was thickening and curving. My lips were bigger, my hair darker. A friend at Choate asked if I was a Jew. I said I thought I was not. I had asked my mother this question once, and she had said *of course not!* I had asked my stepmother; she had laughed: *don't be silly!* Now, a month after my father sat on my bed telling me that truth is all we need, identity is a treasure, I asked him:

"Am I a Jew?"

"Of course not. You're a baptized, confirmed Episcopalian."

"I don't mean that. That doesn't count. Are you a Jew?"

"I'm a confirmed Anglican."

"Was my mother a Jew?"

"She was Dutch, Van Zandt, fine family, Lutherans, I think."

"Your father?"

"Atheist."

"I'm not asking about religion. I'm asking what I am."

"For Christ's sake! You know I'm not an anti-Semite. I wouldn't be ashamed to be a Jew, if I was. I'm not, that's all. Why would I lie to you? Wolff is a German name, Prussian. Your grandfather and grandmother were English. That's all."

So when people asked me, and they asked quite often, I explained that Wolff was a German name, Prussian. Someone at Choate began to call me "Kraut." In Modern European History we read about Himmler's chief of staff, S.S. Major General Karl Wolff. And when I came to class the morning after that reading assignment, half a dozen boys stood and gave me a Nazi salute, *Sieg Heil!* After a week or so the salutes stopped, but "Kraut" stuck. It's right there, in *The Brief:*

GEOFFREY ANSELL WOLFF
"Art"..."Porfirio"..."Kraut"

17

Good grief, why so gloomy? My life was not all sitting on the edges of beds, plumbing the verities. I laughed, graduated, learned. My fourth-form year at Choate I discovered Louis Untermeyer's anthology of American poetry and I read it ragged, till its sturdily bound pages fell away from the spine, and I replaced it. Frost, Dickinson, Whitman, Crane, Pound, Stevens, Williams, Eliot: I had Eliot by rote as I never learned *Eskimo Nell*. On my sixteenth birthday and at Christmas I got Robert Lowell and Theodore Roethke. Then it was Hemingway, who taught me the manners and codes my father had lost the authority to teach me, whose manners and codes meshed perfectly with my father's affections and deepest convictions. O'Neill! *The Iceman Cometh* was my Book of Revelations; there was my father with his pipe dreams; Alice was Hickey, the "Iceman of Death," or I was Hickey, hearing my father's boozy litany, or Choate was Hickey, hearing my blowhard asseverations: *Tomorrow I'll pull it together, get my suit cleaned, find a job, leave Alice, beat the act into shape, shave, sell the Ferrari, work*

*out a budget, lay off the sauce, reform, make the football
team, be a cheerleader, team player, Choatie, good...*

We weren't meant to read O'Neill. We were meant to
read Whittier, Hardy, Cooper, Irving. But I kept
wandering off the reservation, reading rule-breakers to
puzzle out how they did it. I carried my Untermeyer
anthology in the plain brown wrapper of a geometry
textbook dust jacket, but my sixth-form English master
had my number:

> Geof has been building up a resistance to the work we
> have been doing, feeling that a diet of James Joyce,
> Pound, Eliot, Gertrude Stein and others would inspire
> greater interest and value than Hardy and the other
> classics we have been studying. I think Geof would be
> better off to stop dreaming about college courses in
> English and undertake the mastery of something that he
> doesn't think taxes his abilities enough. To sound a loud
> alarm I talked to him straight from the shoulder, alone; I
> must say I have no criticism at all of his behavior for the
> last two weeks. I really think that alarm, or my really
> sound common sense, dictated his quiet but thoughtful
> attentiveness during this last part of the year. He still felt it
> necessary occasionally to exhibit his greater knowledge
> and sophistication to his admirers in the class, but he was
> very careful to keep to himself his former criticisms of the
> course.

To this memo the Head responded: "It's spelled
Geoff!" Yes, I was quiet. Yes, I studied my master. This
man who made his way by books despised books. He
didn't despise me, he despised Joyce and Stein.

John Joseph was another kind of master. He was
swarthy, with heavy features, and we called him "The
Arab." The other masters mostly had diminutives:
Cappy, Ploopy, Porky, Snoopy, Stubby ... The Arab was
serious, tough-headed, irreverent, exacting, ceremonial.
He cooked civilized meals for his friends, and treated me
like a friend. He opened books for me. Long after I left
Choate Mr. Joseph wrote asking about my doings, and

closed his letter asking what had become of my "dapper and youngish sportive father with a sports car." I answered that he was dead, "a bad man and a good father." Mr. Joseph said: "Don't ever again say your father was a 'bad man': there are no 'bad men.'" Now I wish I could believe this.

Mr. Joseph was Boston-born and Harvard-educated. He told me I reminded him of Dexter, in Fitzgerald's "Winter Dreams." I had never heard of Fitzgerald, but I found "Winter Dreams" and didn't know what to make of it, didn't realize till years later that Mr. Joseph had given a judgment neither flattering nor derogatory, just accurate. He saw that I was on the outside of the window looking in, and he knew that this was uncomfortable. Dexter "wanted not association with glittering things and glittering people—he wanted the glittering things themselves. Often he reached out for the best without knowing why he wanted it—and sometimes he ran up against the mysterious denials and prohibitions in which life indulges."

Years later Mr. Joseph confided in me how deeply he hated the "thingness" of American life, our appetites for "glittering things," my father's ruling vice. But I took other lessons from Fitzgerald then, and took him as my master. I read "The Rich Boy" and bought first editions of *All the Sad Young Men, Tales of the Jazz Age, The Beautiful and the Damned*, and of course *This Side of Paradise*. Duke hoped I'd go to New Haven for him, together with more than forty of my hundred thirty classmates; it never entered my mind after I read Fitzgerald, who said that Yale was for bond salesmen, to go there. Mr. Joseph urged Harvard, but that could not be, to Paradise I would go. I visited there, met the great R.P. Blackmur, who spoke to me of his friend Cummings, of his *defects*, as though I were a colleague in letters. Oh, yes: Princeton.

But before I entered the class of 1960 as a freshman I first spent a post-graduate year in England, at Eastbourne College on the Sussex coast, an hour by train from

London. My father was drunk much of the summer of my graduation, and he quarreled with me and with Alice. There were nice moments, playing tennis together, watching tennis at Forest Hills. He had gorgeous style, but never won a set against me. At Forest Hills he favored the oddballs. I rooted for Tony Trabert and Vic Seixas, sobersides who played always to win. Duke liked Sven Davidson and Art Larsen, clowns who broke training but sometimes surprised everyone with a big set or two, seldom three.

The more time I spent near my father the worse I stammered. As I liked him less and less I became more and more like him. I felt trapped, didn't care for myself or Alice, who didn't care for me. I wanted to go far away, but Alice wouldn't send me. She had sent me to Choate and where had it got her? She made plans to leave my father. It was obvious he would never work again, just diddle away the allowance she doled out. The first time she broke camp was over a toy he had ordered from Hoffritz, a tool that had a wrench on one end, pliers on the other and blades and scissors and screwdrivers between. She opened the package, and turned the thing this way and that, and began to laugh, dangerously. She didn't laugh often those days; my father was running her account dry.

She left for New York. I felt premonitions of squalor, and worse—of chaos. I didn't want to be alone with my father. I wanted to be alone with myself. Before Alice returned I remembered my grandmother's legacy. It would free me to go to England for a post-graduate school year with about twenty other American schoolboys, under the eye of the English-Speaking Union.

There was a year! Eastbourne was a new school, less than a hundred years old. No Great Men had gone there, unless you counted the son of Lloyd George, and no one at Eastbourne bothered to count him. The trustees were mostly commoners, with a few men recently knighted. The masters were hard-headed, thick-skinned, and just. The school worked by code rather than common law: the price of everything was given and exacted. Twenty-seven of twenty-eight masters were Oxford or Cambridge men, snobs for merit rather than class. I was their first American and they told me right off that I didn't know anything important.

At Choate I had learned to make a sentence; Eastbourne taught me to make a paragraph, and sense. I wrote as many as six essays a week, and they came back, at first, with insults in the margins: "What *can* this mean, boy?" I had six classes a day, three in history, three in English. An hour of Shakespeare every day, and only two plays all year, *Antony and Cleopatra, Henry IV, Part Two*. We were never obliged to memorize but couldn't help having the plays by rote, and the syntax and meter of blank verse sunk into our own grammars. After class our speech was laced with Shakespeare's conceits: our insults were Falstaff's to Pistol, our teases Antony's of Lepidus.

We read *Paradise Lost*. We read it again to have it down cold for the examinations we would face that coming summer, in competition with everyone else in England who aspired to admission to Oxford or Cambridge. For me the examinations were nominally inconsequential, but to pass them mattered to me supremely.

> The World was all before them, where to choose
> Thir place of rest, and Providence thir guide:
> They hand and hand with wand'ring steps and slow,
> Through *Eden* took thir solitary way.

To *know* something was to be cast into Eden. History was wonderful, the dates were wonderful, accuracy was wonderful. We shared the masters' scorn for ignorant personages, their delight in the charge against James II, booted off his throne for consorting with Jesuits and other wicked people. Quite.

Eastbourne was a curious setting for Eden. A summer resort with hotels of faded grandeur along the beachfront, the town was left to its population of retired clergymen and civil servants when the season ended and school began. There was a cooking school in town, where middle-class girls learned the domestic arts. I met many of them in the town's tea shops and parks, and walked them to Beachy Head to snog in the heather and gorse. Janet, do you remember me? We went to the park at night, even in winter. We would meet and kiss, say not a word. You would sit on my lap, and let me reach under your raincoat and your skirt. Why didn't we ever say anything? Janet was ashamed of her Yorkshire accent, I think, and I was afraid to break the spell. Did I really wear, in accordance with school regulations, a straw boater? Even then, at night, in the park?

I was seventeen, weighed ten stone, boxed for the school, played rugger. Reports went home to the Duke. The housemaster of School House noted that he had made me a house prefect, "which alone is enough to show that we all think well of him." Everything that year surprised me. I was not, for example, ashamed of myself.

A Choate classmate, a blond straight-arrow and football star, ran away from his school in England; he couldn't stand up to the ragging. Other Americans drifted home. I was never homesick, never lonely. My stammer disappeared. I was in love with being in love with a girl I had met coming east on the *Queen Elizabeth;* she was a Denver heiress my age, traveling first class with her mother. They invited me to spend Christmas with them in Florence. Another report went home: "He has made a useful House Prefect and has thrown himself into a host of school activities. He has played vigorous Rugger for the School, scoring often and crucially." My paragraphs seemed to have a reason to exist: "He holds enthusiastically and provocatively to his opinions about literature, and at last is beginning to know enough to justify them. He is learning to write." The headmaster—who described himself as a "benevolent dictator, we have none of your absurd democracy in my school, hope you see things just my way"—let me go to London for weekends.

The food was foul, of course, and the weather. There

was no central heating, and the windows we were required to leave open let the fog drift in. Mercifully it obscured the nights' dramas: we slept thirty to a dormitory, and it shocked me at first to awaken and see twelve empty beds, and everyone present. I wrote letters, ten and more a day; I took piano lessons, learned to use a camera and darkroom. I made lists of things I had done, thoughts I had thought, girls I had kissed, boys punched, cars driven, books read, places seen, anything I had *done*, anything that had weight and mass and reality, anything that added up. Now I knew I was a survivor, in for the long haul.

Once before I had felt this, coming through. Every Choate boy was required to endure Public Speaking, the province of Mr. Pratt, a theatrical character who wore a cape, carried a cane and said the most abusive things I have ever heard a human being say to another human being. The boys hated and feared him, till they left Choate, when they agreed to revere him. We would sit thirty at a time once a week in the basement of the chapel; Mr. Pratt would call on five of us in turn, according to a system of his own devising, so that five times a year, perhaps five weeks in a row, each of us would speak for five minutes on a subject of his choice. If he didn't like what he heard Mr. Pratt would beat his cane and scream; he seldom liked what he heard. My first year I sat trembling week after week for seven weeks before he called on me. I wanted to tell him I stammered, but I didn't want to tell him I stammered. What I wanted most was not to stammer.

Mr. Pratt called on a slow-witted bully, a Lake Forest boy who elected to disarm the ogre with low wit. He began his speech smirking: "Doctor Frood, the infamous" (he said it *in-fay-muss*) "Hun, tells us there is a war between the supernegro and the yid. I'd like to explore..."

Two words into this monologue I heard Pratt mumble; then a sound like a death rattle came from behind us, hitting the silly, blushing boy at the lectern:

"You vile thing! You cur of a child. Where do you think you are?"

As the boy considered a response to this bewildering question, and perhaps developed an alternative presentation—on The Greatness of Napoleon, or Why I'm Proud to Be a Midwesterner—Pratt bowled down the aisle with his cane raised and his cape spread out behind him, showing its blood-red silk lining. He climbed the dais stage left as the boy exited weeping stage right, as though pursued by a bear. Mr. Pratt spoke:

"WOLFF! NEXT! TALK TO ME!"

I stammered an exposition of powerboat racing. I had committed to memory three double-spaced pages, and twenty minutes after I began, shaking my head wildly from side to side to force the words out, *forcing* them out, every word, no substitutes, no cheating on the sadistic plosives, no tricks to push off to a new sentence *(let's see, the fastest hydroplane in the world is, let's see, let's see, Slo-Mo-Shun, let's see)*, just getting it done...after twenty minutes I knew something I had not known before. Doing it is never as bad as not doing it. Before I reached the end of my speech Mr. Pratt held up his hand:

"We have to eat, Wolff. That's enough. Well done."

That was as good as it ever got at Choate, and at Eastbourne it was better than that all the time.

In Florence my Denver heiress turned out to be no heiress, but neither was I what she expected. Her mother had made unwarranted assumptions about a Choate boy Princeton-bound by way of an English public school; she had installed me in the Excelsior, in a room overlooking the Arno. This, I soon learned, was to be my treat, and I was expected to give her and her daughter dinner of an evening. This was careless fortune-hunting; I had three hundred dollars to lavish on my six-week continental holiday, but before I understood I was to pay, and before the heiress and her mother discovered I could not pay, I had the pleasure of a night alone with a beautiful and experienced seventeen-year-old girl.

The next night we fought. I thought that our combat was about love rather than my disappointing Dun &

Bradstreet. I got drunk and morose on grappa at the Grand, where we listened to a bad American pianist play "When Sonny Gets Blue," again and again, as long as I paid for his drinks. The girl unaccountably bit my finger, and caused it to bleed. I thought of myself as Dick Diver even as I slapped her, thinking how lucky I was to have fallen in with someone so interestingly unstable. After I slapped her she even more unaccountably kissed me, languorously. Then she left me, "forever," as she said. I stood on the Ponte Vecchio at three in the morning and contemplated suicide. The following morning I skipped out on my bill at the Excelsior, took the sleeper to Paris, met some American pals and had the devil of a time. Then I spent the spring holidays with them in Spain for six weeks, following the bulls, of course, telling Smith College Junior-Year-Abroaders we were older than we were, which the girls pretended to believe.

At the end of the year I broke a rule much like the rule I had broken at Choate that had put me at the mercy of the Honor Committee. On the Sabbath I went to the cinema. This was serious; I was meant to be at rest or worship. I was caught by a master's wife, summoned to the headmaster.

"Did you worship today, Wolff?"

"No, Sir."

"Do anything?"

"Yes, Sir."

"Tell."

"I saw a film, Sir."

"You're a damned fool."

"Yes, Sir."

"What film?"

"*The Man with the Golden Arm*, Sir."

"Good?"

"Very, Sir."

"You're a double-damned fool if you think so. I should beat you. Instead there'll be no more London weekends for you. Go away."

"Yes, Sir. I'm sorry."

"Of course you are. What difference does that make?"

The headmaster wrote my father: "He has really done a very good year here. It was unfortunate that he made a fool of himself at the end, but that will be forgotten and the good impression that he made will be remembered. He is a good boy."

They even gave me a prize, The Brian Tunstall Imperial Studies Prize, for my paper explaining the colonial insurrection of 1776. The prize came with a book—*The Collected Stories of Ernest Hemingway*—and handshakes from the Bishop of Chichester and Duke of Devonshire, president and vice-president of the school's governing body, The next day I was to leave for a summer in France with my American friends, but Duke telephoned. Alice was gone again, and with her the cash. I was to borrow passage money home, quickest. The phone connection was weak, but I heard for the first time that my father's Oxbridge honk didn't come off, quite, that it went flat on the *a*, which was too narrow, and that it wasn't sufficiently slurred.

I wanted to stay, but said I'd be home "toute suite." I had to go to Paris first, I said, to "fetch up with a chap who owes me lucre." My father instructed me to borrow passage money home from the school, or from his dear old RAF pal, Nick Van Sittart, now Lord.

"Call Nick," said Duke. "He'll give you lunch at White's and a hundred quid till you get home."

I telephoned Lord Van Sittart, and said I belonged to Duke Wolff.

"Never heard of him."

"Arthur Wolff? During the war? An American pilot?"

"Oh *him*. The Yank who liked pilots. Always asking for an introduction to one's tailor. Hardly remember him, sorry."

18

Eastbourne advanced me passage money home on the *Île de France*. By some hook or crook my father got together eight hundred dollars to pay for my first semester at Princeton. After that, it was understood, I was on my own. At Eastbourne I had dreamed fine dreams of Princeton, and of myself. But even before I got there I felt them slipping away. The summer in Wilton before my freshman year was awkward. Alice came and went, always drifting. I understand why she left, but not why she returned. She couldn't bear my father, it seemed, and he seemed indifferent to her. I think she was lonely, but I don't want to condescend to her. Neither do I underestimate loneliness.

At the time I welcomed loneliness for myself, or rather welcomed the state of being alone, the illusion of self-reliance. I felt my father to be a force field of unmakings, and I avoided him. I began to put things together, to remember that alone I had managed to survive, in Niagara Falls, New York, Old Lyme, Sarasota, flying to Seattle, at Eastbourne. No: I had never been alone in those places; what I meant by "alone" was apart from my mother, father, stepmother.

Duke drove me to Princeton. The new scholars wore raccoon coats to our Freshman Week, second week of September, 1956, despite temperatures in the high eighties. Three-by-five-foot felt rectangles hung on their walls, orange PRINCETON against a black field, to remind them where they were spending the night. Most of my friends from the class of 1960, friends through college and now, I met within a week of our arrival. We recognized one another at a glance: no fur coats, no banners on our walls, never a reference to Scott Fitzgerald. The Exeter graduates set the tone: sardonic, smart, quick to laugh and dismiss, "negative" was an honorific. There were Choaties at Princeton, but I kept apart from them.

"We" kissed off the pushers, strivers, tweedbags ("the idiot looks like he was hatched from a madras egg," a friend said about someone who wanted to be his friend), jocks, lounge lizards (one wore his Chesterfield coat to early morning classes, pretending to have just returned from a "do" in The City; everyone knew better, the train schedules didn't fit and the college wouldn't let us drive cars), the greasers, Christers, doers... Kissing off was natural selection. Discrimination. Criticism, judgment: *this* was better than *that*. Here was our education. Choate told me I had been selected from among many good enough for Choate. Now "we" selected from among many good enough for Princeton.

Within weeks the English and the French bombed Egypt, the Soviets crushed the Hungarian freedom fighters, Ike crushed Adlai. We watched history on the tube at the Nass' and the 'Nex. The Nassau Tavern was dark and moist, a ritzy cellar where the Princeton heroes of yore were enshrined on oars and hockey sticks. The Annex Grill was better: Italian bartenders, roadhouse grit.

We drank ourselves silly. Wait: I drank myself silly.

My friends knew when to quit everything. I always went too far.

Princeton was easier than Eastbourne, easier even than Choate, too easy. Everything was first principles, surveys, field requirements. Like everyone I had to take a laboratory science course. There were only two choices for wiseguys: "Rocks" (geology) and "Misfits" (psychology). Chemistry, physics, biology . . . these were exacting, students sometimes flunked them. I chose Misfits, and flunked it. At the final I appeared with my pencils and the professor—Smilin' Jack Somebody—wrote some names on the blackboard of the huge lecture hall; my name was among them, listing the labs I had missed.

Some of the young gentlemen had missed two, four, even six labs. I had missed thirteen.

"Is Mr. Wolff in the room?" I sat in the front row, nodded. "Just wanted to meet you before we say bye-bye," said Smilin' Jack, smiling. "No need for you to take this exam. Your grade is already registered."

Here was trouble, the mighty *seven!* Princeton gave a *one* for excellence, *six* for failure, *seven* for something special, "Flagrant Neglect." I would be punished by a special summer reading course but worse, at the end of my first semester and my father's eight hundred dollars, I was an unlikely candidate for a full scholarship.

Then I flunked another course, but this failure conferred a distinction. Air Force R.O.T.C. was a joke at Princeton, but I didn't know this when I signed up. I wanted to fly, but a month after I entered college I knew there'd be no Eagle Squadron for me. I needed glasses, just like my father. I bought wire rims, just like his. And flunked Air Force. The commanding officer pointed out to my faculty advisor that among other evidence of ill-preparedness (unshined shoes, unpolished belt buckle) were incorrect replies to the following *true/false* first semester examination questions:

The United States of America is the most powerful nation on earth. T or F (circle one)

Scientific and industrial excellence can be achieved as

easily in the yoke of communist repression as in our Free Society. T or F (circle one)

With two failures I was on a sticky wicket. My friends—even the negative, knowing ones—urged me to pull up my socks, drink less, cut fewer classes, play ball. I hadn't applied for a scholarship when I applied to Princeton, and didn't think I was eligible. I asked for a job and got one, washing and delivering my schoolmates' laundry for a dollar an hour, fifteen hours a week. It wasn't enough. I explained my predicament to the bureau of student aid. Despite two failing grades, they went the distance for me: if my father was broke, that was a pity, but I wouldn't have to leave Princeton on that account. Ways could be found, not to worry, do your part and we'll do ours. One thing: ask your dad to pop a financial statement in the mail, so we can work out terms with him.

He wouldn't do it, said his circumstances were no damned business of Princeton's. I asked him not to visit me in the Mercedes, wearing bespoke suits and hand-lasted Lobb shoes. He visited in the Mercedes, wearing bespoke suits and the rest, what he always wore. My friends were charmed by him, and called him The Duke, though not to his face; they thought him to be quite the most swank (or most risible) dad they knew. He was sometimes invited to parties, and came.

Three weeks after I entered Princeton the bursar of Eastbourne wrote the headmaster of Choate about an "awkward" matter.

The fees for the Michaelmas Term, and the extras for that term and fees for the Lent Term were paid, but no payment has been made for the extras for the Lent and Summer Terms, or the fees for the Summer Term. We had to advance the boy considerable sums for the Easter holidays and also had to advance his fare back to America. The result is that the parent now owes us four hundred eight pounds, eighteen shillings and fourpence. I have written to the parent without reply, A.S.A. Wolff,

Esq., "Driftways," Nod Hill Road, Wilton, Connecticut on July 18th, August 15th, and September 10th. What should I do?

St. John wrote my father, with a copy to me:

I have just received through the English-Speaking Union a most disturbing letter from Eastbourne College . . . I am naturally concerned on several counts: your and Geoff's good name, our good name, and our relationships with England . . . Eastbourne says it is writing this letter as a last hope—before taking legal action . . . Geoff apparently did such a good job at Eastbourne, and has such a happy future ahead of him, that I should feel terribly to have it blighted in any way . . .

I wrote St. John the truth. Tuition and fees were twelve hundred dollars a year at Eastbourne, third-class passage back and forth another four hundred, and this left about eight hundred from my inheritance, which my father promised to deal out as bills came in. Other people promise that the moon is made of cheese.

"Dad said he had received NO BILLS from Eastbourne. He said this as recently as this weekend. I fear I now know a different truth. What can I do? I have no money. I shall call Dad immediately. I fear he has none. Needless to say, any pride I might have taken in what I accomplished is more than outweighed by this disgrace to my family and my country." Dear me.

St. John answered compassionately. He was relieved to report that my father had assured him a check was in the mail. It must have gone astray. I paid the debt three years later. But meantime, to mark the "disgrace to my family and country," I got falling-down drunk and was shaken awake on the steps of Palmer Physics Laboratory by a student, on his way to a 7:40 A.M. engineering class, who half carried me to the infirmary. It was thought that I had fallen from a height, but I had in fact fallen my own height, to lie six hours in the mid-October rain. A doctor noticed that I was incoherent; perhaps there had been a blow to the head? There were X-rays, a blood test. I was drunk. The following morning I was still drunk. That afternoon I was sent to the Assistant Dean of Students. He observed that there was a pattern here of self-destruction. I saw that this was so, and said it was so. How did I explain it? I tried, I really tried to explain it. I explained about predetermination, being a father's son. The dean explained fresh starts, clean slates. Self-pity blocked my ears; also, a fast slide downhill is sometimes exhilarating.

I began to run up bills, why not? I couldn't travel to Poughkeepsie and Northampton wearing rags. We'd drive eleven hours in a roommate's ancient and illegally registered Buick convertible, in violation of Princeton's injunction against student driving, so I could take a Smith girl to Rahars and three hours later kiss her (maybe) on the steps of her house, while her housemother watched, an hour before midnight. Then we'd spend the night on someone's cousin's friend's floor at Amherst, and the next day drive back through the rain. This we called "dating."

My other "dates" were perquisites of my baritone crooning with a singing group called The Tigertones, a close harmony chorus of a dozen or so. We sang funny songs and we sang sad songs. During the winter of my freshman year I had Langrock fit me with a suit of tails, so I could sing at coming-out parties. Spring vacation we Tigertones flew to Bermuda to sing at the Belmont Manor. There were fewer girls than boys in Bermuda when we were there. Surprisingly, singers did not seduce them. Football players, in Bermuda ostensibly to play Rugby but in fact for spring football practice, seduced them. Football players shaved their ankles before they taped them. That was how you recognized them as football players, by their shaved ankles. I shaved my ankles. This was a metaphor, the kind my father had understood for many years. I was learning, nothing to it, soap and a razor, jubilee.

That summer I went to Colorado with a quartet of Princeton singers, The Boomerangs. We sang "Sweet Adeline!.," "Mavourneen," "Bandoleros" ("We are brave and happy Ban-do-laaaayrose;/ We con-quer, or diiie!") and "Teasin'." We wore striped jackets and boaters. The bass, son of an undertaker, taught me to drink martinis in the Mineshaft Bar near Central City, where we sang at the Glory Hole Saloon for meals and tips. We didn't sing very well, in part because of the martinis. We went broke and broker, and now when we passed the boater for tips we salted it with a fiver, till one night we got it back with less than two dollars. I borrowed money first from the second tenor, and then from the first. I was supposed to bring back at least a thousand to help me through Princeton my second year. I came back empty-handed, with a hangover. My friends helped me, and wanted me to be other than who I was. Who? There was a saying at Princeton they should have embroidered on samplers and sold at the U-Store: "Be yourself at all times, and if that isn't good enough—be someone else."

The fall of my sophomore year a friend from Philadelphia came to our house in Wilton. Duke was about to get the gate for nonpayment of rent, and he wanted to shut down in style, with a party. It was the weekend of the Yale game, and some of us went. Yale won. When we returned from the game Duke said he was sorry for Princeton but happy on his own account.

My Philadelphia friend was an oddly tenacious fellow; he was inquisitive, and willing to bore in for answers to his questions. He was not exactly a snob and not exactly not, a St. Paul's man who despised social fakers, and loved to ferret them out. I knew this. When my father made his harmless remark about Yale's victory I said to my friend:

"Dad went to Yale. Right, Dad?"

My father blushed. He had not invited this.

"He was Deke, Bones too. Right?"

"Bones men don't discuss Bones," my father said.

My friend was interested. "Which one is Skull and

Bones? The Palladian or the Georgian building?"

My father was silent.

"How about Deke? Where's it located?"

My father said nothing, and began to shake his head. His face was deep red. My friend, almost seven feet tall, was not in the least intimidated by my father's frown.

"Which college faces Trumbull Street?"

"Saybrook," my father said.

"You're wrong," my friend said. For all he or I or Duke knew, my father was right.

"It's been a long time," my father said. "The memory's not so hot."

"The truth is," my friend said, as my father walked away, "he didn't go to Yale."

He said this loud enough for my father to hear it. My father left the house, walking slowly and erect, with his shoulders back. My friend, anxious not to embarrass me further, turned his back to me. I hated them both. I hated myself.

The section from *This Side of Paradise* called "Spires and Gargoyles" is Princeton's public shame and private pride. It accurately evokes a certain Princeton of my day, lush and soft, delicate, beyond the grip of time. Fitzgerald characterizes the eating clubs:

> Ivy, detached and breathlessly aristocratic; Cottage, an impressive mélange of brilliant adventurers and well-dressed philanderers; Tiger Inn, broad-shouldered and athletic... Cap and Gown, anti-alcoholic, faintly religious and politically powerful; flamboyant Colonel...

At the end of sophomore fall semester my friends and roommates didn't dream of Tiger Inn, and even less of Cap and Gown, though these were two of the Big Five of twenty-some eating clubs on Prospect Street. They had eyes for the Big Three, Ivy, Cottage and Colonial, in that order, though there were sometimes crossovers by men bid by Ivy who went to Cottage or Colonial because of a father's or brother's membership, or to hold together in one club a band of friends.

The process of club selection, known as "Bicker," was complex and debasing. After the night of Architectural Tour (the first time underclassmen were meant to have seen the clubs), groups of roommates were visited in their dormitory "suites" by clubmen. Every club came once at least to every suite, but the winnowing was quick and ruthless. Club members recognized their types, and after each interview gave a grade to the sophomore, from the highest (1: "ace") to the lowest (7: flagrant neglect, "fleg-neg," "lunchmeat," "banana," "wonk," "wombat," "turkey"). It frequently happened that from a room of six sophomores only one was wanted by a particular club, or three were wanted, or five. The desirables were courted avidly, sometimes double-teamed, while the unwanted was treated to small talk by a specialist at dumping.

"Are you a legacy anywhere?" (Did your father, grandfather, cousin belong to a Princeton club, other than ours?) "No? Pity. Where did your father go to college? *Maybe* Yale? Never heard that one before. Say, could I have a glass of water? What do *I* major in? I thought I was asking the questions. Oh, well, I major in English. Yeah, it's pretty interesting. Do you like sports? Yes? That's nice. Where did you get the jacket? New, isn't it? Well, I'll say this: you've taken good care of it, it looks brand-new to me. Really, you *never* use wire hangers? Good idea, I guess wire hangers *do* stretch the shoulders out of shape, thanks for the tip, time to roll, I guess the other guys are talked out too."

My roommates were: the son of a diplomat, son of a textile magnate, son of the senior partner of an investment banking house, son of an insurance company president. They were very much wanted by Ivy, Cottage, Colonial, for many reasons. The other clubs recognized these men to be beyond their dreams, and quit their visitations to us. Sometimes when visiting Ivies, Cottages, and Colonials left our room we heard loud laughter from beyond the shut door. This was not understood to bear on my roommates. People, friends, whispered in my ear that I was thought "odd," not "serious" about the enterprise of Bicker, not "polite." It was accurately rumored that on the night of Architectural Tour I had told the president of Cottage that I would like less to see the library, dining room, pool tables, and television room than the kitchen, basement, plumbing, heating plant, and circuit boxes. And that when I left I told the Cottage president: "It's sound; I'll buy it." This had not been a politic jape. It was said that I had a reputation for savage, and sometimes conspicuous, drunkenness, for want of purpose. It was said I had run up debts. I was held to laugh abruptly, from no evident or reasonable motive.

After a week only three clubs came to our room, and I was spending five and six hours a day in small talk with imperious and condescending young gentlemen. There would be another ten days and nights of this. Not for me there wouldn't.

I walked away from a chat with a Grosse Point Ivy boy who wondered aloud, again, how the hockey team would "fare" this year. I explained, again, that I couldn't skate and didn't care. He could not believe that I could not skate and did not care. I just took a walk, enough now. It was January, snowing. I followed Washington Road toward Route One. Every dormitory window was lit. Washington Road was dark. I stopped at the corner of Prospect Street, considered putting a brick through an Ivy window, something dumb like that. It was cold. I walked downhill about a mile, to the bridge over Lake Carnegie. The snow was falling thick; far off I could see the spires, imagine the gargoyles. My roommates would worry; they had worried for days, unable to look straight at me or think straight at me or think what to do. They wouldn't patronize me. I stood on the bridge looking into the dark below. I thought this was it, end of the road, end indeed of Prospect. The bridge railing was wide and low, and I stood on it, then sat on the edge looking down into the water I couldn't see. Now and then a car passed, throwing dirty light on the hunched figure so out of place and expectation. A car stopped. A man asked if I was all right, did I need a ride? I waved him away. I couldn't see the water, but it was down there, almost nine feet below me, three feet of water covering a foot of muck. I thought of my grandfather Loftus' suicide attempt in the reflecting pool in Washington. I wouldn't drown, for sure. I wouldn't even freeze: I was wearing a coonskin coat; Duke had given it to me for Christmas, had told me it had been his "at university." I began to laugh. I shook with the laughter from my chest. I couldn't stop the laughter; it almost rolled me off the bridge. I lay on my back on the bridge, letting the snow hit my face. Then I lay in the middle of Washington Road. I'd lie there till the count of a hundred. That was it: let someone else decide. Thirty-two, thirty-three, thirty-four ... forty-one, forty-two ... I was counting fast ... f'r six, sen ... I saw low beams coming out of Princeton, past Prospect Street. I stopped counting, held my breath, stood slowly with plenty of time to spare, and walked home to my room. I shared a six-pack with my friends, who looked at one another relieved as I told them my decision. They didn't argue with it. I packed, and the next day withdrew.

The deans were kindness itself. I'd be welcome back anytime after twelve months had passed, on condition I settled my outstanding accounts. Counting my debt to Eastbourne, I owed twenty-five hundred, give or take a hundred. I said I might not be back, ever, but I'd pay my bills. I wasn't a college boy, I said. Well, they said, you may feel differently later. Good luck.

Duke drove down to get me. He kissed me, and said whatever I wanted was fine with him, "fuck 'em." Would I live with him? I didn't have to, of course, but he hoped I would, he had missed me. Sure, I said, sure. Was Alice at home? No, she'd just left again that morning. Oh, I said, she didn't look forward to her stepson's return? Not that at all, he said, just one of those things, you know Alice.

My father was aces that day. He took me to "21" for dinner, and paid in cash. People made a fuss over me, he must have kept his account there current. He told me I had done the just, wise, courageous, defiant, honorable, only possible thing.

A couple of weeks later he ran into his cousin Ruth Atkins in Hartford. Her late brother Art Samuels, president of Cottage half a century back, came into their conversation.

"Tried to get Geoffrey to go Cottage for the family's sake," my father told Ruth. "No dice, he went Ivy, wanted to stick by his friends, what can I say?"

19

The new place was in Newtown, on Birch Hill Road. There were no birches in sight, but it perched on a hill my father's car couldn't climb my first snow-blown night home. The sprawling ranch house was unfinished, as though its builder-owner, two weeks before the house-warming, had remembered he had forgotten his hat in a restaurant somewhere and had been looking for it ever since.

A swimming pool out back was full to the three-foot mark with rain water, now skimmed with ice and dirty snow. With the spring thaws, mud sluiced down Birch Hill and dammed up along the neighbors' sagging snow fences. I never met anyone who lived in a house contiguous with ours until I went with my father to court. A neighbor had charged him with dumping garbage beside our road, and this was true. He was fingered by his name on the envelopes of unopened bills, fined fifty dollars, and scolded. I paid the fine.

I paid for everything that year. Food (after our grocery accounts were closed), rent (for the first few months, a

hundred ten a month), cigarettes, and booze. I didn't want
to pay. I wanted to save what I earned to settle my debts.
But if I didn't pay, no one would.

It was the time of the Eisenhower recession; Newtown
is near Danbury, a depressed community if ever there was
one, and at first I couldn't find work. My father got it for
me at Sikorsky, a helicopter manufacturer in Bridgeport
for whom he had twice worked. He got me my job, he
said, by selflessly withdrawing his own job application
there, making room for me. Five years later, taking a leaf
from my father's résumés, I described my work at
Sikorsky to a prospective employer:

> In charge of distribution of all engineering data. Did an
> analysis of the efficiency of the system and recommended
> a complete change in the various processes of distribu-
> tion. This proposal was accepted, resulting in more
> efficient distribution methods.

Sikorsky called me "Engineering Communications Co-
Ordinator." I was the mail boy, at two-seventy a month; I
dressed for work in overalls, and lugged dusty canvas
sacks from place to place. My résumé was accurate, to a
point. I had encouraged at least one procedural change,
that someone be hired to help me. Nick—a tall, proud
Pole about my age—got twenty dollars a month less than
I, and toted heavier loads, so he looked up to me. He
covered for me while I read novels in the can, and I
covered for him while he slept there. He didn't mind that I
read my employers' private communications, and I didn't
mind when he threw into the shredder letters he didn't
wish to deliver.

My immediate supervisor was an émigré Russian
prince who hired me because his son was at Choate, which
had improbably written him testifying to my "excellent
character." Sikorsky made the ubiquitous H-58 helicopter, choice of the Armies, Navies, and Air Forces of our
country and others'. Many blueprints and parts diagrams
were required, with notations in dozens of languages. It

was in part my responsibility to guard the blueprint cage and ensure that diagrams were returned and replaced in their proper folders after they had been checked out. There were so many drawings that many of them seemed to me frivolous or expendable, and the diagrams I least highly prized I tucked beneath my shirt and took home. There I boiled them. They were gelatin on cloth, made to survive eternity, and when the coating had been boiled off its Irish linen backing, one was left with glue stuck to the sides of a pot and with handkerchiefs twelve inches square, soft and tightly woven.

My father taught me this trick. So I owed him, as he owed me. Our arrangement—his arrangement—did not comfort me. I was to keep an account of what I earned (twelve months times two-thirty or so, after withholding), give it all to him to use as he wished, and in twelve months he would repay me in full. Sure. My situation seemed to me hopeless. I would care for him, as Alice had, and there would be an end to it.

Our days and nights in Newtown settled into routine. We rarely saw anyone or went anywhere. Sikorsky was more than an hour's drive; as I was due at the plant by eight I rose at six, while my father slept, and came home after dark, just as he had in Saybrook, when he worked at Sikorsky. Birch Hill's elevation gave us irreproachable television reception, and we watched Westerns, cops, game shows, anything. That winter of 1958–59, my father drank and played with his toys, an electric train and a gruesomely expensive model of a supercharged Bentley he built during six months of spare time. Since all his time was spare time, he invested a lot in the car.

We burned up time. We smoked Camels, and I remember fumbling drunk with their cellophane wrappers, swearing at them. The beast on the Camel logo was mysteriously reduced and paled, made less aggressive in response to marketing advice. We were enraged, and wrote R.J. Reynolds so scalding a letter that they returned their camel to its dark color, and full complement of humps.

My father was meant to clean the house and cook, but didn't. I cooked TV dinners and hash out of cans, and he complained about the food. We listened to Bessie Smith—"Gimmee a Pigfoot and a Bottle of Beer" and "Up on Black Mountain"—and my father played an upright in the storeroom. The storeroom was cold, and as time passed it filled with stacks of magazines and the garbage no one would collect because we didn't pay to have it collected, and finally it got too high in there, especially in warm weather, to enjoy music.

Sometimes I'd announce that I had a date in New York for the weekend, or wanted to go alone to a movie, or have a drink with Nick after work. Then my father would pout, and get ugly-drunk, and visit my bed to tell me how I'd screwed up his life, how he'd given up everything to get me through Choate, had married a woman he couldn't bear to send me to Choate. And what had I done? I'd kicked his ass, that's what I'd done. Then he'd talk big, he was pulling out, he didn't need me or Alice or anyone, he had put up with all the crap he could take, he'd had it, and this time he really meant it, he was washing his hands of me, see how I did on my own, for a change . . .

Some nights we would read quietly, and be friends. Other nights, listening to rain leak through the roof into plastic buckets, we'd laugh and fume and be friends; we'd telephone the landlord (owed four months' rent) to complain about his shoddy upkeep of the place. Dishes piled up in the sink, and empty bottles everywhere.

"Tomorrow," my father would tell me, "I'm going to get cracking."

We listened to *Sounds of Sebring*. Yes: racing car engines recorded winding up at Sebring. We also listened to *Sounds of Monaco* and *Sounds of Silverstone*. We listened to *Whistles in the Night*, trains going from somewhere to elsewhere, till the power company cut the switch on us.

Alice returned briefly in April. She and my father
quarreled at once, but she cleaned the house anyway, and
seemed to dig in. She let me borrow her car; it was a
chance to get off Birch Hill, and I took some time off from
work *(sorry, got the grippe)* to drive north to Stowe to ski
with Princeton friends. I slept in the parking lot of their
lodge and met John, a Harvard boy. He was my first
hipster and I was his, he thought. I had never taken to
anyone as quickly, and he became the chief witness to that
Newtown year, for when I returned home Tootie packed
and left, yelling: "All you do is read! The trouble with
both of you is your damned books!"

No, that was not *the* trouble with us. I saw my
stepmother two years later for the last time; I'd like to see
her again, if she's alive, and tell her I know she deserved
better from her golden years than what she got from my
father and me, but when she left her husband for good,
while he lay sick with pneumonia in California, she went
to deep cover, where no Wolff could find her.

Only one girl visited the place in Newtown. I had met
her about the time I left Princeton, in Philadelphia, where
her mother asked the father of my roommate during
lunch at the Gulph Mills Club whether his houseguest,
that young man so interested in her daughter, was a
"gentleman or a Jew." My roommate's father said he
didn't understand the question, its purpose or its
either/or construction. (Still, I learned of the question,
and his response, from him.)

This girl, whom I had busily courted at Smith, washed
up at our house by an unexpected circumstance, a missed
train from New Haven, a phone call to me, a ride from
New Haven to Newtown with my father. It was May.
When she arrived I was shoveling leaves and frogs from
the swimming pool. There was something else in there,
too. This was a woodchuck, I think, a long time dead. I
was fishing for it when my love arrived with my father,
who had stopped for "fortifications" at a joint called The

Three Bears Inn. I was paddling with the shovel, my trousers rolled up to my knees, and then I had it, something soft, white, rancid, unspeakable that I flung down the hill toward the neighbors who had complained about my father's garbage disposal. I greeted the girl and went inside to clean up.

The wonderful, tall, skinny, sporting, rebellious Smith sophomore did not wrinkle up her nose at dinner (chicken croquettes with instant mashed), but I could smell the dead thing on myself. My father was peppy, told college jokes on himself, anecdotes about stolen bell clappers and painted sundials and saplings murdered by sophomores—"no names, please"—who pissed out windows upon them. These were *my* stories. My father had become so careless in his fictions, so indifferent to them, that he forgot their provenance. I looked at him sharply, and he blushed. Drinking a demitasse with my pinky extended crooked, I used the word "attractive."

"Jesus!" my father roared. "*Attractive!* What a word! Scottsdale is 'attractive,' Mimsy is 'attractive.' Mimsy has an 'attractive' dog, polo pony, husband, chess set..."

The lovely girl was abruptly "fagged out, done in, dead tired." I put her in the "guest room" and slept with my father. He snored, and sucked his thumb. I lay awake. I went to the bathroom, saw what the girl had seen, my father's false upper teeth ("choppers," he called them) stewing in an effervescent broth in a pewter beer mug beside the sink. I noticed the fake brass towel rings that swiveled through Neptune's mouth. I drove that girl to the Bridgeport station next morning wearing my work clothes.

No. I wanted better. I wanted to escape to Princeton, from my father. I wanted not to be like him, to let him sink alone. I wrote Princeton, and Princeton welcomed me back come January, just pay the bills.

I didn't tell my father about this exchange of letters, but he sensed it. He knew me.

*   *   *

John came often to visit. He liked my father; my father liked him. John didn't like Harvard, or the conventions. He had been raised in a huge Lake Forest house at the water's edge, and lived summers in another huge house with its own beach on Martha's Vineyard. John wanted something different—Bohemia—and Newtown provided it, definitely.

Cars united the three of us. John owned an Austin-Healey with a Corvette engine, and tinkered with it in our garage. Duke had a folly called an Abarth-Zagato, a tiny maroon coupe that cost many thousands of someone else's dollars. It could uncomfortably seat two and was capable, when it ran, of the top speed of a stock Chevy six. Its 850cc Fiat Toppolino engine had been bored out from 600cc, which raised its compression ratio so high it often blew head gaskets. When they blew the head had to be shaved to seat the new gasket, which raised the compression ratio higher, which provoked another blown gasket. The car seldom ran.

Which was just as well, for my father and I owned between us a single set of license plates, and these had been stolen from yet a third party, my stepmother. We moved the plates from car to car according to need, a procedure that John regarded as pleasingly subversive, my father as routine, and I as a nuisance.

I had my own folly, a 1937 Delahaye, a car longer than a Cadillac, with a cockpit smaller than the Abarth-Zagato's. Its fifty-five gallon gas tank gave it a range of about three hundred miles, and it had four speeds in reverse. This was a car for the *corniche* drives between Nice and Monte, but my father chose it as just the car to carry me from Newtown to Bridgeport and back. When it went at all it would not self-start, which made our birchless prominence a necessary convenience; in the parking lot at Sikorsky, armed with jumper cables, I was at the mercy of strangers with twelve-volt electrical systems and a few moments to spare.

John invited my father and me to Martha's Vineyard for a summer week. I was apprehensive. John's father was

Ike's Secretary of the Air Force, and I dreaded the opportunities this would afford my father for self-celebration. So John adjusted the invitation to include my father out, but he showed up anyway toward the end of the week. He brought along a suitcase made of wood; when this was unfolded it became a boat, which he paddled around the harbor at Vineyard Haven, serving me right, I know.

My father was a mystery, or as crazy as crazy can be. His schemes were insane. He would go to law school, become an expert on wheat speculations, advise the Algerians or Venezuelans on oil refining. He decided the jazz pianist at The Three Bears in Wilton was a genius, as good as King Cole. During the early forties in California he had "discovered" Cole playing piano in a bowling alley, and the King, responding to my father's enthusiasm, asked the Duke to manage him. My father had laughed at the notion. *This* chance my father wouldn't miss, he would produce a record for this pianist, they'd both have it made. He brought the man home, recorded his work on our out-of-tune upright using a top dollar Ampex, shot publicity snaps with a Rollei (white dinner jacket, pencil-line mustache, and rug), and led him to the mountain top. The man was my father's age, with more or less my father's prospects, with one greater skill and one greater vice. The piano player could play the piano better, but he was always drunk; my father was drunk only once—maybe twice—a week.

Duke charged ahead. He charged and charged ahead. There was something about him, what he wanted he got. Salesmen loved him, he was the highest evolution of consumer. Discriminating, too: he railed against shoddy goods and cheapjack workmanship. He would actually return, for credit, an electric blender or an alpine tent that didn't perform, by his lights, to specification. He demanded the best, and never mind the price. As for debts, they didn't bother him at all. He said that merchants who were owed stayed on their toes, aimed to please. Dunning letters meant nothing to him. He laughed off the vulgar thrustings of the book and record clubs, with their absurd threats to take him to law. People owed a bundle, who brought out their heavy artillery, got my father's Samuel Johnson remark: "Small debts are like small shot; they are rattling on every side, and can scarcely be escaped without a wound; great debts are like cannon, of loud noise but little danger." He was slippery: he used the telephone to persuade the telephone company he should be allowed a sixth month of non-payment without suffering disconnection, because he needed to call people long distance to borrow money from them to pay his telephone bills. He was cool, but not icy. He owed a Westport barkeep a couple of hundred, and when the man died in a car accident my father was sorry, and told his widow about the debt, not that he ever paid her.

Finally it got out of hand. It had nowhere to go but out of hand. I wearied of telling people on our stoop or through the phone that they had the wrong Arthur Wolff, that my father had just left for the hospital, or the Vale of Kashmir, or Quito. I tired of asking "How do I know you're who you say you are?" when people asked questions about my father's whereabouts and plans. I hated it, wanted to flee. It was October; there were months still to get through, too many months but too few to cobble up a miracle of loaves and find the twenty-five hundred dollars to buy my way back into Princeton.

My father and I were watching the Giants play the Colts in the snow for the championship when two Connecticut State troopers arrived during the first sudden death overtime. They watched with us till the game ended, and then took my father to the lockup in Danbury. He had left a bad check at The Three Bears; they were pressing charges. I found a mouthpiece who went bail, made good the check and got the charges dropped. Duke had talked with him. The old man hadn't lost his touch at all, only with me. With me he had lost his touch.

A week before my birthday he wrecked my Delahaye. I loved the dumb car. I was in bed when I heard him climb the driveway cursing. He was blind drunk, drunker than I'd ever seen him. He railed at me as soon as he came in, called me a phony. I feigned sleep, he burst through the room, blinded me with the overhead light, told me I was full of crap, a zero, zed, cipher, blanko, double-zero.

"I'm leaving you," he said.

I laughed: "In what?"

A mistake. His face reddened. I sat up, pretending to rub sleep from my eyes while he swore at my car, said it had damned near killed him swerving into the ditch, it could rot there for all he cared. He was usually just a finger-wagger, but I still feared him. Now he poked my bare chest with his stiff yellow finger, for punctuation. It hurt. I was afraid. Then I wasn't afraid; I came off my bed naked, cocked my fist at my father, and said: "Leave me alone."

My father moved fast to his room, shut the door, and locked it. I was astounded. I don't believe he was afraid of me; I believe he was afraid of what he might do to me. I sat on the edge of my bed, shaking with anger. He turned on his television set loud: Jack Paar. He hated Paar. There was a shot, a hollow noise from the .45. I had heard that deep, awful boom before, coming from the black cellar in Birmingham, a bedroom in Saybrook. I thought my father would kill me. That was my first thought. Then that he would kill himself, then that he had already killed himself. I heard it again, again, again. He raged, glass broke, again, again. The whole clip. Nothing. Silence from him, silence from Paar. A low moan, laughter rising to a crescendo, breaking, a howl, sobs, more laughter. I called to my father.

"Shit fire," he answered, "now I've done it, now I've *done* it!"

He had broken. No police, the phone was finally disconnected. I tried the door. Locked. Shook it hard. Locked fast. I moved back to shoulder through and as in a comic movie, it opened.

My father had shot out Jack Paar; bits of tubes and wires were strewn across the floor. He had shot out the pretty watercolors painted by Betty during their Mississippi rendezvous. He had shot out himself in the mirror. Behind the mirror was his closet, and he was looking into his closet at his suits. Dozens of bespoke suits, symmetrically hung, and through each suit a couple of holes in both pant-legs, a couple in the jacket. Four holes at least in each suit, six in the vested models.

"Hell of a weapon," my father said.

"Oh, yes," I said. "*Hell* of a weapon!"

November fifth I turned twenty-one. My father had a present for me, two presents really, a present and its wrapping. He gave me his gold signet ring, the one I wear today—lions and fleurs-de-lis, *nulla vestigium retrorsit*—wrapped in a scrap of white paper, a due bill signed *Dad*, witnessed and notarized by a Danbury real estate agent: *I.O.U. Princeton.*

"How?" I asked.

"Piece of cake," my father said, "done and done."

I was due at Princeton January 15th. By then the Abarth had been repossessed and the Delahaye was still and forever a junker. I rode to Sikorsky with Nick, who drove twenty miles out of his way to pick me up and return me in his Edsel. After work the day following New Year's I found a rented black Buick in the driveway. My father told me to help him pack it, we were leaving pronto and for good; what didn't come with us we'd never see again. I asked questions. I got no answers, except this:

"It's Princeton time. We're going by way of Boston."

I almost believed him. We packed, walked away from everything. I wish I had the stuff now, letters, photographs, a Boy Scout merit badge sash, Shep's ribbon:

Gentlest in Show at the Old Lyme grade school fair. My father had had his two favorite suits rewoven; he left the rest behind with most of his shoes, umbrellas, hats, accessories. He left behind the model Bentley that cost him half a year to build. He brought his camera, the little Minox he always carried and never used ("handy if someone whacks you with his car, here's the old evidence machine," he'd say, tapping the silly chain on the silly camera). I brought my typewriter and my novel. While my father had watched television I had written a novel. I worked on it every night, with my bedroom door shut; my father treated it like a rival, which it was, a still, invented place safe from him. He made cracks about The Great Book, and resented me for locking it away every night when I finished with it, while he shut down the Late Show, and then the Late Late. I made much of not showing it to him.

On the way to Boston we stopped by Stratford, where Sikorsky had moved. I quit, told the personnel department where to send my final check, said goodbye to no one. When I returned to the car my father said to me:

"Fiction is the thing for you. Finish Princeton if you want, but don't let them turn you into a goddamned professor or a critic. Write make-believe. You've got a feel for it."

Had he read my stuff? "Why, do you think?"

"I know you."

We drove directly to Shreve, Crump & Low, Boston's finest silversmith. Duke double-parked on Boylston Street and asked me to help him unload two canvas duffels from the trunk. He called them "parachute bags"; maybe that's what they were, parachute bags. They were heavy as corpses; we had to share the load.

"What's going on?" I asked. "What's in here?"

"Never mind. Help me."

We sweated the bags into the store, past staring ladies and gentlemen to the manager. My father opened a zipper and there was Alice's flat silver: solid silver gun-handle knives, instruments to cut fish and lettuce, dessert spoons and lobster forks, three-tined forks and four-tined forks, every imaginable implement, service for sixteen. In the other bag were teapots, coffeepots, creamers, saltcellars, Georgian treasure, the works polished by my father, piles gleaming dangerously in the lumpy canvas sacks.

The manager examined a few pieces. He was correct; he looked from my face to my father's while he spoke.

"These are very nice, as you know. I could perhaps arrange a buyer... This will take time. If you're in no rush..."

"I want money today," my father said.

"This will be quite impossible," the manager said.

"I won't quibble," my father said. "I know what the silver is worth, but I'm pinched, I won't quibble."

"You don't understand," the manager said.

"Let's not play games," my father said.

"This is quite impossible," the manager said. "I think you'd best take this all away now."

"Won't you make an offer?"

"No," the manager said.

"Nothing?" my father asked.

"Nothing."

"You're a fool," my father told the manager of Shreve, Crump & Low.

"I think not," said the manager of Shreve, Crump & Low. "Good afternoon, gentlemen."

We reloaded the car. I said nothing to my father, and he said nothing to me. There we were. It was simple, really, where everything had been pointing, right over the line. This wasn't mischief. This wouldn't make a funny story back among my college pals. This was something else. We drove to a different kind of place. This one had cages on the windows, and the neighborhood wasn't good. The manager here was also different.

"You want to pawn all this stuff?"

"Yes," my father said.

"Can you prove ownership?"

"Yes."

"Okay," the pawnbroker said. He sorted through it, scratched a few pieces and touched them with a chemical.

"It's solid silver," my father said.

"Yes," the man said, "it is."

"What will you loan us, about?"

I heard the *us*. I looked straight at my father, and he looked straight back.

"Will you reclaim it soon?" My father shrugged at this question. "Because if you don't really need it, if you'd sell it, I'd buy. We're talking more money now, about four times what I'd loan you."

"What would you do with it?" my father asked. "Sell it?"

"No," the man said. "I'd melt it down."

My father looked at me: "Okay?"

"Okay," I said.

My father nodded. While he signed something the man took cash from a huge floor safe. He counted it out, twenties bound in units of five hundred dollars. I looked away, didn't want to know the bottom line on this one. There were limits, for me, I thought.

We checked into the Ritz-Carlton. Looked at each other and smiled. I felt all right, pretty good, great. I felt great.

"What now?" I asked my father.

Years later I read about the Philadelphia cobbler and his twelve-year-old son said to have done such awful things together, robbing at first, breaking and entering. Then much worse, rape and murder. I wondered if it could have kept screwing tighter that way for us, higher stakes, lower threshold of *this, but not that*. I thought that day in the Ritz, sun setting, that we might wind up with girls, together in the same room with a couple of girls. But as in Seattle I had misread my father.

"Let's get some champers and fish-eggs up here," he said.

So we drank Dom Perignon and ate Beluga caviar and watched night fall over Boston Common. Then we took dinner at Joseph's and listened to Teddy Wilson play

piano at Mahogany Hall. Back at the Ritz, lying in clean
linen in the quiet room, my father shared with me a
scheme he had been a long time hatching.

"Here's how it works. I think I can make this work, I'm
sure I can. Here's how it goes. Okay, I go to a medium-size
town, check into a hotel, not the worst, not the best. I
open an account at the local bank, cash a few small
checks, give them time to clear. I go to a Cadillac
showroom just before closing on Friday, point to the first
car I see and say I'll buy it, no road test or questions, no
haggling."

My father spoke deliberately, doing both voices in the
dark. When he spoke as an ingratiating salesman he
flattened his accent, and didn't stammer:

"How would you care to pay, sir? Will you be financing
your purchase? Do you want to trade in your present
automobile?"

"This is a cash purchase. (The salesman beams.) I'm
paying by check. (The salesman frowns a little.) On a local
bank, of course. (The salesman beams again.)"

"Fine, sir. We'll have the car registered and cleaned.
It'll be ready Monday afternoon."

"At this I bristle. I bristle well, don't you think?"

"You are probably the sovereign bristler of our epoch,"
I told my father.

He would tell the salesman he wanted the car now or
not at all, period. There would be a nervous conference,
beyond my father's hearing, with the dealer. The dealer
would note Duke's fine clothes and confident bearing;
now or never was this customer's way, *carpe diem*, here
was an *easy* sale, car leaving town, maybe just maybe this
was kosher. Probably not, but how many top-of-the-line
cars can you sell right off the floor, no bullshit about
price, color, or options? Now the dealer was in charge, the
salesman wasn't man enough for this decision. The dealer
would telephone Duke's hotel and receive lukewarm
assurances. Trembling, plunging, he would take Duke's
check. My father would drive to a used car dealer a block
or two away, offer to sell his fine new automobile for

whatever he was offered, he was in a rush, yeah, three thousand was okay. A telephone call would be made to the dealer. Police would arrive. My father would protest his innocence, spend the weekend in a cell. Monday the check would clear. Tuesday my father would retain the services of a shyster, if the dealer hadn't already settled. With the police he would never settle. False arrest would put him on Easy Street. How did I like it?

"Nice sting. It might work." The Novice.

"Of course it will work." The Expert.

The next morning we checked out and my father mailed the Buick's keys to a Hertz agent in Stamford, telling him where to find his car. Then a VW bus materialized. My father had taken it for a test drive; maybe he paid for it later, and maybe he forgot to pay for it later. My father called this "freeloading."

We drove to Princeton in the bus, with my novel on the back seat beside a cooler filled with cracked ice and champagne, a cash purchase from S.S. Pierce. We reached Princeton about four and parked on Nassau Street, outside the Annex Grill, across from Firestone Library.

"How much did you give me last year?"

"About twenty-five hundred," I said, "but a lot of that was for my own keep."

"I don't charge my boy room and board," my father said. He pulled clumps of twenties from a manila envelope. Five packets, twenty-five hundred dollars, there it was, every penny, just as he had promised, precisely what I owed. "And here's another five hundred to get you started."

"Thanks," I said. "Where will you go now?"

"New York for a while. Then, I don't know. Maybe California. I always had luck in California."

"Sounds like a good plan," I said. "Stay in touch," I said.

"Sure," he said. "Do well, Geoffrey. Be good."

"Sure," I said. "I won't screw up this time."

"No," he said, "you probably won't. Now don't be *too* good. There's such a thing as too good."

"Don't worry," I said laughing, wanting this to end.

"Don't forget your book," my father said, while I unloaded the van. "I'll be reading it someday, I guess. I'll be in touch, you'll hear from me, hang in there."

He was gone. An illegal turn on Nassau headed him back where he had come from.

20

My first afternoon back in Princeton I walked the streets paying debts, peeling off banknotes, getting receipts and handshakes.

"Congratulations, son. I'll tell you, I never thought I'd see this money. You're a man of your word. Your credit's good here anytime."

"No, sir, thanks, I don't think I'll be charging any more."

I cabled twelve hundred fifty to Eastbourne, gathered my *paid-in-fulls* and climbed the steps of Nassau Hall to the assistant dean's office.

"Welcome home," he said.

Colonial Club invited me to join, and I joined. I moved into a new suite of rooms in Holder Hall with old friends. I took my novel to Richard Blackmur. The book was three hundred pages about a young man, sometimes called "Tony" and sometimes "Anthony" and sometimes "the boy." Tony was in Europe coming—as the author of *Certain Half-Deserted Streets* put it—"into season." He was of a sensitive disposition, an unflagging enemy of

vulgarity and convention, tetchy, proud, and quick to
dismay. He fell in love (twice he got laid) and refused to
respond to letters from his father (whole chapters here), a
Bones man, lawyer, OSS hero, blond with fine hair and
blue eyes. He sent Tony timely checks, but as he was a
success, a "clothes-wearing man," Tony regarded him as a
fool and villain.

The book was good, I knew it. Had I not sweated it out
after a day hauling mail sacks? After cooking and washing
dishes? I submitted one copy in application for the F.
Scott Fitzgerald Prize (for distinguished undergraduate
fiction) and another copy for Richard Blackmur's
consideration. The prize went elsewhere, to my surprise,
but Blackmur I knew would love the book. I had a
question to ask him: Knopf or Scribner's? Oh, I realized
that Scribner was a Princeton man and Princeton's
publisher of choice; still, hadn't the house slipped
recently? I saw Blackmur every week for our conference
but he never gave me occasion to ask this question, or any
other about *Certain Half-Deserted Streets*. Three weeks,
four, six . . . Finally:

"I wonder—have you had a chance to glance at my
novel?"

"Of course: I read it." Blackmur was tiny and exact and
mysterious, a heavy drinker at his most lucid before noon
and his best after lunch. We were eating lunch at
Lahiere's, at his special table.

"What's your advice?"

"Put it in your desk drawer."

"Ah, I know, put it away a few months, come at it
fresh."

"No," he said, "that is not my advice to you. My advice
is to put it in your desk drawer, lock your desk drawer,
lose the key to your desk drawer. However, keys are
sometimes found, returned to their owners. This could
happen, so I would set fire to your desk. I recommend the
sole, though the chops are edible."

Not much of *Certain Half-Deserted Streets* remains. I
pretty much followed Blackmur's counsel, but not before

I let *The Nassau Lit* print a couple of sections, including the first chapter, set in England and in Paris, where "the boy" goes to a party:

> The two apaches sectionated towards one another from opposite sides of the loft. One was a gargantuan buck nigger with a toosmall head and serpentine grace; the other a French girl, surly, with bobbed hair and neither chest nor waist. Her skin was very white. So very white.
>
> They danced not with but at each other. Soon it was over and they parted without a word. It was not always that way, but one must not think back. That is what they had told me. I must not think back.

Hang them, and what they told him. Tony thinks back:

> There is an old waiter at the Ritz Hotel and his name is Albert. He had brought me tall glasses of lemonade and drops of water from the condensation had fallen ouch! on my bare knee when I was short trousers years old. And I had been with my father and I had loved him. And I remembered going through the lobby with him and the whole world had loved looking at us. He was so big and I was so little and I had almost to run to keep up with him and I am still running but now I am very tired and not keeping up so well.

I wrote these words in Newtown, with *Leave It to Beaver* and *Gunsmoke* clamoring in the room beyond the thin wall, where my father, needing a shave, sat in his underpants chain-smoking Camels, fiddling with his Colt automatic.

The last chapter, "A Piece of Bone, a Hank of Hair," finds Tony in an Italian jail, charged with killing a whore he has thrown down a flight of stairs. In fact she fell, but Tony won't defend himself. At seventeen he's "too tired now to care." He wants only to write his memoirs on a roll of toilet paper, and flush them away. The consul-general wants to help the boy, whose father was his classmate: "Everyone wanted to help the boy save the boy himself."

Why don't you mind your business? All of you. The girl is dead . . . very dead . . . I understand . . . and I suppose it was my fault. So why don't you just leave me alone and let me sleep here in peace till the trial is over and then they can do whatever they want to do with me. I don't care. I really just don't care . . .

The reason I lied as a young man, I think, was the same reason my fiction was so awful: I didn't know that anything had happened to me; I forced my history, just as my father forced his. Blackmur made me scruple to form it, to make it count. I cannot overestimate my debt to that man. I was in awe of his precision and his daring. His speech was elliptical, inclining toward the runic, but his lectures were legendary—Poetics in the fall and Aesthetics in the spring, the same course, what he happened to bring to class in his Harvard bookbag—and once an hour he would come awake as from a private reverie with a dazzling penetration of test or motive. To have him as a weekly presence in my life, to meet with him one-to-one every week for two years, was everything. He was the most luminous of the New Critics, and his special province was diction. Words were like rubies, emeralds, diamonds, dogshit. They had their weight, each one, and this was where I learned to begin.

Princeton was wide open to any student who would use it. The English department had its stiffs and tailors' dummies, but it also had Walt Litz, a courtly Joyce, Eliot, and Stevens scholar with a soft Arkansas accent and a taste for students who were oddballs and outlaws. Larry Holland was the James man, and spoke in the circular rhetoric of The Master, brilliantly, his periods folding into one another like bolts of bright silk. Holland was not a lecturer from whom a student could take notes, and so he wasn't popular as a lecturer. He saw me through a thesis on the grammar, language, and point of view of *Absalom, Absalom!* written two years after *Certain Half-Deserted Streets;* I did not set fire to the thesis and

THE DUKE OF DECEPTION

can read it without embarrassment. I had come to
Faulkner from Fitzgerald and Hemingway, to a preoccupation with words and grammar from Fitzgerald's
artifacts and manners, Hemingway's rites and codes. My
affection for Faulkner represented a deliverance from my
father's affections, and affectations.

My father loved *The Great Gatsby* (he identified with
Nick Carraway!) and despised *This Side of Paradise*. But
there is a sentence in the Princeton novel about Amory
Blaine that fixed my father exactly: "It was always the
becoming he dreamed of, never the being." My second
shot at Princeton I became what I became by being in the
present. My college life was governed by an almost
unvarying routine: I rose at twelve-thirty, ate lunch at
Colonial, went to an afternoon seminar or to my carrel in
the library, ate dinner and shot pool from six to
seven-thirty and returned to the library until it shut at
midnight. Then I drank and played poker till dawn,
making about three hundred a month at seven-card stud
roll 'em and a Princeton invention we called "legs," draw
poker played with three cards. My grades were good,
which I hardly noticed. I was lost in books, beside myself
with critical measurements.

The first few months back I heard nothing from my
father. Then he called me at Colonial during dinner. He
was drunk, and told a sad, confused story about a fight
with a banker. My father had been hit in the eye with a
poker, he said, but I should see the banker, the banker was
in the hospital. *How was his eye?* The eye was swollen
shut, but it would be okay. The banker was a "nibshit."
My father said he needed to see me, he was in trouble.
Where are you? My father said he was in Gloversville,
New York, would I come up? A couple of my clubmates
were waiting to use the telephone. I looked past them to
the cheerful fire in the club library, heard quiet voices and
serene laughter, realized I had left my dinner on the table,
wondered if the waiter had removed it.

"I can't," I told my father. "I have a paper due."

Then I heard my father make a kind of coughing noise, as though he were choking. I realized he was sobbing, or laughing.

"Sure," I said. "I can come. Tell me where to come."

My father had hung up. Later I learned about the banker. He had held the note on the Abarth-Zagato and the Delahaye and he hired my father to repossess cars for him, *set a thief to catch a thief,* the banker told my father when he hired him. The banker financed cars for soldiers, who often failed to meet their monthly payments. In return for a one-room shack in Gloversville, expenses on the road and fifty dollars per repossession my father went on bounty hunts in a truck equipped with a tow-bar, with a set of master ignition keys, as far as Virginia. The banker treated my father like an indentured servant, which he was, and finally took an excessive liberty. The Gloversville police wanted my father on an assault charge.

So, like a hurricane that goes out to sea, beyond sight and mind, only to sweep back on shore with redoubled fury, my father blew back through Princeton. A few days after his call to Colonial I returned to my room to find a letter from Seymour St. John and a bill from Langrock. Later there were bills from Douglas MacDaid, The University Store, Lahiere's and The Princeton Inn, all my father's work, "bill my boy." The letter from St. John said he was "as relieved as I am sure you must be" by my repayment of Eastbourne College, "this evidence of good faith and integrity which involves not only you and your family, but American schools and our country."

That was the first paragraph. The second paragraph said "I have just had word from one of our local merchants, Mr. Mushinsky, that you owe him a bill for clothes of nearly $500. Is that true? As you know, this sort of thing follows you all your life. Your good name and your credit are more valuable to you than anything else you possess, and you just don't have it as long as you leave bills outstanding. How any boy could have run up any bill such as that is beyond me."

I hadn't. Duke was moving around. I didn't hear from him again for more than a year. He went west with his Princeton booty, putting in to Chicago's best hotel, owned by my Choate roommate's father. He stayed ten days, put everything on the cuff, even his amphetamines. He was running now on Dexamil. When his bill rose past a thousand, the management requested something on account. The Duke said he was waiting for a grain transaction to clear the Chicago Wheat Pit, and flashed some papers that seemed to confirm this fiction. He got my roommate's endorsement on a few big checks and vanished, leaving a roomful of clothes from Langrock and Mushinsky. He had come into Chicago driving a Triumph sports car and left in a Mercedes sedan. Trading up all the way, heading for the gold fields, "I always had luck in California."

But I didn't know then where he was. And after St. John and Dean Lippincott cleared my good name and my credit, "more valuable" to me than "anything" I possessed, I didn't care a fiddler's fuck where my father was, alive or dead, as long as he wasn't near me.

I orphaned myself. I had lost track of my mother and Toby, hadn't seen nor heard from them for five years. I knew my mother had left Sarasota abruptly and gone to Salt Lake City, where the cost of living was said to be low. (So was the standard of living, but unemployment was high.) Then she had gone to Seattle, then somewhere else, then somewhere else. When people asked about her I was vague, ashamed to admit that I didn't know where she lived. I used Duke's techniques of inference, managed to suggest to half the people who asked that she was a Russian princess exiled to Spain, and to the other half that she was a Spanish communist exiled to Russia. She was gone, leave it there.

From the moment I went on my own my situation at Princeton and in the world improved. This is a blunt paradox, but many people, friends, and their parents, took many pains on my behalf. My friends' mothers and fathers interested me because their enthusiasms and anxieties were fresh for me. I always had a place to spend vacations, usually a sumptuous place. One day, as I stood in the marble-floored entrance hall of Mr. Lippincott's huge house on the Main Line, I made small talk with a delivery boy who just then noticed an oil portrait of a bewigged eighteenth-century grandee: "Mr. Lippincott, I presume." How my father would have relished such a confusion! I felt a frisson of loss, as though a cold breeze had made me tremble, but it vanished.

For my part I enjoyed the company of my friends' fathers because I was accustomed to adults and sought, perhaps, a replacement for my own father. I seemed old for my age and took pains to look even older than I seemed, a custom of the fifties that I pushed too far. I wore double-breasted suits and wire-rimmed glasses. A friend warned me that my affection for maturity was morbid, that I should have a care about inviting death, nature's way of telling us we are mature enough. People saw me as a blank sheet: be bold, be cautious; settle down, stay in motion. Be a writer, teacher, diplomat, broker, banker, barkeep, spy.

There was no need to listen to them. I was the luckiest boy I knew at college. I owed no one an explanation, was free to come and go where I could afford, be what I wished to be without regard for anyone's judgment.

John and I discussed opening a restaurant/bar/art gallery/bookstore in the South of France, and decided not to. I took Foreign Service examinations, passed the written test, and failed the oral in New York. At the time I was spending the summer watching baseball and daytime soap operas on a Princeton roommate's Gramercy Park television set. We lay on mattresses on the floor of his air-conditioned apartment drinking Bud and letting one day slip into another. We hadn't twenty bucks between us but a deli at Third Avenue and Twenty-third Street delivered, and his father, in Europe, had an account there. The apartment was as cool as a cave with the shades drawn.

That summer we read *Lucky Jim,* saw *Look Back in Anger* and wallowed in *The Ginger Man.* "I think we are the natural aristocrats of the race," the Ginger Man tells his horny sidekick Kenneth. "Come before our time. Born to be abused by them out there with the eyes and the mouths." How we loved that, cocking a snoot at Them as we drank ruinously expensive and flat bitter at Churchill's, where we tried to scandalize ladies. We wanted to be bully boys, but were merely naughty. Only a couple of friends *took gas,* were *deep-sixed* from Princeton prematurely and against their wishes. One was addicted to television Westerns—he watched them wearing chaps, spurs, a black ten-gallon hat, a spangled vest, and a six-shooter. He learned to raise the volume by hitting a dial with his bullwhip, and he shot himself in the foot quick-drawing a Colt Peacemaker in the basement shower. When Princeton sent him home to his mom and dad he left us with a homily from *Maverick:* "Never forget," he said, "a coward dies a thousand deaths; a brave man dies but one thousand to one odds are pretty good."

Another friend we called Pixie. He missed the consolations of his native California beaches during the long New Jersey winter, and during his senior year emptied his living room of furniture and filled it with sand. He installed a plastic swimming pool that leaked on us living beneath him in 1879 Hall. He drank piña coladas beneath potted palms, and let many sun lamps burn him purple. His roommate, distracted by such perpetual holiday, failed to finish (or to begin) his required thesis. He contrived a Good Plan. He set fire to his room and told the dean his thesis had been consumed in flames ignited by the sun lamps.

"You have suffered a double tragedy," the dean told him. "You are without insurance, so you and your family are down the cost of your possessions, your roommate's possessions and the cost of repairing your room. Also, as your thesis burned, you won't graduate. Good afternoon."

* * *

One thing for sure: we would never, like Them, like saps, work. That's what we promised ourselves, till something changed our minds. The summer of 1960 I stayed with a friend and his parents in Westchester County and commuted to a New York job another friend's father had secured for me as a "research trainee" at Auchincloss, Parker and Redpath, a brokerage house near Wall Street on Broadway. I was sent to "due diligence" meetings at which executives explained to brokers their company's business, trying to lie up the price of stock by provoking its recommendation. When I was not at these meetings I was meant to perform a survey of oil investments.

I shared an office with Pencils and Fast Eddie, at the antipodes of research philosophy. Pencils was an historian of the market; he would tell you where you were going if you would tell him where you had been. He used graphs, charts, econometric models, all in the service of prophecy about a textile stock, Collins & Aikman, which moved from 10 1/2 to 11 to 10, in small blocs, all summer. I plunged for ten shares (Pencils said it was the chance of a lifetime), though I can't imagine how I afforded them on fifty-seven dollars a week. Given the respectable character of my employment I had bought a broker's suit, a navy pin-striped worsted three-piecer that sweated off fifteen pounds during subway rides from Grand Central to Wall Street and back. I had tried to charge the suit, but either the name Wolff was known to F.R. Tripler, or I lacked the Duke's panache. I spent the balance of my salary on commutation, *Wall Street Journals* and movies. I went to many movies, especially favoring double bills at the Fourteenth Street RKO when I was supposed to be detailing the fortunes of the oil industry.

Fast Eddie finally explained to me the secret of investment research. His girlfriend, a secretary at a huge brokerage firm, told him by telephone what her boss, also a research wizard, planned to boost the following week. Fast Eddie always got there first, and he wasn't obliged to know anything about the stock, which always rose on the huge firm's buying. He had awful contempt for Pencils, and so did I when I sold my Collins & Aikman for what I had paid for it, less commissions coming and going.

The managing partner of Auchincloss, Parker & Redpath looked over my survey of the oil industry the week before I returned to Princeton for my last year. I hoped he would offer me a place with the firm. He suggested instead that I enter a profession that made no use of numbers. Nevertheless I caught him regarding my suit with undisguised admiration.

I would miss the cool, clean office and its cool, clean employees, the company letterhead and toll-free calls. You could fall asleep at your desk, or die, and no one would ever disturb you. Before I left Wall Street I got a call from tourists from the state of Washington, friends of my mother who had tracked me down. Could they see me? They had photographs of Toby and Rosemary. We ate at a place frequented by middle-rank brokers poised to become partners. I carried an attaché case filled with novels, and wore my suit with a Panama hat. It was mid-August, touching a hundred, but the tourists stood in such awe of the composite picture I presented that they never asked if I was hot in my wool vest. I showed them "The Exchange" as I called it, and while bells mysteriously clanged I retailed anecdotes and explicated the symbols on "The Big Board," as I called *it*. How, asked the head of the family, did a fellow make money on Wall Street?

"Quite simple, really. I always say: Buy cheap and sell dear."

I inventoried my portfolio, suggesting a go with Collins & Aikman. The husband looked thoughtful, and then showed me my mother. Rosemary was standing beside a black Labrador on a hilltop, wearing a buffalo-plaid lumberjack's shirt, with a high-powered rifle crooked in her arm.

"She's a crack shot," I was told. "A fine woman, everyone loves her."

I asked about her husband. I had just that moment learned she was married again. The tourist's wife shrugged: "I guess she's happy enough. Look, here's Jack."

It was Toby, with a new name. He was fourteen, looked like I had looked in Seattle, training to be a greaser.

The tourists took my picture. I wrote my mother on Auchincloss, Parker and Redpath letterhead and enclosed a photocopy of the final chapter of *Certain Half-Deserted Streets,* the *Nassau Lit* version of "A Piece of Bone, a Hank of Hair." Toby says they were impressed, thought I was a financier, I looked like a financier. And the story?

"Bewildering. I was proud not to be able to understand a word you wrote us."

I sent him a Choate T-shirt and Princeton necktie.

My last day at "work" I ran into Alice, walking with another lady in front of the Biltmore. She pretended she hadn't seen me from across the street but I yelled at her—"Hey, Toots!"—and there we were. We walked under the clock where I had clotted with other tweed bags during Thanksgiving holidays from Choate. Alice asked me:

"Aren't you hot in that wool suit?"

"Not at all." I ordered tea. The Palm Court waiter brought iced tea and I sent it back, "I want *hot* tea." I decided Alice's friend was sneering. Alice remarked that she had left my father forever. "Where is he?"

"In California."

"Where?"

"I really wouldn't know."

"I'd like to know where he is."

"I can't help you."

"Try. Where did you see him last?"

"I won't sit here and be cross-examined by you, young man."

"Where is he?"

"Don't raise your voice."

Her friend interrupted: "It so happens that your father is a drug addict."

I said: "Fuck you both," and neither saw nor heard from my stepmother again.

I was in love that summer with a gangly blonde who spoke in riddles and too softly to be understood. I thought I wanted to marry her; we talked about this and she decided I was too erratic for her taste. I understood, after a while. At first I thought I was heartbroken; maybe I was, but losing her had the effect of driving me deeper into books and work. I prospered at college and soon met a Louisville girl so wild that her previous boyfriend, Hunter Thompson, had given her up as a bad job. She had a flat near Columbia in New York, and studied piano at Juilliard. She would play for me, play away whole afternoons. She had a broken nose and smart eyes. She could tap dance, and because I thought this the most piquant practice I had seen, she tap-danced for me when I asked. She drank a quart of Early Times every day (with a bit of beer and champagne) but she was never more drunk or less than the first time I met her. She kept her flat impeccably clean; we sent out for food, never left the place, laughed, made love and did monologues. She was incapable of conversation. She would listen to six or seven paragraphs, then speak six or seven that had no bearing on mine. Her place was sanctuary. She had the palest skin, as though she had never been outside her room. I loved her Kentucky accent. She chewed bubble-gum, and blew bubbles. We lived together every weekend for several months in complete happiness until she tried to stab me. This was unexpected. She said she was going to march the following weekend with Bertrand Russell to protest nuclear proliferation. From where to where would they march? From somewhere to somewhere. I said I hoped it didn't rain. She asked why. I said she wouldn't go if it rained, I knew her, wouldn't leave her place to march, she was her own prisoner there, who was she kidding? This was our first dialogue, and she tried to stab me that night in bed. She had warned me: "Don't touch me." I had touched her foot with mine. The knife shone in its arc through the spill of a streetlamp's light, so I ducked in time and the blade only tore my pillow apart. I left, and never saw her again. She wrote me once, but I couldn't decipher her script or her meaning.

At Princeton I enjoyed a boon companion, Stephen, a great athlete and elegant gent in what we wistfully believed to be the manner of the eighteenth century. Larding our conversations with liberal *sirs* and quotations from Samuel Johnson—"Most friendships are formed by caprice or by chance—mere confederacies in vice or leagues in folly"—we would watch, over a bottle of rancid port, the television series *Hong Kong*. This series followed the pleasures and perils of an American intelligence agent masquerading as something he was not, a journalist as I recollect. Stephen and I, sitting in the darkened television room of Colonial Club, watching this fellow so laid back and well-laid, resolved to become him. And by degrees, as senior year progressed and we came to grasp more and more Hong Kong's manifest superiorities to Mercer County, New Jersey, we *swore* we would make our fortune abroad as . . . adventurers! That's what we called what we would be, living by our wits, which we were confident would carry us far, at least to a house hung from a prominence above Hong Kong, looking across to subtle and perilous Macao. Hang the consequences! We would make a life, Sir!

To this end we planned to work for a time in a salmon-canning factory in Alaska, where we thought we knew we could quickly knock down huge sums. Then with our bundle to the South Seas, lazing our way from the Marquesas to Tonga in the copra and sisal (whatever they were) trade. And so to Hong Kong, where we would set up as journalists or whatever, and as spies.

In the event, Stephen met a fine Smith girl from Lake Forest, married her immediately, and fell into the arms of IBM, which instructed him to wear a hat, gloves, and white shirt to his place of employment, which he did, Sir. When Stephen jumped our ship to become a good citizen for "them out there with the eyes and the mouths," I grabbed the first job that would take me abroad. I was half an hour away from a final interview with the foreign training program of First National City Bank when I got a cable inviting me to teach in Turkey, so Turkey it was.

I left Princeton with some final advice from Richard Blackmur. I ran into him outside the library late that June afternoon. He had had a long lunch at Lahiere's, and I told him I was soon away to Turkey. I knew he had lectured there, did he have suggestions, people or places I shouldn't miss? Perhaps, I thought, he would send me on my way with an epiphany, or at least a rune, words I could study and someday perhaps comprehend.

"Never," said Professor Blackmur, "have sexual congress with Near Eastern melons. I'm told they put the foreskin in jeopardy."

A friend planned to spend the summer sailing the New England coast on his father's forty-foot cutter. I was invited to join him, and wanted to. At the end of our first week cruising, Duke tracked me down. There was a message from Princeton at my friend's house when we called home ship-to-shore, and ship-to-shore I got through to my father in California. Would I come to La Jolla for the rest of the summer?

"No," I said.

But he had heard I was going to Turkey, just as he had gone. It was a last chance to see each other.

"No," I said.

"I have a wonderful job," he said. "Toby's coming. Wouldn't you like to see him?"

"Yes," I said.

My father promised to send the air fare at once.

21

Father. He promised to send Toby bus fare to La Jolla, and after some foot-dragging he finally did; he stiffed me, so I borrowed bus fare from a friend. Toby left first, looking forward to seeing his father after seven years, hard years for my brother. Rosemary had gone here and there across the country, looking always for some improvement in her circumstances, never finding it. Sometimes Duke, or Alice, sent support payments, but usually my mother was on her own.

She married someone, another of the mean, violent men she seemed drawn to. This one, a house painter in a town of temporary dwellings raised for dam workers near Washington's Canadian border, mistreated Toby and finally tried to choke my mother to death. Perhaps it was desperation that led her seriously to consider Duke's proposal, in 1961, that they live together again in California, perhaps even remarry. "I've always had sand between my toes," Mother says. Toby came south as a kind of scout for this improbable arrangement. "He was a blue-sky artist," Mother says of Father. Mother too.

Toby was fifteen. A few months earlier he had called me at Princeton and begged me to help get him a scholarship at some boarding school, anything to spring him from Newhalem Camp, Washington, and Concrete High School. I wrote some schools, even Choate, and asked Princeton friends to help. A friend put Toby together with The Hill School in Pottstown, Pennsylvania, and my brother won a full scholarship there, to begin the fall after our La Jolla reunion. I was proud. Eleven years later Toby told me he had won the scholarship by forging letters of recommendation from teachers at Concrete High School and by forging a letter-perfect transcript on a stolen form. The James Gang, The Wolff Boys. Hill was puzzled by his uneven academic performance: he could not perform long division or do sums. After two years of puzzlement the school put Toby on its retired list, and he never did get an American high school diploma, though Oxford gave him a First in English.

But now he was on the brink of rescue, coming south, full of hope for an overdue reunion.

"All the way down the Pacific coast I bullshitted everyone on the bus," Toby remembers. "I told them I was a Princeton man, and whatever else I wanted to tell them."

When he arrived at the San Diego terminal he looked around for his father, and didn't see him. He waited on the sidewalk, looking up and down the street till he saw someone who might have been his father, a big, bald man wearing heavy glasses. Toby smiled; the man smiled back. Half an hour later Toby went to the men's room, and the man followed him.

"Really," my brother remembers, "this was so confusing."

Duke, when he finally came for his son, was drunk, though Toby didn't understand this at the time. They went together to a small efficiency apartment near Wind 'n' Sea Beach, and Duke sat in his underpants, fiddling with a lighter, talking about how Rosemary had "kicked him in the ass, but maybe he'd forgive her."

He had a job, of sorts, with General Dynamics Astronautics, manufacturers of the Atlas missile, but it was Toby's impression that his father hadn't worked for a while, and the day after his long-absent younger son came "home" he explained that he had to go for a few days to Nevada with a lady friend. He left Toby some cash, a rented Chevrolet, a cupboard filled with Cokes and canned soup, a television set and the telephone number of a Navy officer who would look in on him. Then he drove away in his Abarth-Allemagne, a more expensive and less comfortable and dependable version of his Newtown toy, the Abarth-Zagato.

"I didn't know what to make of it all," Toby says.

He made use of the rented car, though he didn't know how to drive; he took it straight down the San Diego highway, almost to Mexico. When he finally figured out how to head it north again he returned to the apartment and waited for me to arrive, or his father to come home.

I was coming west, also bullshitting the passengers. I taught a marine to play the Princeton poker game called "legs"; in Pittsburgh, where he and I were to part, I stuck with him, continuing the course of instruction. I won two hundred dollars by the time we reached El Paso, and I decided to run with my winnings; I lay over in Juarez, during a down-and-out-under-the-border-town-volcano routine for a couple of days. I telephoned Toby from a cantina, and he filled me in on our dad. Toby had had another disappointment. The Navy officer had stopped by. He was friendly, very friendly, and Toby had had to lock him out of the apartment. He had tracked our father to a Las Vegas hotel and telephoned him there. Duke sounded annoyed to be disturbed, and suggested that Toby deal with the amorous sailor by shooting him dead: in the bottom drawer of his dresser, under the sweaters, there was a .223 Air Force survival rifle that folded into its stock, Toby could use it on the guy, anything else? Toby told me he hoped I'd hurry west, he'd certainly appreciate some company.

I got there two days later, just after midday of a Sunday. They were at the bus station, in the Chevrolet. My father looked twenty years older than when I had last seen him on Nassau Street two years back. He had flabby jowls and liver spots on his bare skull. He had lost mass, taken on a pot. He moved awkwardly now, uncertainly. He wore thick-framed eyeglasses like Barry Goldwater's and his clothes—I couldn't believe this—were on the flashy side. He was a retired Senior Citizen by the seaside. We embraced, all said how great it was to be together, what a great summer we'd have. Toby was a rube; I looked him over, decided he'd need grooming for The Hill, and some improvement by a tailor.

Driving to the apartment my father seemed to have lost more than his youth. He was distracted, coarse, not very bright. He seemed like an imposter. We stopped somewhere, at a woman's small house. She was a shopkeeper or realtor, I forget. It seemed important to my father to have her meet me, at once. She was friendly, but ill at ease. He made me dig out my Princeton diploma.

"See," he said, pointing, "*summa cum laude*. That's highest honors. Princeton University, like I told you."

She counterfeited amazement. I caught Toby's eye: What was going on? He shrugged. My father told me to take the car and Toby home, he'd be along soon with his friend. I protested, said we should stay together, next day was a workday. Our father waved us away. Toby said the woman had been in Nevada with Duke when the Abarth had some kind of mechanical trouble, it had all been quite unsettling, and unpleasant. We sat for an hour on the beach, catching up; I was avuncular, told Toby he'd have to run fast to catch up at The Hill, that I'd push him along, set him a course of reading. I sounded talking to him as I had wanted Richard Blackmur to sound talking to me.

We waited in the one-room flat for our father to come home for dinner. We waited. Toby didn't know the woman's name or telephone number. We waited. We decided we couldn't find her house and cooked dinner, and waited. The landlord came to see us. The rent hadn't been paid for months; we'd have to leave in the morning. The telephone rang. The woman was hysterical.

"I can't get him to leave! He won't even leave that chair he was sitting in when you left. He won't move. He won't talk. He just rocks back and forth crying. I don't know what to do with him. Get him out of here, help me."

I telephoned the police. They were there when I arrived, without Toby. It was as she had said. My father was catatonic, sobbing, terrified even to move from the chair. He couldn't speak, or wouldn't. He moved only to shake his head, *no no no no no no* . . . The police were gentle, practiced. They called an ambulance, held everything low key. The woman calmed herself, said she hoped there would be nothing in the papers, she was divorcing her husband, her husband could be difficult. I noticed her earrings, silver and turquoise, with complicated loops and pendants, the kind of jewelry my father despised. She said my father had been *very* difficult. So I could see.

"A man with his educational attainments, what a pity!"

"Yes," I said. "It is a pity."

They led my father to the ambulance. He was not too far gone to walk. The woman said she thought he might have been using pills, maybe tranquilizers. He had been drinking a great deal in Nevada. The ambulance attendants and the police wrote down the woman's musings.

But my father didn't seem drunk, or drugged. He seemed dead. I followed the ambulance to a hospital in La Jolla. The police came in with me, asked if they could help in any way. They told me my father was probably just overtired.

I signed him in. He was snuffling like a baby, shaking his head like a baby refusing to eat or sleep or stop doing something. Back and forth, deliberately, no . . . no . . . The next day, about eleven, my father could talk. He wore what soldiers call a thousand-yard stare, but he could talk. He said he wanted to see the woman, and I called her. She said she'd rather not see my father, didn't want "to open that can of worms again. He really spooked me last night," she said. "He's one sick guy."

I told my father that the woman would not be able to see him that morning, maybe a little later. My father began to weep.

"She's wonderful. I need her."

My father didn't ask how Toby was getting along, or where he was, or what we would all do with our lives here in La Jolla. He was past caring about these things now. Now he was deep in the woods, and he knew it, and no use pretending he knew the way home.

I took him to a sanitarium south of San Diego. It was bucolic, high in the hills looking down on the Pacific. The patients were mostly self-admitted, like my father. The question of payment was raised, and dropped when my father produced a Blue Cross card. Surprisingly, he was covered. He seemed happy to be removed from me by a nice young orderly. He asked, before he disappeared into a ward, when he could expect to see the woman he wished to see.

"Soon," I lied to him. "She'll be in touch soon."

I borrowed another couple of hundred from another friend back east, and this got us out of one apartment and into another, even closer to Wind 'n' Sea Beach. I gave the Chevrolet back to Budget, who had missed it, and bought a Ford convertible with no money down off a used car lot. I drove it to General Dynamics Astronautics, and walked out after half an hour in the personnel department with a job as an engineering writer, eight hundred a month, cost-plus again. It was the job my father had had, at less than eight hundred a month.

There was a training program. I was put in front of a movie about the marvels of rocket technology and then told by an executive that America could, if America wished, put an Atlas slap into Khrushchev's bathtub. I saw one of them on the assembly line, a stainless-steel thermos, fifteen stories high.

My work, what they called my work, was done in a

hangar with about two hundred other engineering writers. We sat in rows translating English into technical jargon. The engineering reports were given to us with certain words underlined, and these words were to be replaced with other words, which were listed in a loose-leaf dictionary. The single skill required for my job was a knowledge of the alphabet, and I finished a day's labor in about two hours. The other six I sat at my desk, staring at my hands. I was not permitted to bring anything—a book, say—into the hangar. I was to be at my desk from punch-in to punch-out, in case government inspectors came around to check on the cost-plus arrangements.

While I was at the missile works I obliged Toby to read a book a day and write a thousand words. I must say he was sporting about this intrusion into his holiday hours. But then, as I often reminded him, I was paying the rent and buying the food. I had a feeling sometimes that Toby wished he were elsewhere, but I was too angry about the outcome of our reunion to care what Toby wished.

Toby had my father's gestures and facial tics, and certain maneuvers with his hands and voice that made him resemble our old man more than I did, as he still does.

"It scares me to death," he says.

We visited our father in the sanitarium. He was placid, capable of gallows humor. He didn't mention the woman now, a couple of weeks after his treatment had begun. He said he had been "tuckered out." He didn't apologize for having put us to some inconvenience, but he was friendly enough. I did think he showed unfeeling indifference toward Toby, but he was beyond the reach of our judgment now, and I thought Toby understood this, though had I reflected a bit I would have realized that this was asking a lot of understanding of my fifteen-year-old brother.

Duke had a couple of new friends. One was a Milton scholar getting electric shock therapy. He was a skinny, red-haired fellow, very cheerful, said it wasn't all that bad. He read *Paradise Lost* once a week now, every time as though for the first time. All the patients were nice, like a sewing circle of the damned. My father made me a briefcase out of leather, and burned my initials into it. It took him a week to make, and he was proud of it. I assured him his job was waiting for him when he got out; I had been instructed by my father's therapist to tell this lie. My father only made me tell it once; I think he knew the truth.

Two things obsessed him during our twice-weekly visits: his car (which had been repossessed) and a silver cigarette lighter he said had been given to him in England by RAF friends. My father described this to me with affectionate care, and said Jimmy Little's and Mike Crosley's names were inscribed on it.

"You remember it, don't you? I always kept it with me."

I didn't remember it, was sure I had never seen it. My father said this object had been in the apartment we had had to vacate. I asked Toby if he remembered it and he said no, he had never seen it. My father wanted it. He was very firm about this. He asked his doctor to instruct his sons to look hard for it. He needed it.

Toby helped me look for it, in the new apartment and the old, in the rental car we had returned, through every box and pocket and drawer. We couldn't find it. I decided it had never been, and even if it had existed was just a fake inscribed with some sentiment of my father's own devising and names off a roll of lost friends and scant acquaintances. Finally, the day my father was released, five weeks after Toby had arrived, we reached the bottom of this mystery. Toby confessed under my father's inquisition that he had lost it; he had taken the lighter while my father was in Nevada and left it on the beach. He had been afraid to tell us, of course. The old man broke down in rage, and so did I, remembering the hours Toby had let me spend with him while he pretended to look for the damned thing, while he gave helpful suggestions where to look for it. I saw then, in a stroke, how much Toby must hate us both, and why. We put him on a bus north the next morning and my father and I spent two days and nights together looking at each other, rarely speaking.

He asked once if I would give up my job in Turkey to stay with him till he got back on his feet. He asked me when he was drunk, and I soberly said no.

The last time I saw my father was in the San Diego jail. He had borrowed my Ford while I sat around drinking and trading summer stories with a Princeton friend who had just driven across Mexico in a Cadillac hearse. My friend had started off with five fellow travelers, and now was alone. He had frightened off the others with serious drinking, a quart a day first of gin and then tequila and then mescal. There had been consequential mischief: my friend had spent a week in a Mazatlán jail after a misunderstanding with a pack of mariachis and a taxi driver, and he had a deep cut under his eye when he rolled in tired, drunk, hungry, and broke.

While we prepared for bed my father called. He wanted me at once, at the jailhouse. He told me over the phone that he had been "wronged." I found him in a holding tank among hookers, sailors, the usual Saturday night gang in a municipal jail. He explained: he had made an illegal U-turn and a cop had pulled him over. He had just bought some bacon and eggs, my father said, check for myself, they were in the car, he was just shopping for breakfast food for my guest. The cop had been abusive, so my father had stammered at him, abusively. The policeman assumed that my father was drunk, which he was not. It was surprising that my father was not drunk, but in truth he was not.

The police evidently now believed that my father had not been drunk, and they prepared to give him back to me. It would be a few minutes, the desk sergeant said. I explained this to my Princeton friend, waiting outside in his Cadillac hearse. He seemed befuddled, asked several times where we were, what was going on. I didn't understand then how far gone my friend was, that in a couple of years it would take weeks to dry him out in the violent ward at Bellevue, that he had been walking the line since Freshman year. I thought he was just like me, a fun-loving, spit-in-their-eye kind of chap, an outlaw like my father at our age.

The police called Sacramento. They checked routinely on everyone they booked; it was regulation procedure. They seemed sheepish about the episode, "just a misunderstanding." My father, I thought, was unusually indifferent to the injustice, unusually willing to let bygones be bygones and be on his way.

The call to Sacramento was answered with urgency. My father was—resonant word—"wanted." There was a warrant outstanding for his arrest; the charge was Grand Theft Auto. The auto was an Abarth-Allemagne, "so pretty" my father explained, nine thousand 1961 dollars. He had done his car scam after all. He had bought the thing off a showroom floor with a check. The check had his true name stamped on it but otherwise, in the assurances it made—the implication that the Bank of America had some loose association with my father and would exchange the piece of paper for cash—the piece of paper was misleading. Just as my father had predicted, the salesman and dealer had struggled against their better instincts when he faced them with a choice: I'll take the car now, at once, for this check. Or I won't take it at all. Consumers in the San Diego area had been learning to get through one week and then another without owning Abarth-Allemagnes; greed had triumphed over prudence, once again. My father had taken the car into Nevada as soon as he "bought" it, when Toby arrived. He had driven it flat out till it caught on fire, and then its pretty paint was sandblasted by a desert storm. The car, now in the hands of the dealer, was a disappointment to the dealer.

Most of this I learned from the police. My father was returned to the tank, and I talked to him through the sturdy wire mesh, above the bedlam of San Diego street folk. I asked my father if the story I had just heard was true. He shrugged. I asked again, and again he shrugged. "Never explain, never apologize"; he liked to say that. I told him that what he had done was wrong. I had many times suggested such things to him with sullenness and despairing sighs, but I had never before directly charged him with doing wrong. When I told my father that what he had done was wrong he stared at me, as though I had at last truly puzzled him.

"Don't you understand me at all?" he asked. "Do you think I care what they think is wrong?"

I spoke with a bail bondsman. I would be obliged to guarantee my father's appearance in court. I would remain in California, right? But I was due at a job ten days later, out of the state, half way around the world, as far from the San Diego jail as it was possible to travel and still stay on this earth. This was not interesting to the bail bondsman, who repeated his conditions.

I woke up my Princeton friend. He still didn't know where he was, and didn't understand the dilemma except that it was serious. He began to moan, as though he had a terrible bellyache, so I let him sleep it off in the back of the hearse, untroubled by this particular complication.

I yelled at my father through the mesh. Would he appear in court if I stood bail for him? I explained to him the bind I was in, the bind he had put me in. He did not seem sympathetic. Like the bondsman, he did not seem interested in the delicate character of my choice. I asked him bluntly: If I went to the edge for him, would he promise to come to court? He would promise nothing. He said I should do as I pleased, that he owed me no promises, he owed me nothing.

I did not make bail. I crossed the country with my Princeton friend, and flew away to Turkey. My father conned the bondsman out of ten thousand, plus ten percent, the bondsman's vigorish. Then he jumped jurisdiction, and was caught. And he was punished. They paid him back with interest for the space he had occupied, the airs he had put on, the fictions he had enacted. He had told me he hoped I'd never be a reviewer, a critic. I understand. Out in the real world the critics have teeth, and use them.

22

I taught two years in Turkey, at Robert College and Istanbul University. I couldn't have asked for a better hideout. I read and sent long letters home which, taken together, made the best fiction I had written. I sailed in Greece, skied in Austria, spent the summer of 1962 in Paris, house-sitting a flat at 50 rue Jacob. My father reached me there with a letter forwarded from Turkey: he was free, what could I do for him? He wanted money, a job, a place to live. What were my plans for him?

I tried. I telephoned friends and their parents. I wrote Sikorsky. I asked the Princeton placement office for help. I sent a little money. But the case was hopeless, no one could help my father. I wrote him a letter brimming with fond recollections, but without my return address in Paris. I had a friend mail the letter from Italy. Still, I expected him any minute, waited for his knock. Waiting spoiled my Paris holiday. Tough luck. I had come to the Left Bank to write. I wore a beard and rheumy eyes; I dressed in tatters, drove a black motorcycle. After my father's letter I took to wasting hours at a stretch, whole

days. I played solitaire sitting cross-legged on the parquet
floor of my drawing-room, while outside the world went
about its sunny city business. Smoking hashish, I'd listen
to the Jazz Messengers or the MJQ, *No Sun in Venice*. At
such moments my mind was as empty as I could will it to
be, but it was never empty of my father. A letter to my
mother from this period sighs that "every backward look
reveals a body hanging from the family tree." I think I
must have stolen the line. It doesn't sound like mine, and
it has too much zip for the time of its composition.

In the winter of 1963 I shaved off my beard the better to
impress a Fulbright interviewer at the American consu-
late in Istanbul. When I met the interviewer he was
wearing a beard like the Great Emancipator's. He gave me
the Fulbright anyway, and I went to England, to
Cambridge, to study with George Steiner. My father was
proud of this attainment, and when he congratulated me
on it he told me the book he was most enjoying in prison
(he was back) was *The Wind in the Willows*. I had sent it
to him to cheer him up; he especially liked Mr. Toad's
escape from jail in the disguise of a washerwoman. In
response to my father's letter of congratulation I asked
him a simple question: was he a Jew? He wrote back: "I
am weary unto death of that dumb question. Don't ask it
again."

It was by now a serious question. During a visit to New
York at the end of my first semester at Cambridge I had
met someone I wanted to marry, who wanted to marry
me. Her parents did not approve, for many reasons. They
had noticed dirt beneath my fingernails when I dined with
them, they knew I had nothing to commend me other than
a scholarship at a foreign university, they knew my father
was a yardbird, and they believed I was a Jew.

Their daughter and I wished to prevail, and finally we
did. But her parents were relentless in their opposition. I
nevertheless gave George Steiner our good news. My wife
has the Yankee Christian name Priscilla, and a New
England surname.

"Is she a gentile?"

"Yes," I answered, puzzled by Steiner's question.

"Well," he said, "don't underestimate the difficulties."

"What difficulties?"

"Of a Jew marrying a gentile." Steiner was not legendary for his patience with slow thinkers, and he was losing patience with me.

"I'm not a Jew," I said.

"Of course you are."

"No," I said. "My father says I'm not."

Steiner laughed. "I don't care what he says. I'm a Jew, and so are you. Anyone can see it. Don't be silly. Of course you're a Jew."

"My mother is Irish, and she says my father is not a Jew."

"Your mother is mistaken."

And then Steiner, thank Christ, changed the subject to tragic literature.

I left Cambridge after a year. I don't know why I left. I meant to return after a summer working at *The Washington Post*, but the summer ended, and I didn't leave. My mother now lived in Washington, and so did Toby, sent down from The Hill to a public high school. I had last seen my mother when I was fifteen and she was thirty-four; now she was forty-five and I was twenty-six going on forty. Our first night together, as soon as the dinner dishes were cleared away, I began to ask questions:

"Is my father a Jew?"

"Not that I know of. He never went to a synagogue."

"Was his father a Jew?"

"Not in the regular sense. He didn't believe in God."

"That isn't what I mean. You know what I mean."

"Well, roughly speaking, I guess you could call him a Jew, yes. But not your grandmother, I'm quite sure of that, so you're only a quarter Jewish."

"My grandmother wasn't a Jew?"

"Well, maybe she was. Yes, I guess she was. She was in Hadassah, a wonderful lady."

"Why didn't you tell me?"

"I promised your father I wouldn't."

"But *why*, dammit!"

"I don't know, maybe to spare you the pain he felt. There never seemed to be a right time for it. When you were with me you were so young. Then it was his problem. I don't know."

Even before he knew what *schlemiel* meant Toby announced that he wanted to leave for Israel and a kibbutz; later he said he wanted to fight Arabs in the Six-Day War, but then the sixth day came, and the seventh, and he was still here. I went around for a few weeks after my talk with my mother telling all my friends I was a Jew. I thought I was; I had long ago converted to Jewish habits of mind, as I understood them from books: melancholy, acid humor, skepticism. These attitudes suited me, just as British manners had suited my father. When I told my friends I was a Jew most of them said *sure, of course, so what?*

A member of Priscilla's family flew four hundred miles to tell her, a month before we were married, that if she didn't care herself about the consequences of a "mixed marriage," she should "think of the children." They'd never be welcome in Hobe Sound, or Delray, or some other place on the Atlantic coast of Florida. My wife laughed, and became my wife.

Ten years later my older son, Nicholas, came home from school with a question I had asked my father:

"Am I a Jew? What's a Jew?"

I tried to answer him seriously. I explained that Jews didn't think of me as a Jew because I didn't worship as a Jew and wasn't raised as one. Israel didn't think of me as a Jew: under the Law of Return you are a Jew only if your mother is a Jew. My mother was Irish Catholic . . .

"You're talking about Granny?"

"Yes."

Then I explained to Nicholas that his paternal great-grandparents were a German-Jewish believer born in Scotland and an atheist Jew born in England. His mother's people were of gentile English stock. His question was difficult to answer. But he answered it,

telling his little brother, who had been listening:
"Hey, Justin, you're a mutt."
"You too," Justin said.
"Me too," I said.

My mother and brother were at our wedding; my father was in prison again, bad checks or grand theft or defrauding an innkeeper. Toby was in the Army. I sent my father rent money, one hundred fifty a month when he was free, and California merchants dunned me for his debts. I bought a uscd Volvo to get me to work at *The Washington Post*, where my father wrote telling me he wanted a BMW, "a damned sensible vehicle." He could get one with only a thousand miles on it, a "demo." I could make the down payment, carry the monthlies, what did I say? I said no, and stopped writing. The letters kept coming in from strangers around Los Angeles. My father set beds on fire in the fleabags where he lit from time to time. An ex-cellmate called me at the office collect to sell me information, he knew a "fairy actor" who knew who killed Kennedy, how much was it worth, "your old man said to call."

I got a letter from Mrs. Ira Levenson. She had known all us Wolffs during the war, when we lived in Manhattan Beach and shopped at her husband's grocery store. She had just seen my father:

Dear Sir:

Mr. Levenson and I made our first visit in our lives, yesterday, to ANY jail, and the impact of what we saw, and experienced in the L.A. County Jail, where we saw your father, caged and bewildered, sick in mind and body, is indeed an indelible impression and memory, not easy to forget or erase. We talked; I should say we bellowed at one another through the heavy wire, over the noise and din of hundreds of inmates and their visitors clawing their fingers, straining their eyes and ears against the caging.

I told your father of our telephone conversation, and explained to him that you believe he can and will best be served and assisted if you do not at this time attempt to clear away all the criminal charges against him by paying off his bad checks and all the other indebtedness he has incurred, by charges and unpaid rents and damages to property, etc., etc. I told him it would be wise and desirable for him to co-operate with you in your effort to gain medical care and hospitalization for him. He is a lost soul, and he wailed "What can I do? Can't I go East to my son?"

I further tried to explain to your father that this would be quite impossible all things being as they are today and then he asked me "Do you believe my son will get me out of here?"

I tried to assure him that you will make every effort to help him to help himself, and that you may even find it possible to come to Los Angeles yourself. My opinion is that unless your father's dilemma is forthwith dealt with through channels of kinship, understanding, and human kindness and if your father's physical and mental failings are not given first consideration over and above the many other failings that undoubtedly are the result and outcome of these failures, then my guess is that Arthur S. Wolff III can be written off right here and now, with all his fine education, background and various degrees etc., etc.

Because we knew your father many years ago, Geoffrey, and the sight of him handcuffed in the courtroom first, and the sickening visit I had with him in the jail yesterday, I found it impossible to write you just a brief note about all this. The fact that you phoned as soon as you heard about your father is a gratifying and honorable gesture. All of us here are pleased for your father's sake that you called. In fact, when I told him yesterday that I came to see him on your request, and gave him your message and said you would write him immediately, his bulky frame shook as the tears left his eyes...

I asked Ben Bradlee to help, and he did. He arranged for *Newsweek*'s Los Angeles bureau chief to visit my father. What Karl Fleming saw in jail is what the Levensons had seen, the wreck of a desperado. Fleming gave him pocket money, and tried to cheer him, but no one could set him free, of prison or himself. He served a year, was released.

Toby stopped off to see him in Manhattan Beach on his way to Vietnam in 1967 as a first lieutenant in the Green Berets:

"The first time I saw him I didn't know it was him. He was just an old geezer, staring at the surf, with white stubble on his face and little white globs of hair sticking out of his ears. What did I feel about him? I felt pity. I wanted to give him a nice couple of days. We had a pretty good time, a couple of laughs. He was very seedy, hesitant. He'd lost his power. I wasn't afraid of him anymore. His clothes were tacky, and not clean. He was no Tom Buchanan, just an old Hebe. He had B.O. He said you were a sell-out suburbanite. He deplored many things. He had met Joe Pyne. You remember Pyne, the television patriot? Pyne also deplored many things. He seemed to like the old man, from a distance. The old man took me to meet Pyne at a marina. Pyne was scouring the teak decks of his yacht. He looked like he hoped the old man would offer to help, but he didn't."

He was using assumed names now. His favorite was Saunders Ansel-Wolff III. He opened an account at the Bank of America under the name, and used a bad check to buy a watch. He was caught, tried, convicted. Sent to Chino. He had his hand almost cut off at the wrist after a fight with another Chino inmate about whether to watch *I Spy* or *Run for Your Life* on the cellblock television set. I thought he'd kill himself. What else could he do? I tried to imagine the desolation of his life. Books and movies with their dialogues must have been an awful affront to a solitary, sociable man. No hope. I thought he'd kill himself because he never shot off at his mouth about killing himself.

But he didn't, and he didn't, and he didn't. One day I got a rational, blunt letter. It came from prison, said I had sold myself at discount writing book reviews for *The Washington Post*. Never mind, the letter said: he could be released immediately into my custody, two years early, it was up to me. My father didn't beg, all he said was this: "I'd like to leave here, now, and live with you and Priscilla. What do you say?"

A District of Columbia probation officer came to see us. He was a black man, soft-voiced and gentle. He said that while the District of Columbia had no special appetite for my father's presence, he was no grave menace to society. Here was an opportunity for my father, if I wanted to take it. My father would have to live with us. The parole officer noticed that my wife was pregnant:

"Maybe the place would be too crowded with a father-in-law under the roof?"

The probation officer gave me my father's "rap sheet," as he called it, his record. It reported my father's sworn statement to the probation officials of the state of California that he had "graduated from Deerfield Academy when he was 17 years old and subsequently obtained a degree at Yale University, matriculated at the Sorbonne in Paris, France in Aeronautical Engineering, obtaining a master's degree, he states."

It also remarked that he had been committed in 1963 to Norwalk State Hospital as mentally ill. The defendant was diagnosed by a Metropolitan State Hospital psychiatrist as psychoneurotic reaction, depressive reaction. He states he recently had surgery at Los Angeles County General Hospital that involved the blood circulation from his waist to his knees. He has no religious preference. He has not been a member of any organizations other than the Racquet Club in New York and spends his leisure time hunting, playing golf, and reading. Attached to this report is Defendant's written statement in which he says in part that the last five years have been a great disappointment to him . . . He states he has two sons, one of which is the Editor of *The Washington Post* and the other is awaiting his commission in the Airborne Special Forces, so he does not feel that his life has been entirely inadequate. The first one is named Geoffrey.

*   *   *

Under the rubric "Interested Parties" my father's record included a letter from the chief psychiatrist of Norwalk State Mental Hospital. For the sake of the record this letter appeared in the language of abbreviation, thus:

"First mental hospitalization [sic] June 11, 1963, some history excessive use of Dexamyl and Doriden, possible alcohol excesses, at least two suicidal attempts drug ingestion (1962 and 1963) and two to one arrests for failure to pay bills [sic]. Course in hospital: group and individual therapy, Thorazine 101 mgm daily, ineffectual industrial performance in warehouse. Two assaults on other patients and much lying during interviews." (My father had been told by his young analyst that the only way out of the deep hole he was in was by way of the truth. Now, asked the analyst, what was my father's most recent line of work before his arrest?

"I was a psychoanalyst, actually," my father told the psychoanalyst.)

The profile continued: "Left arm now healed and functions normally. Patient is suitable for unskilled labor. Long range prognosis is poor for social and economic rehabilitation. Discharge to self. 6-16-63: Social Service Note: Approved by the ward team for discharge—patient advanced many excuses for remaining in the hospital. He was given $5 by the hospital and a referral card to the Bureau of Public Assistance. Patient had become an irritant on the ward, and there were many complaints from patients and ward staff about his provocative personality traits. Discharged improved, nonpsychotic."

"In other words," I asked the probation officer, "they sent him away from the state mental hospital because his behavior was abnormal and unpleasant?"

"More or less. You want him here?"

The probation officer looked at his watch. It was dinnertime. I looked at my father's record. There it was, his biography, in part:

10-15-41   LAPD—TRAFFIC WARRANT—NO DISPO.

7-30-42   SO, SAN DIEGO—DRUNK—7-30-42, $25 OR $2 PER DAY.

12-21-45   PD, BURBANK—APPLICATION CHIEF PROJECT ENGI-
NEER.

12-28-45   PD, HERMOSA BEACH—DRUNK DRIVING—RELEASED
$250 BAIL.

4-23-54   PD, NEW LONDON, CONN.—DRUNK DRIVING—NOT
GUILTY, FINED $60 ON RECKLESS DRIVING.

9-13-58   PD, WESTPORT, CONN.—FRAUD CHECKS—12-1-58
DISMISSED.

3-11-60   LAPD—23102 (DRUNK DRIVING MISDEMEANOR)
—3-11-60 $250 OR 10 DAYS, $125 OR 5 DAYS SUSP.
PAID FINE.

8-14-61   LASO—487.3 (GRAND THEFT AUTO); 10851 VC (UN-
LAWFUL TAKING OF VEHICLE)—10-20-61, 10851 VC
SENTENCED TO TIME SERVED, COUNT ONE DIS-
MISSED.

10-20-61   LAPD—WARRANT, TRAFFIC, 21453A VC; 537 PC
(NEWPORT BEACH)—10-23-61
SENTENCED TO ONE DAY. $10 OR 2 DAYS SUSP.

10-26-61   SO, SANTA ANA, CALIF.—537 PC WARRANT— 11-1-61
CASE DISMISSED.

11-9-61   PD, SAN DIEGO—GRAND THEFT, DEFRAUDING INN-
KEEPER—11-10-61 RELEASED, GRAND THEFT.

12-15-61   PD, SAN DIEGO—ILLEGAL U TURN & FAILURE TO
APPEAR—NO DISPO.

4-17-62   SO, SAN DIEGO—TRAFFIC, 8 VIOLATIONS—NO DISP

7-1-62   PD, DOWNEY—TRAFFIC WARRANT FROM LAPD—
POSTED BAIL.

9-27-62   PD, SANTA MONICA—WARRANT SAN DIEGO,
TRAFFIC BAIL POSTED.

1-3-63   SO, SANTA ANA, CALIF.—484 PC (PETTY
THEFT); 487 PC (GRAND THEFT), WARRANT—
HOLDING FOR THE D.A. 7-1-63 DISMISSED.

1-23-63   PD, SANTA MONICA—INTOXICATION, GLUE
SNIFFING—6-5-63 DISMISSED.

9-19-63   LASO—DISORDERLY CONDUCT & DRUNK—
ARRESTED BY CHP; NO DISP.

9-9-65   LASO—476A PC (CHECKS NSF); ON WARRANT
FROM LAPD—PRESENT OFFENSE.

*   *   *

There it was, up to date except for UNLAWFUL FLIGHT TO
AVOID PROSECUTION after he jumped bail in 1961, and his
conviction for littering in Newtown, Connecticut. The
"present offense" was the purchase of a wrist watch from a
jeweler, Donavan & Seamans, with a check for $248.70
from an account that had been closed more than four
years. My father didn't need the watch—he had a dozen
others—and he finally gave it to Toby on Toby's way to
Vietnam. The watch cost him two years in Chino.

In the summer of 1968, when my father was free of
crime and institutional punishment for the last time, I
wrote a novel, *Bad Debts;* it suggests with considerable
accuracy how I (or the cruel cartoon of myself I called
Caxton) felt about a prospective association with my
father (Freeman) in Washington, D.C. The following
scene is set at a dinner party. The hostess is a Georgetown
legend for her dinner parties:

There was not a person there (wives excluded) whose face
Caxton did not immediately recognize and there was not a
person there to whom Caxton had previously been
introduced ... The guests included an associate justice of
the Supreme Court ... the Secretary of State, three
senators, an ambassador and five journalists (one
managing editor and four columnists) ... The hostess'
manner when she introduced Caxton implied that they
were very old friends indeed. That they were not, she
seemed to promise him, would be their secret. She
prodded him for his opinions, encouraged him to talk
about himself. Yet she was perfectly discreet; she never
asked for information that might possibly compromise
his work or injure his feelings. She asked no questions
about Caxton's opinion of his colleagues, no questions
about where he was born or whom he had by way of
parents. The party represented perfectly what Washington at its best gave the illusion of being: a meritocracy.

And Caxton had been forewarned of the bounds

within which he would be expected to confine himself: no sham humility, no ungoverned laughter, no strongly held opinions forcefully expressed. By the fish course Caxton was secure... There had been no ruptures on the plain cloth of his discourse, he had refused a third glass of wine (to the evident satisfaction of the managing editor) and he was about to enjoy the company of the younger of his two attractive companions when the table turned with a change of courses. Then the butler went to the hostess. And she said, "Caxton dear, your father seems to be at the door."

It was a holocaust. The hostess insisted that Freeman be brought to the table and served wine ("Why didn't you tell me your father would be here? You are very wicked—we would have been honored to have him.") And Freeman, without the slightest hesitation, dressed in khaki trousers and a tweed jacket (and wearing Caxton's Princeton tie—black with orange tigers dancing upon it...), pulled up a chair as though he were joining a poker game and shook hands all round.

Caxton remembered asking, choking the question past his furious blush, when Freeman had arrived. And his father, smiling cheerfully, replied that he had hitched a ride up from Charlottesville with a truck driver. He had found the hostess' invitation stuck in his son's mirror. "What took you to Charlottesville?" someone asked him. "Passing through when the Bentley blew up on me," he replied. "Damned nuisance, really."

It got worse. Caxton had never heard him talk so much... or heard his inventions come forth so fantastically unfinished. At the table were half a dozen men known by Caxton to have been in the OSS during the war: Freeman spoke obsessively of his secret assignments and near escapes. The managing editor was a trustee of Yale, and the same age as Freeman. So Caxton's father spoke disdainfully of an imaginary colleague in "Bones" whose imaginary name was an amalgam of the family names of two of the men who sat with him at the table...

He asked the hostess whether she got to New York often (he called it "The City") and when she said that she did not much go there, he said, "Pity. You're missing fine theater, music, best food in the world." When he was asked what at the theater had entertained him recently he had no answer, didn't even try to bluff out an answer. He shrugged . . .

Caxton insisted that he and his father had to leave. The hostess did not urge them to stay longer. She saw them to the door (her face a mask of hospitality), where Freeman, to Caxton's unspeakable shame (nothing would ever again wound him so grievously), slipped into a raccoon coat. And said "Cheers!" as they took their leave.

Of course, as I tumidly instructed my father, *Bad Debts* is a fiction. Freeman should not be imagined as a replica of Wolff. After all, Freeman is an anti-Semitic Jew passing as an Anglican, and Wolff was not much of an anti-Semite. *Bad Debts*, I explained to my father, "is both kind and cruel." I told him by mail I hoped it was more kind than cruel, and was encouraged in this hope by an advance reading in which James Baldwin admired the novel's "loving lack of pity." How I hung to that reading, wanting Baldwin's judgment to be right on the money. Three months before publication I tried to justify myself to my father:

I don't know whether you will like my book. Parts of it will infuriate you, I'm sure. It is, for example, in part a story about being Jewish and not wanting to be. It could cause you pain. You will reflect that this or that is not "true" which is precisely, of course, the point of the exercise. It is not you, or even *about* you—it is about a single problem that has troubled me for a long while. This: I have for some years taken an obsessive interest in truth. Bullshit drives me wild with anger, from whatever quarter it comes. I am not sure, to be blunt, that truth, *qua* truth, deserves such affection. At one point in my book Freeman shouts at his son that truth is a bully and a fraud. Freeman has a history wholly of his own invention, and it is a solace to him. The problem is this: be careful who you pretend you are lest you wind up becoming your pretense.

For example (let me be blunt, again): who you in fact

are is someone far greater than the person you have, from time to time, pretended to be. Yale graduates are a dime a dozen. Your history is more interesting, has more spice and wit and reach. Suppose for a moment, thinking back to your fictons, that you could will them to be true. Would this make you happy?

It wasn't till much later that I realized where I had first heard some of these locutions: *Who you in fact are is someone far greater than the person you have, from time to time, pretended to be... Your history is more interesting...* My father had told me these things to save me from crucial turns toward falsehood, and in these terms precisely.

To my question—Would this make you happy?—I got no answer. I never heard from my father again. He died a year after I mailed this letter. The letter was inside his copy of *Bad Debts*. He had told me to write a novel. He had read this one. There are coffee rings on some of the pages, and the corners of many other pages have been folded down. The letter and the book, together with twelve of my checks for one hundred fifty dollars—a check a month, all uncashed—were stored in the basement of his apartment building at 2420 Manhattan Avenue in Manhattan Beach. They were in a shoe box with some fake driver's licenses and identification papers and a couple of bills. One bill was from an irate Hong Kong tailor, Jimmy Sung ("Gentleman, We wrote on 20 October last year for which we have not as yet have your reaction. We expect US$299.25 from you. US$150 means returned check drawn on Bank of New York because of 'signature unknown' and US$149.25 being balance if it has not paid to Jimmy. Hoping to hear from you soonest...") and the other was from his milkman for US$123.38 for sixty-seven quarts of white milk, two pounds of butter, four gallons of orange juice, six dozen eggs and an ice-cream bar.

The milkman, smelling something unpleasant, found him on the last day of July, 1970. Later my father's neighbors remembered that they too had smelled something unpleasant. No one knows precisely when he died. The official estimate held that he had been dead about two weeks when he was found. No one had missed him while he lay there falling apart. He had no friends, and when no one called him anymore he had had his telephone number unlisted, just like Benjamin Freeman.

Through the Open Door

I had never seen kindred dying or dead. No one I knew well was killed in a car or a war. None drowned, or fell from a great height, or was shot hunting. My dead were strangers. When I was a cub on the night police beat for *The Washington Post* I was sent to a tough neighborhood near Howard University to look at someone who had been hurt. It was raining, late at night. A cop said something about knife wounds, and gestured. The thing lay covered by a piece of oilskin, with its feet in a brimming gutter. The cop obligingly pulled back the poncho, for the merest instant, like a stripper flashing the last bit just at the blackout. He grinned at me while I scribbled in my notebook: *coal in a croker sack . . . blood: pretty, a dash of red on a blackbird's wing.* (I assumed the corpse was black: the bad street, the knife, the late hour, the law's indifference, even the rain suggested that the corpse was black, and it was.) I returned to the newsroom to compose a memorial drenched in mist and metaphysics, but the night city editor was interested only in the man's name and address, age and occupation, and I knew

286

none of these. I should at least have asked his name.

And once I saw a stain on Route 301, on the Eastern Shore of the Chesapeake Bay Bridge. It was said by gawkers to have been a man changing a tire. A truck highballing north had whacked him; the stain was still wet in the low October sun, more rust than red, and greasy. The remains of the man who had been changing his tire formed an imperfect disc, about four feet across. The first rain would clean him away.

Just those two experiences of death, or just those two close up. One of my best friends killed himself a few days after I had spent a merry week with him. I had come to America from Cambridge to visit him at the Harvard Business School, where he was a student and not performing as well as he had expected himself to perform. A few days after he announced his engagement to a girl he seemed to love, who seemed to love him back, he parked his car near the emergency room of a hospital near his family's house. He lay across the front seat, stuck the muzzle of a pump gun in his mouth, and pulled the trigger with his toe. I had come home for the engagement party but was back in England when he did it.

I don't know why he shot himself. People spoke of a dark history I knew nothing about, and a few mentioned the confusions of love, but most people believed he was disappointed by his performance at the business school. None of these reasons seemed much like reasons to me.

Now, driving home from Kay's terrace where I had just learned of my father's death, trying to think of my father, I thought instead of Kay's husband. He wore a wooden leg, got around well on it, elaborated jokes about it. He had flown wearing it in the Air Corps, and had escaped from a German POW camp wearing it. People who knew this man loved him, while he was alive. But he shot himself in a spectacularly cruel way, perhaps not calculated to do maximum hurt to his four children and three stepchildren, but having that end, and the damage he did to his wife was incalculable. Driving to my in-laws' house I thought of that suicide. Why would anyone choose so casually to empty so much life from himself?

There was a message to telephone the police in California. There would be an autopsy; they suspected suicide. In the room where my father died, the police told me on the telephone, were many empty liquor bottles and empty barbituate pillboxes. Much later the police told me that the general squalor of the scene—my father lying on his stomach naked, his head under a chair, "legs and feet together pointing eastward" in the language of the death report—combined with the awful smell of the dank, tiny room to argue, even to case-hardened cops, hopelessness. This suicide was no mystery. It made sense to me. I thought my father had every reason to welcome death, and I had always assumed he would try to control his history to the very end. *It's nothing.* But the autopsy a few days later revealed a death from congestion of his arteries; probably, when he died, he wanted to live forever.

From my in-laws' house I telephoned my mother, and told her as much as I knew, and for the first time I heard my mother weep. I telephoned Ruth Atkins, and when I had finished with the telephone about suppertime, Priscilla asked me if I wanted to eat. I said I wasn't hungry. She said she was sleepy, and would go to bed. I followed her to the guest room, expecting her to mourn with me. She wouldn't. I grew angry to the point of violence. I didn't understand her coldness, but I do now.

I had felt ashamed of my father in her father's house, and now I was ashamed of my shame, and ashamed to be there at all, under that roof. It was as though to accept their hospitality were to collaborate in their judgment of my father. I thought I knew what they thought of him, and I knew what they thought of me. Sometimes in that house I felt Priscilla look at me through her parents' eyes, and I thought that house in Narragansett was a place where my father would not have been made to feel welcome. I tried to forget the night of his death that neither had he been welcome those past ten years in my own house, and in my eagerness to forget this I repudiated all of them, my wife and her parents, and now Priscilla says she has never seen me so cold or so angry. She withdrew, would not dishonor any of us by seeming to feel what she did not. I wanted her to love my father now. I wanted to love my father now. How could she, if I could not? She had never seen him, had heard his voice once across telephone wires. We had promised him and ourselves a visit to California, but we never went. Every time we settled on a date to show my father his first grandson, and then his second, something happened, he got put away again or pulled a fast move on me or we decided we'd rather visit Madrid, ski in Austria.

I think that for a few hours that night I hated my wife. I drove to a seedy Narragansett roadhouse, a rough bar with a tropical motif where surfers hung out. I wanted a fight. I sat at the bar drinking whiskey chased by beer, scowling and muttering at friendly strangers wearing cut-offs and clean, jokey T-shirts. The beachboys were tan, pacific, easy; surfers had no beef with me. I shut the place down and drove flat out to Kay's house. I wanted to explain to her, at once, why I had thanked God that my father was dead. I wanted her to know that my words were not an atheist's unfelt exclamation, and that they did not only display relief that my children were alive. They also meant what they seemed to mean, that I thanked someone that my father had been delivered from the world, and I had been delivered from him.

I woke my friend three hours before dawn. I had first met Kay at her California ranch nine years earlier, the day after I left my father in the San Diego jail. Two of her daughters were Priscilla's lifelong friends, and one of them I had courted. Like everyone who knew him I had idolized her husband, and he and I had traveled in Spain together. One night he had crawled out the bedroom window of our Madrid hotel room, swaying drunk on a narrow ledge ten floors above the street because I had just told him a sad story. A couple of his children helped me snag his good leg and haul him to safety, and the way they looked at him that night I guessed they had had to save him from himself many times before. A few days before he shot himself, with his wife and children as witnesses, Kay had written me to wish me well in my courtship of Priscilla, and her letter was full of energy, wit, love, and delight with the future.

It was too cold to sit on the terrace, but my friend lit the Japanese lanterns out there so we could see them from the living room. Above the fireplace a motto was cut into the mantel: *Kind friend, around this hearthstone speak no evil of any creature.*

The morning with Kay changed me. She spoke of her dead husband and I told of my dead father; we traded scandal for scandal, and soon we were laughing. I told how my father despised prudence, savings accounts, the *idea* of savings accounts, the *fact* of savings accounts, looks before leaps. Yes, her husband too, hobbling along the pitching deck of a sailboat he had chartered to sail solo before he taught himself to sail. It had been fun to be her husband's wife, and my father's son. This was important to understand.

Kay led me through my father's history, let me begin to apprehend him as a critic of the conventions, a man who caricatured what he despised. *Is it Yale men you like? Okay, I'm a Yale man, see how easy it is? Nothing to it but will and nerve.* My father led me to understand how lucky I was to be free, that there was a benign side to my father's dishonor, that I had never had to explain or apologize to him any more than he had had to explain or apologize to me. Much of this, of course, was casuistry. I don't believe now that my father was truly a critic of society, or that his life was any more happy than it was defiant.

Never mind. I had come into that night alienated. I was becoming handy with repudiations of every kind, and learning to nurture anger solicitously. I had felt betrayed by my father, and wanted to betray him. Kay turned my course. She had the authority of someone who had passed through the worst of fires. I listened to her. I saw again what I had seen when I was a child, in love with my father as with no one else. He had never repudiated me or seen in my face intimations of his own mortality. He had never let me think he wished to be rid of me or the burden of my judgment, even when I had hounded him about his history, had quibbled with its details like a small-print artist, like a reviewer, for God's sake! He didn't try to form me in his own image. How could he? Which image to choose? He had wanted me to be happier than he had been, to do better. He had taught me many things, some of which were important, some of which he meant, some of which were true. The things he told me were the right things to tell a son, usually, and by the time I understood their source in mendacity they had done what good they could. I had been estranged from my father by my apprehension of other people's opinions of him, and by a compulsion to be free of his chaos and destructions. I had forgotten I loved him, mostly, and mostly now I missed him. I miss him.

When I finally left Kay's house I felt these things, some for the first time. I drove home slowly, and stopped at stop signs. The door to the room I shared with Priscilla was open when I came in, but I didn't go through that door that night. I went to my children's room. I stood above Justin, looking down at him. And then my son Nicholas began to moan, quietly at first. They did not know their grandfather was dead; they knew nothing about their grandfather. There would be time for that. I resolved to tell them what I could, and hoped they would want to know as much as I could tell. Nicholas cried out in his sleep, as he had so many times before, dragging me out of nightmares about his death with his own nightmares about his death, his dreams of cats with broken legs, broken-winged screaming birds, deer caught in traps, little boys hurt and crying, beyond the range of their parents' hearing. Sometimes I dreamt of my son bleeding to death from some simple wound I had neglected to learn to mend.

Now I smoothed his forehead as my father had smoothed mine when I was feverish. Justin breathed deeply. I crawled in bed beside my sweet Nicholas and took him in my arms and began to rock him in time to Justin's regular breaths. I stunk of whiskey and there was blood on my face from a fall leaving Kay's house, but I knew I couldn't frighten my son. He ceased moaning, and I rocked him in my arms till light came down on us, and he stirred awake in my arms as I, in his, fell into a sleep free of dreams.

CHILDREN OF POWER

The shocking and critically acclaimed novel by

SUSAN RICHARDS SHREVE

Natty Taylor is a child of power.
Daughter of one of Washington's top
liberals, she knows the power of politics;
girlfriend of the city's star athlete,
she knows the power of her own
blossoming womanhood.

But Natty's in trouble. Her father's
inexplicable friendship with the ruined
Senator McCarthy has unleashed a
vicious campaign of terror, a nightmare
proving that the hatred of her parents'
generation is far surpassed by the
violence of her own.

Bestsellers from Berkley
The books you've been hearing about—and want to read